# MUSIC AND HUMANISM

# Music and Humanism

AN ESSAY IN THE AESTHETICS OF MUSIC

## R. A. SHARPE

OXFORD
UNIVERSITY PRESS

# OXFORD
UNIVERSITY PRESS

Great Clarendon Street, Oxford OX2 6DP

Oxford University Press is a department of the University of Oxford.
It furthers the University's objective of excellence in research, scholarship,
and education by publishing worldwide in

Oxford New York

Athens Auckland Bangkok Bogotá Buenos Aires Calcutta
Cape Town Chennai Dar es Salaam Delhi Florence Hong Kong Istanbul
Karachi Kuala Lumpur Madrid Melbourne Mexico City Mumbai
Nairobi Paris São Paulo Singapore Taipei Tokyo Toronto Warsaw
and associated companies in Berlin Ibadan

Oxford is a registered trade mark of Oxford University Press
in the UK and certain other countries

Published in the United States
by Oxford University Press Inc., New York

British Library Cataloguing in Publication Data

Data available

Library of Congress Cataloging in Publication Data
Sharpe, R. A.
Music and humanism: an essay in the aesthetics of music / R. A. Sharpe.
Includes bibliographical references and index.
1. Music—Philosophy and aesthetics. 2. Music—Psychology. I. Title.
ML3845.S417 2000 780.1′7—dc21 99-050261
ISBN 0–19–823885–1

1 3 5 7 9 10 8 6 4 2

Typeset by Best-set Typesetter Ltd., Hong Kong
Printed in Great Britain
on acid-free paper by
Biddles Ltd
Guildford and King's Lynn

# *Preface*

If music is for you, as it is for me, a serious passion, then from time to time you will probably have been confronted with this problem: How do you distinguish between what is alien to your taste and what is not? Furthermore, how do you tell what music merely demands extra time and hard work in order to appreciate it and what music is not worth the effort, either because it is music which is technically competent but dead, or because it is music which is good but which will never appeal to you? I have also been exercised, as any lover of the arts ought to be, by the dictatorial nature of my own taste. I cannot see anything but crudity in the famous counterpoint in the *Mastersingers* overture. The Liszt piano concertos strike me as commonplace in ideas and invention. On the other hand, that any music-lover could not worship Berlioz seems to me astounding. I am not thinking of music which once moved me but does so no longer, such as the Brahms symphonies (with the exception of the second). I am thinking of music that has generally left me cold—for example, nearly all of Handel. This is music, like the operas of Wagner, which is of the highest quality, but music which I fail to appreciate. Am I so entrenched in my taste that I cannot give a fair hearing to this? Was I born a devotee of Bach rather than Handel?

Any reader will be able to find examples from his or her own taste. Are such differences primitive, irresolvable, like basic differences in sensitivity to others? Or are they merely the result of adventitious differences in circumstance and upbringing, of associations and ideology, bearing on a taste which is initially unformed and uniform and which, left to itself, would enable us, like Oscar Wilde's auctioneer, to admire the best in everything. Even if this latter were a possibility, it is, I believe, a matter of evident fact that beliefs and ideas do affect our appreciation of music. This book is, *inter alia*, about such matters.

My examples are largely from Western classical music from Josquin des Prez to Arvo Pärt. There is both a cause and a reason for this. The cause is that this happens to be the music with which I am familiar and which I love—I have a much less extensive knowledge of jazz, rock, and world music. The reason is that this is an essay in the philosophy of the arts. I believe that central to our concept of art is the concept of interpretation. Where improvisation is at the centre of a musical practice, then the question of interpretation in that sense in which we speak of the way a performer chooses to play a certain piece of music cannot arise. We do not compare 'covers', as they are known, of the song 'Yesterday' in the way we compare interpretations of Beethoven's 'Eroica' by Toscanini and by Klemperer. Music, of course, is interpreted in another sense. As well as the interpretation of the performer, choosing just how fast and how loud to play and how to phrase it, the significance of the music is explored in various critical essays. The importance of Lutheranism to the music of J. S. Bach or the relationship of Berlioz to nineteenth-century ideas about the classical world are examples.

As a result of decisions as to which rock albums of the vinyl era to re-release on compact disc, a canon of rock music is beginning to emerge, and this will change matters. In the sense of being discussed and written about, such music will be interpreted.[1] Already the critical discussion of rock music is burgeoning. But, as matters stand, classical music is the standard subject for the aesthetics of music, and virtually all philosophical writing about music has taken it as the locus of discussion.

This 'privileging', as the jargon goes, of Western music is often criticized as élitist. Philip Tagg speaks of the 'aesthetic dictates of elitist European bourgeois music culture with its canonisation of some musics and its deprecation of others'.[2] Frith quotes Bourdieu's remark that such privileging displays the pleasures of superiority.[3] This ignores the passionate desire of many musicians to educate the public; they want more people to share the richness of the classical heritage. Not of all us subscribe to Schoenberg's dictum that 'if it is for all it is not art'.[4] It is also a mistake to think that this exclusivity is to be found only amongst the admirers of classical music. The division between that rock music which its devotees take seriously and that which they scorn is very marked.

[1] Nicholas Cook, *Music: A Very Short Introduction* (Oxford: Oxford University Press, 1998), 106.
[2] Philip Tagg, Open Letter: 'Black Music, Afro-American Music and European Music', *Popular Music*, 8/3 (1989), 285.
[3] Simon Frith, *Performing Rites* (Oxford: Oxford University Press, 1998), 9.
[4] Ibid. 65.

Bob Searle remarked: 'I would be suspicious of a record or song that appeals to everyone.' If classical music is élitist, it is not differentiated from rock on that account, and its restricted appeal is something many of us regret. This music is too important to be a weapon in class warfare, and there is no reason why it should be.

So it is classical music which is at the centre of this book, and it is important for another reason that my examples are from the great composers. It is the stability of classical music that gives it its role in our culture, a role at present denied to jazz and rock, even though they declare the nature of modern culture more effectively.

General philosophical questions about the arts, the discussion of which is indifferent to the particular art-form in question, are, on the whole, set aside here, though I shall discuss the nature of the work of music and its performance; problems here connect with problems in other performing arts. There are two major questions in the aesthetics of music. First, there is the familiar problem of expression, of how we can justify calling music grave or optimistic. This is, I think, a special problem for music; it does not arise in the same way in the representational arts, where at least the subject-matter offers an initial way of answering the question. A picture may be sad because of what it depicts. The second problem does have parallels in the other arts, but is peculiarly acute with respect to music; it is the question of the role of pleasure in artistic judgement. For in music, pleasure has always seemed to play a more direct role in explaining why we think a piece of music good. When should I discount my pleasure, and for what reasons?

The problem of expression for a start. I begin by considering the view that music is expressive inasmuch as it causes certain states in us. Even sophisticated versions of a causal theory fail, because they underestimate the cognitive element in our response to music. We have ideas about music, ideas which lead to an appreciation of its structure; these are integral to our experience of it. This view I shall describe as 'cognitivism'; but 'cognitivism' will be used in two ways. First, it is the view that primarily we recognize music as grave or optimistic, rather than feel those 'psychological' states which we ascribe to the music. This book is also about the way that certain general ideas about the music and its relation to its times affect our judgement. It is about ideology and appreciation. So, second, I shall also describe as 'cognitivism' the notion that our experience of music is infected and deflected by ideas about the music.

There is a certain atheoretical quality about my conclusions. First, I argue in Part I that no general theory can be found which will explain why we describe music in terms such as 'joyous' or 'sad'.[5] Secondly, as I argue in Chapter 4, I do not believe that any general theory can be given of the ontology of music, the relationship between work, score, interpretation, and performance. Such an ontology, I shall argue, is impregnated with assumptions and values on which there is no universal agreement, though there are, as one might expect, varying degrees of overlap. This scepticism about the availability of general solutions reflects the influence of Wittgenstein on my thinking. Chapter 6 continues the discussion of ideology. In the closing chapter I take a still broader view. Music has been thought of as a language, and this metaphor has deeply affected the way we think about it and the way we hear it. We think of music as something we understand and, furthermore, as something which we can think of as expressive. These two ideas underpin our thought that it is a humanist art. But music has changed markedly in this century. Does it still make sense to think of it as at all like a language? Our conception of music as capable of expressing human psychological states is deeply enmeshed with our sense that it is a humanist art-form in a way that mere pattern making is not. So, more generally, is it still a humanist art, or are our major composers nowadays no longer composing music which we can, in any sense, regard as humanist?

Only one substantial part of this book has been previously published, and that is a large section of Chapter 4, which appeared in the *British Journal of Aesthetics* in January 1995 as 'Music, Platonism and Performance: Some Ontological Strains'. But parts of it have been read to philosophical audiences at the universities of Liverpool, Essex, Kent, Southampton, Leipzig, Wales (Cardiff), Crete, and London, and at a conference on musical aesthetics in Budapest. I am indebted to questioners on these occasions. Two major intellectual debts are to Peter Kivy's series of books on the aesthetics of music and to Lydia Goehr's *The Imaginary Museum of Musical Works*. I owe an immense debt to Colin Lyas who read the book at a point when I was beginning to have serious doubts about it, and not only made numerous suggestions, but encouraged

---

[5] Compare Francis Sparshott, 'Music and Feeling', *Journal of Aesthetics and Art Criticism*, 52/1 (Winter 1994), 23.

me to publish it; to Professor Lydia Goehr who also read the manuscript and made many valuable suggestions; and to an anonymous reader for Oxford University Press. Finally, it has been read in its entirety by Professor Peter Williams, whose knowledge of both the history of music and performing practice set me right at many points, and saved me from some rash historical judgements. Those that remain, remain despite his admonitions. I also acknowledge with gratitude the help of Kathy Miles in the Library of the University of Wales, Lampeter, and of Connie Gdula in the Computer Department.

R.A.S.

# Contents

# PART I

*Naturalizing Music*

# I

# *Naturalizing Music*

Imagine aliens visiting the earth for the first time. Much of what they see they could explain if they had some grasp of the laws of physics and some knowledge of evolution and natural selection. Thus they might be able to offer some explanation of the cycle of the seasons, why birds pair off, build nests, and sit on eggs, and of the growth and decay of plants and animals. They might not always get the explanation right, of course; but what is going on need not be unintelligible. They might even come to see that human beings need family groups to nurture the young. They might find it odd that rites of passage should take the form they do, but that there should be crises in people's lives might not be so surprising.

But they would, I suspect, be surprised to see large numbers of people converging on buildings in which up to a hundred or so sit before them, scrape at strings stretched over shaped wooden boxes, blow through various sorts of tubes, and bang at various things with hammers, whilst, with his back to the crowd, somebody waves a thin wooden stick.[1] They might be even more mystified at the reactions of the listeners, ranging from tears to cheers, and they might be startled to be told that the 'players' started training in early childhood and that the training went on for years. (Always supposing that they could make sense both of human reactions and of what was said.)

The point of this imaginary picture is to impress upon you just how surprising the phenomenon of music is. We need buildings for shelter; architecture is in some sense a primitive requirement. Given the initial expectation that there will be close ties between members of a family, it is not surprising that the art of making representations of the human form in the form of portraits has developed. There was a need for pictures long before good likenesses became possible. I think as well that human beings have a need to

---

[1] See Jonathan Swift, *Gulliver's Travels*, pt. III, ch. 2.

tell stories, and that story-telling is natural for them. It connects with the development of the imagination, which is so important in morality.[2] I am not for a minute suggesting that you can 'explain away' the arts in such a fashion, reducing them simply to what we need in order to live and reproduce our kind. I simply suggest that there are continuities, perhaps tenuous, between some of the arts and the form our life has to take.

But music is problematic. It mimics the sound of the cuckoo or the steam train, but not much else besides. Its capacity for representation is limited and of marginal interest. Its connections with life are slim. For this reason alone, we can see the attractions of Platonism, the idea that music proper belongs to a suprasensory world of pure structures. In our culture, at least, music seems an art apart, having freed itself in the last few centuries from a dependence on words, drama, or dance. 'Pure music' has become thought of as the pinnacle of the art.[3] For millennia music has seemed to bear a close relationship with mathematics, and the aesthetic appeal of mathematics to be analogous to that of music. Those formal properties which both display may be both beautiful and satisfying.

However, Platonism, though currently popular as an account of the nature of a piece of music, merely gives up as far as the question of the power and attraction of music is concerned. If our interest in music is an interest in an abstract Platonic object, then it remains a mystery why such sounds should move us, and why we should characterize music as grave, or sad, or exuberant. If music is to be related to our interests, it has to be naturalized. By this I mean that we need some sort of explanation of its appeal in terms of a connection with human life. If music can be said to be joyful, we need an explanation of how this can be. Such a 'naturalization' does not preclude the intimate and complex relationships music bears to the received ideas of a particular culture, a matter I shall be increasingly concerned with as this book progresses. But I share with other analytic philosophers a conviction that there are some very basic questions to be settled, and in this chapter I shall try to lay a foundation for what follows.

[2] See R. A. Sharpe, 'Moral Tales', *Philosophy*, 67 (1992), 155–68.
[3] Cf. Lawrence Kramer, 'The Musicology of the Future', *Repercussions*, I/I (1992), 5–18, for a very different view. Also Charles Rosen, 'Music à la Mode', *New York Review of Books*, 23 June 1994, 55–62, for some penetrating criticism of the 'new musicology'.

Now the Platonic view is, in part, an expression of a vision of an order which goes beyond life; Henry James expressed this on more than one occasion: 'Life has no direct sense whatever for the subject and is capable, luckily for us, of nothing but splendid waste. Hence the opportunity for the sublime economy of art'.[4] Such a 'sublime economy' is properly part of the appeal of music; but music also connects with human passions in ways which I shall try to show, though I take the connection to be slender.

So music is, largely, an art apart. Yet it moves us so profoundly. Marghanita Laski's observation that ecstasy is generated more by music than by anything else reports common experience, and I don't suppose that anybody who has picked up this book will be unaware of it. In Hanslick's words, 'Even if we have to grant to all the arts, without exception, the power to produce effects upon the feelings, yet we do not deny that there is something specific, peculiar only to it, in the way music exercises that power. Music works more rapidly and intensely upon the mind than any other art.'

These generalizations are clichés; still, it is perhaps salutary to question whether they are true. Copland thought drama more powerful still. Whether or not he is right, the ecstasy music engenders seems almost unique, and it remains a puzzle as to how such a supposedly abstract art can affect us so deeply. Should we not be engaged, rather, by something which more obviously relates to human interests and concerns?

## CAUSAL THEORIES

The problem which faces the alien in my opening fable has puzzled terrestrial philosophers. How can music move us and absorb our attention in the way it does? Why do we value it so highly? One obvious answer to my principal question would be to say that music, as a matter of fact, causes certain states in us, states which, also as a matter of fact, we value. Such a claim is an integral element in what are known as 'expressionist' theories of art; so our first task will be to examine, briefly, expressionist theories of music.

---

[4] Henry James, 'Preface to the Spoils of Poynton; A London Life; The Chaperon', in *The Critical Muse; Selected Literary Criticism* (Harmondsworth: Penguin, 1987), 530.

## (i) Expressionism

The history of the aesthetics of music has oscillated between two poles; on the one hand, the study of music has been seen as the study of a purely mathematical relationship, and the audible experience of music has been thought at best irrelevant and at worst a hindrance. This Pythagorean perspective is beautifully caught by Keats in the *Ode On a Grecian Urn*: 'Heard melodies are sweet but those unheard are sweeter.'

The other approach argues for the capacity of music to arouse and involve our passions, and this eventually developed into the thesis that music is a language of the emotions, possibly the most widely held form of expressionism. Thomas Mace, writing in 1676, seems to have been one of the first writers to consider music a language; by the eighteenth century what was known before as the doctrine of the affections had become central. A writer in the *Monthly Review* of 1796, whom Schueller suggests may have been Burney, classifies the passions that music can represent as the 'bold, courageous, merry, joyous, magnanimous, calm, cheerful, contented, tender, plaintive, compassionate, solemn, devotional'. More recently, Deryck Cooke[5] has not only embraced the thesis that music is a language of the emotions, but has provided a sort of glossary whereby predicates in English are matched with intervals, harmonic progressions, and melodic shapes. Now the role played by the model of language in our thought about music is another issue which will become increasingly prominent as this book progresses. But for the present, we will concentrate on the notion of expression which includes, but is not coextensive with, expression through language.

There are two elements in an expressionist account of music. One is the claim that music can express the passions; the other is that the way it does so is through causing certain states in the listener. Let us consider, first of all, the question, does music express the passions? Few writers seem to have much doubt about this. We may speak of music as 'poignant' or 'calm' or 'tempestuous'. Music is said to express these characteristics, and these examples of what are now called 'expressive predicates' are from the common stock of examples used by philosophers. There are others which may be

---

[5] Deryck Cooke, *The Language of Music* (Oxford: Oxford University Press, 1959).

more inventive and informative about the music. How about some of the following:

feline, intellectually dazzling (Haydn), bombastic, demagogic (Wagner), grandiose (Handel), fey (Schumann), violent, threatening, aggressive (Stravinsky), nostalgic, tub-thumping (Elgar), sparkling (Prokofiev), sarcastic, bitter (Bartók), acid (Shostakovich), exotic (Szymanowski), sardonic, ironic (Liszt), ambiguous, companionable, affectionate, warm-hearted, ambivalent (Schubert), self-indulgent (Berg's Violin Concerto), over-emotional (Tchaikovsky), *faux-naif* (Mahler)?

Some of these are debatable and are none the worse for that. They encourage us to argue over the character of the music, and may challenge us to see it in a different light. But, it is commonly thought, they are all phrases which apply principally to the character of human beings and are, by extension, applied to music.

Granted that music can be expressive, the most widely canvassed candidate for the explanation as to how music moves us has been that it affects our emotions, a view which, from the seventeenth century on, was so widely accepted as to be a cliché. This thesis has dominated the history of the aesthetics of music inasmuch as most sophisticated writers have felt it necessary to distance themselves from it. They have rejected even more strongly the sort of expression theory of art advocated by Tolstoy amongst many others. Tolstoy[6] advocates what has been called the 'infection' theory of art. Good art conveys the emotions the artist feels so effectively as to re-create them in the listener. So the expressive properties of art are expressive in virtue of their being a causal medium whereby the emotions of the artist are re-created in his public.

It is a cliché of modern aesthetics that it does not follow from the fact that we apply expressive predicates to music that either the composer was sad when he composed sad music, that the performer is sad when he performs it, or that the audience is sad when they hear it. Biographical data confirm what is obvious on a little reflection. Tchaikovsky, of all people, denied that he felt the emotion his music expressed, and Berlioz admitted to feeling the emotion which characterized his music on one occasion only, in the composition of his song 'Irlande'. Such biographical evidence should be taken with a pinch of salt perhaps, but it seems obvious

[6] L. Tolstoy, *What is Art?*, The World's Classics (Oxford: Oxford University Press, 1930).

enough that a composer may be asked to provide a funeral march for a state occasion and, knowing how to do so, produces something appropriate. A slow tempo, a steady pace, and a subdued and dignified melody with no great leaps in the melodic line are what is required. A good composer may produce an excellent funeral march without feeling any grief at the death of the person being commemorated. Likewise, a composer may write suitable music for a stage play or for the dramatic events of an opera without experiencing the appropriate emotions. Indeed we can easily imagine that he might be exhilarated by his success in producing a really good funeral march. No more does an actor need to feel the emotions he portrays or the performer the expressive qualities of the music she performs. Indeed, she might find that to be moved interferes with the performance.

There is another difficulty. Irony in music depends upon presenting music with one face whilst implying another. It can be brutal, as in Bartók's Concerto for Orchestra, where he mercilessly guys Shostakovich's 'Leningrad' Symphony, or it can be more subtle, as in Shostakovich himself. Once we grant this, we can open a gap between the 'expressive surface' of the music and what the composer is expressing through it. Shostakovich may compose sentimental music, but, by distancing himself from it, he ensures that it does not express sentimentality. Mahler's Wunderhorn Lieder may be naïve; sometimes, as in the rather bad interpretations by Schwarzkopf, they sound *faux-naif* (both characteristics which it is hard to think of the listener mirroring). Which are they? Mahler certainly was not naïve in composing them.[7]

In general, then, we cannot conclude from the fact that a particular piece of music expresses a particular quality that that quality properly characterizes the composer at the time of creation. On the other hand, there are some, relatively neglected, expressive epithets of a different kind which do entitle us to draw inferences about the state of the composer or the performer. If the music is witty or ironic, then the composer was witty or ironic in composing it.

What I have said so far applies equally to performer and listener. As my analogy suggests, just as the actor need not suffer grief in expressing grief, no more need the performer suffer grief whilst

[7] See E. T. Cone, *The Composer's Voice* (Berkeley: University of California Press, 1974), and Wayne C. Booth's *The Rhetoric of Fiction* (Chicago: University of Chicago Press, 1961), to which Cone is indebted.

playing Chopin's Funeral March. The performance may lose nothing from the fact that the pianist is not in paroxysms of tears as she plays. Neither should we think that to be moved by music is to suffer whatever emotions the music apparently expresses. If I, whether performing or listening, identify a certain expressive character in the music and am moved by it, it does not follow that I suffer the corresponding emotions. If the music is tempestuous, I may simply register that fact. Impressed with the music, I may be calmly satisfied. My reaction is in no way deficient. I react with perception to what I hear. To summarize, then, when a piece of music is sad, we are not justified in thinking that the composer was sad when he created it, the performer sad when she plays it, or the listener sad when she hears it. It is the music itself which is sad.

The view that it is the music itself which is sad is known as 'cognitivism'. In the aesthetics of music, cognitivism is the theory that our descriptions of music tell us what properties the music has, rather than how the music affects us or what the composer was expressing by means of it. So a description of a piece of music as stormy describes the music itself. Historically, cognitivism has allied itself with the view that music is, essentially, a formal art of decoration and pattern, and that its value lies in that, rather than in its power to conjure up or relate to the extra-musical.

The opposition to cognitivism is complex and varied. There are writers who point to the way in which music is integrated into the patterns of our social life, into its rituals and practices; they may argue that the relative isolation of music is a modern Western phenomenon, something local and particular, and does not represent the situation of music in other societies or in the West at other times. Other musics, other metaphysics! Or they may argue that the picture of music as a formal art misrepresents the significance of music for us in this Western society. In particular, there is a movement amongst 'humanistic musicologists' which advocates understanding music as drama and narrative; in the words of Anthony Newcomb, music is 'a composed novel';[8] such stories or 'programmes', spun around the music by earlier writers on music and scorned by formalists, have become respectable once again.

---

[8] Anthony Newcomb, 'Once More between Absolute and Program Music: Schumann's Second Symphony', *Nineteenth Century Music*, 7 (1984), 234. See also Jenefer Robinson (ed.), *Music and Meaning* (Ithaca, NY: Cornell University Press, 1997).

Then there are those who believe that we value music because
it infects us with its passions. Many philosophers of the analytic
persuasion will argue vehemently for this, and it is to them that we
must now turn.

### (ii) Arousalism

Although I think that there is a consensus that expressionism is
false as a description of composer or performer, there has been a
recent move by Colin Radford, Aaron Ridley, Derek Matravers,
and others to re-establish one element of the classical expressionist theory: the thesis that what music expresses is mirrored in the
hearer. They believe that the power of music can be explained in
this way. For example, many have been persuaded by Colin
Radford's argument that if a grey wet day can make me feel sad,
then there is no reason to deny that slow, subdued music can make
me feel grave. Even the arch-cognitivist Peter Kivy wavers.[9]

There is a second route to arousalism. Consider this question:
Does the fact that a piece of music has a particular expressive character have anything to do with its value? If there is a connection,
arousalism offers an explanation of the link. Malcolm Budd, for
one, thinks that the expressive qualities which a piece has are
grounds for valuing it. Prima facie the claim seems strange. The
oddness of the claim that the grave quality of the opening movement of Beethoven's Op. 101 sonata is a reason for valuing it lies
partly in the fact that there is a mountain of bad, grave music. The
fact is that there is poor sad music and poor joyful music. Indeed,
the possibilities of the latter are much explored by musical ironists
like Shostakovich. Budd implies that a good-making characteristic
like gravity can be offset by some failings,[10] so that the work need
not be good overall. But this does not dispose of the fact that to

---

[9] Colin Radford, 'Emotions and Music: A Reply to the Cognitivists', *Journal of
Aesthetics and Art Criticism*, 47/1 (1989), 69–76; *idem*, 'Muddy Waters', *Journal of
Aesthetics and Art Criticism*, 49 (1991), 242–52. Aaron Ridley, 'Musical Sympathies:
The Experience of Expressive Music', *Journal of Aesthetics and Art Criticism*, 53/1
(1995), 49–57; *idem*, *Music, Value and the Passions* (Ithaca, NY: Cornell University
Press, 1995); Derek Matravers, *Art and Emotion* (Oxford: Oxford University Press,
1998); Peter Kivy, 'Auditor's Emotions: Contention, Concession and Compromise',
*Journal of Aesthetics and Art Criticism*, 51/1 (1993), 1–12; see also *idem*, *Music Alone*
(Ithaca, NY: Cornell University Press, 1990), ch. 8; Alan Goldman, 'Emotions in
Music (A Postscript)', *Journal of Aesthetics and Art Criticism*, 53/1 (1995), 59–69.
[10] Malcolm Budd, *Values of Art* (London: Allen Lane, 1995), 146.

say of a work that it is grave seems to be no reason at all for thinking it good.

However, we could certainly concede to Budd that there are
cases where a certain expressive character is necessary for a work,
and without which the work would be less successful. Just that
expressive quality, a sort of troubled wistfulness, is what is required
for the finale to Beethoven's Quartet in A minor Op. 132. This is a
matter of what expressive character is required for a given context.
But, more generally, we might, I suppose, value that music of,
say, Mozart or Schubert which displays an equivocal quality just
because of its ambiguity. I am thinking of some of Schubert's
dances for piano or of some of those movements by Mozart which
are sometimes rather sentimentally described as 'smiling through
tears'. In such cases it is also true that a failure to grasp the expressive character will be a crucial failure on our part to comprehend
them, and may render us incapable of the important judgements
that perceptive listeners need to make. But such cases are comparatively rare. I do not generally prize music for its expressive
qualities. As an unqualified assertion, Budd's thesis is wrong.

The general problem here is that we slide very quickly into that
old difficulty with criteria for value in the arts. If the possession of
an expressive character can be characterized sufficiently generally
to count as a reason for valuing a work, then the objection arises
that qualities such as gravity will be found in works both good and
bad. But if the criteria are made precise enough to fit an individual case, they end up as not reasons at all (for reasons are general),
but mere pointings. They register what attracts the speaker about
this particular work. But if we cannot characterize the piece so as
to reveal its expressive character without simply pointing at the
particular work, then what is the relationship between the expressive character of the piece and its value? How does one stand as a
basis for the other? Arousalism, is, of course, one answer. It is
because experiences we value match the expressive content of the
music that we can base an evaluation of the music on that expressive content.

However this may be, it is a sufficient rebuttal of the arousalist
thesis that it is one thing to characterize music in terms of such
expressive predicates and quite another to think that we generally
experience these emotions ourselves as a result of hearing the
music. What we recognize as the character of the music is not

usually what we feel. Music moves us, and moves us powerfully. But it is a mistake, and a central mistake, in Aaron Ridley's version of arousalism[11] that he assumes that when we are moved by music, we are moved to whatever expressive character the music bears. I may agree with Ridley that the slow movement of the 'Eroica' is 'heavy-hearted but resolute', but I deny that I feel heavy-hearted or resolute when I respond. It is also a mistake to think that we are regularly and typically moved this way. Most of the music I enjoy, follow, and appreciate I do so without such emotional involvement, and my reaction, I maintain, is in no way deficient. I listen to the classic performance of the Fauré Violin Sonata by Grumiaux and Crossley, music which we might describe as 'reticent'. It absorbs me, and I shall listen to it again and again, following the flow of the music, but at no time am I 'reticent' (whatever that might be). Again, my reaction seems to me to lack nothing important. Indeed, I find it very difficult to recognize in myself the states of yearning, anger, and melancholy which arousalists claim music sparks in them. Like Peter Kivy, I am prepared to 'swear by the dog' that sad music does not make me sad. Indeed, if music does affect me, it might be grounds for objecting to it. Sometimes I find a work objectionable because of its expressive qualities; I might dislike a piece because it is sentimental, for example, and my revulsion is compounded if it actually makes me sentimental as well. I may object because I am being manipulated, and that is at the very heart of the discomfort some of us feel about two composers of very different stature, Puccini and Wagner.

As a general thesis, arousalism will not do. Of course, music moves me. It always has and, I hope, always will. Berlioz described his experience thus,

My whole being seems to vibrate; at first it is a delightful pleasure, in which reason does not appear to participate at all. The emotions increase in direct ratio with the force or grandeur of the agitation in the circulation of the blood. My pulses beat violently, tears, which usually give evidence of the crisis of a paroxysm, indicate only a progressive stage, and a greater excitement and agitation is to follow. When the crisis is really reached there occur spasmodic contractions of the muscles, a trembling in all the limbs, a total numbness of feet and hands, a partial paralysis of the nerves of vision and hearing. I no longer can see and can hardly hear. (from 'The Art of Music', 'A Travers Chants')

[11] Ridley, *Music, Value and the Passions*.

Trust Berlioz to overstate. Still, my own reactions are powerful enough. My first experience, as a teenager, of a live performance of the Sanctus from Bach's B minor Mass was unforgettable. I trembled, tears ran down my face, I shivered. Was this emotion? I was certainly moved. But I did not feel what the music expressed. Other occasions are, well, occasions: listening to Curzon playing Mozart and guessing that he had not too long to live, Janet Baker faltering at the words 'Farewell Brother dear' in a memorial performance of *Gerontius* for Barbirolli, Lotti Lehmann's last recital when she was unable to complete Schubert's 'An die Musik' (whose words, 'I thank thee, holy art' would be a fitting epitaph for any musician). In such cases the music combines with extraneous factors to move us, and I might be moved even though I find *Gerontius* a tedious work.

Is there an alternative form of arousalism? In a recent book Derek Matravers[12] offers various formulations which differ from the sort of account preferred by Ridley and Radford. Thus he claims that we experience music as sad,[13] or, elsewhere, that we hear sadness in the music.[14] (These locutions fit rather uneasily with the more unabashed arousalism to be found in remarks such as 'a piece of sad music causes feelings which cause the belief that the music is sad'.[15])

Now we do not say that we experience the grass as green. What could be the reason for saying that we hear the music as sad, rather than saying that we hear that the music is sad? The talk of 'hearing as' implies an analogy with 'seeing as'; so the suggestion might be that just as we can see Wittgenstein's famous drawing as a duck or as a rabbit, so we might hear music as sad or as something quite other. But no reflection at all is required to convince us that this is not so. The music *is* sad, and in most cases there is no other defensible way of hearing it. There is music which has an ambiguous quality, and it may be necessary to call our attention to the fact that this finale by Schubert is not in fact jolly and carefree after all. But such cases are certainly not typical, and are not what Matravers, for one, has in mind.[16] The problem, then, is that talk of hearing the sadness in the music seems to oscillate between two alternatives: first, that the music makes us feel sad—a proposition which looks unacceptable as a general principle inasmuch as many musically

---

[12] Matravers, *Art and Emotion.*  [13] Ibid. 115, 190, 199.
[14] Ibid. 170.  [15] Ibid. 188–9.  [16] Ibid. 176.

experienced listeners deny it—or it collapses into cognitivism, in which case 'I hear the music as sad' simply means 'I recognize that the music is sad'.

Something else is perhaps afoot. In that memorable final interview, the writer Dennis Potter, within a month of his death, said that never had the apple blossom seemed so white as it had that spring. 'The whitest, frothiest, blossomest blossom.' Most of us have had such comparably intense experiences, and there are occasions when a performance of music moves us particularly. This might tempt us into trying to find some other description for what is going on. Critics sometimes say of a performance that it is revelatory, and they may go on to say that it showed something about the work which they had not heard before. One thing is true about our experience of music and our experience of the other arts: namely, the question 'What was it like for you?' is always a pertinent question. In that sense the experience may be a 'rich' or 'thick' experience.[17] But I believe that a proper answer in the case of music might just be 'fascinating', 'absorbing', 'interesting', or, indeed, 'boring'. Now here the question of value which Budd and others think is intimately connected with the expressive character of music is at issue. The problem is that different issues have been confused: first, on what basis we describe music as sad; second, what the content of our experience of music is; and, third, on what basis we value music.

A restricted and more plausible form of arousalism is proposed by Jenefer Robinson, who argues: 'music can make me feel tense or relaxed; it can disturb, unsettle and startle me; it can calm me down or excite me; it can get me tapping my foot, singing along or dancing; it can maybe lift my spirits and mellow me out. . . . I am myself emotionally involved in the music.'[18]

I agree with Robinson's list. I think she catches with precision the range of reactions we have to music. None of them, of course, implies a positive evaluation by itself, and, more significantly, these reactions do not generally match the expressive character of the music. They do not necessarily 'mirror' it. Syrupy Christmas music unsettles me, as does a great deal of pop music, especially when I am unfortunate enough to catch the lyrics. Nor do I see why I

[17] See R. A. Sharpe, 'The Empiricist Theory of Artistic Value', *Journal of Aesthetics and Art Criticism* (forthcoming).

[18] Jenefer Robinson, 'The Expression and Arousal of Emotion in Music', *Journal of Aesthetics and Art Criticism*, 52/1 (1994), 18 ff.

should say that I am emotionally involved. Of course, I might be, but just to be startled or calmed is not *ipso facto* to be put in an emotional state.

So what is to be said here? Musically sensitive writers claim that music arouses the feelings it expresses in its listeners. But the objections to this seem terminal. The critic has a couple of options. First, he can say that Radford and Ridley, like others, misdescribe their experience of music. Or he can say that they do describe their experiences, but what they describe is merely one form of musical experience (a form which used to be described in a derogatory way as 'wallowing'). This second is compatible with Kivy's conclusion, that musical experiences vary. Perhaps my musical experience, like my taste in music, simply differs from that of Radford. He has nothing to say here about musical texture, architecture, or the pleasures of watching a master manipulating his materials. In which case he omits what is central to the interest of sophisticated listeners.

Of course, Radford might respond, 'What's wrong with wallowing?', and object, with some justification, to the pejorative tone. The answer must be that if an emotional reaction (if that is what it is) precludes recognition of the skill of the composer and performer, and if it replaces following the musical argument, then it obscures from the listener an important part of the music. In the worst case, the music is being used to arouse a state in which the listener luxuriates. In such cases other music might do the job as well. A sophisticated arousalist like Ridley will then counter that the mirroring state has to be an analogue of the precise expressive nature of the music, and may be too exact to be captured in words. In such a case the arousalist will argue that the response is fully equal to the individuality of the music. As for the phenomenological point that an overwhelming sense of lassitude which mirrors the musical character of *Prelude à l'après midi d'une faune* or the energy which matches the expressive content of *The Rite of Spring* does get in the way of appreciating other features, the arousalist will counter that an intellectual appreciation of the music cancels out a vivid emotional response and is, in its way, as restrictive. That this is a popular move amongst the unsophisticated does not rob it of force. At this point honours might seem even.

But the force of the last reply does, I suspect, depend upon the erroneous assumption that to be aware of the structural qualities of music is somehow incompatible with being moved by the music.

## 1. NOS SOIRÉES/1. НАШИ ВЕЧЕРА

**Moderato** ($\downarrow$ = 80)

This is not my experience, or the experience of cultivated musicians and music-lovers with whom I have discussed the matter.

There are other problems. It is often not easy to characterize music. It is a gift which even people who are both musical and articulate may lack. Arousalists often recall Mendelssohn's contention. 'The thoughts which are expressed to me by music that I love are not too indefinite to put into words but, on the contrary, too definite.'[19] But to substantiate the thesis that the character of the experience matches the character of the music, it is necessary to describe both. But if you asked me to describe the precise expressive quality of, say, Janáček's opening number in the piano suite 'On an Overgrown Path' (Ex. 1) I don't think I could. Is it quietly happy or quietly sad? I cannot say. So far, we might seem to be following Mendelssohn. The precise quality of this music is ineffable; it cannot be put into words. However, if Mendelssohn is right, we ought at least to agree about these more general qualities before finding that we cannot settle the issue of the more fine-grained predicates. That is, if music is 'expressing' something more definite

[19] Quoted in S. Morgenstern, *Composers on Music* (London: Faber and Faber, 1968), 140.

and more precise than sadness, then we ought at least to be able to agree that the music is sad before we surrender any attempt to render the character more precisely. Almost certainly there will be a very broad level at which we can agree. However, between the very broad and the unsustainably precise there will be a whole range of predicates on whose application competent listeners cannot settle. Indeed, a good critic may be one who can find just the right phrase to help a listener to see a different character in a work. This is a gift which is particularly valuable when introducing music to a general audience whose members cannot read staff notation. Thus, to describe a Haydn finale as 'high-spirited' tells us not very much, and is hardly a description over which people will take issue. To say that it is 'high-spirited with a hint of menace' may be better. There may be disagreements between good listeners as to whether this accurately describes its character, but it is a focus for attention. In this context we see what use 'expressive predicates' can have; one valuable role begins to emerge just at the point when they cease to be straightforward descriptions; either their metaphorical content becomes more prominent, or—and the upshot is the same—they become subjects for dispute. Still, these considerations notwithstanding, the argument favours Mendelssohn. At least sometimes, what music expresses may not be put into words. Of course, we can give up the attempt too easily. Is there any reason to suppose that when a section of a work by Mozart hovers between smiling and tears, this cannot be captured in words? In fact, I have just done so. The adaptation and juxtaposition of existing terms does the trick. The fact that no single word suffices does not imply that the state is ineffable.

I shall need to return to the question of ineffability in a different context later in this chapter. But, in the interim, there is another possibility to be considered, one which does not carry the consequence that the music has a content which is ineffable. Suppose for a minute that I cannot describe the exact expressive content of that piece by Janáček. I need not conclude that there is an expressive state for which I lack the vocabulary but which the music does characterize. I might equally assume that there is no further content awaiting description. The assumption that there must be one confuses the individuality of the music with a distinct expressive content. Indeed, if there were a state incapable of being captured in words, we might also have prima-facie arguments against supposing that it could be instantiated in the listener, and this would constitute a further objection to arousalism.

A stronger argument might run along these lines. We share with animals a certain repertoire of mental states: anxiety, curiosity, etc. Refinements of these take their precise form from intensional features, the beliefs which are integral to them and the objects which they take. A dog can be aggressive, but not malicious or resentful. Such peculiar mental states require beliefs, motives, and a consciousness of objects peculiar to human beings, as far as we know. My resentment depends upon a belief that I have been deliberately injured. So the refinement of moods and emotions which we find in human beings depends upon certain beliefs and objects which are constitutive of these moods and emotions. They cannot be discriminated phenomenologically. The greater the variety in the species of generic moods or emotions, the greater the role of such intensional elements. In order to discriminate very minutely a mental state, we need just that apparatus of objects, context, and associated beliefs lacking in music. Music has no beliefs, therefore music will not possess such refined states. Of course, it can be broadly characterized, but narrower characterizations may be arbitrary.[20] There is no determinate yet ineffable content in the music which arouses a determinate yet ineffable content in the listener.

We may recall, too, the argument rehearsed earlier. Irony in music relies upon the music having a surface which belies its real character. Shostakovich writes deliciously sentimental music in the slow movement of the Second Piano Concerto, but we do not take it at face value. The sense that he is, gently and affectionately, guying the genre makes us reluctant to describe it as simply sentimental. Once this is granted, arousalism faces further difficulties. Which is the state to be mirrored: that on the surface of the music or what the composer expresses through it? I assume that I can be moved to sentimentality, but I am not sure what it would be to be moved to irony. Arousalists owe us an answer.

Music has many faces, and perhaps it is the restricted diet of examples which philosophers use which has prevented them from seeing this. It is proper to describe Spohr's delectable Double

---

[20] Cf. Alan Tormey, *The Concept of Expression* (Princeton: Princeton University Press, 1971), 136.

Quartet Op. 65 as charming. But though we are here, as so often, shifting a predicate normally descriptive of human beings to music, 'charming' is not a mental state. However, 'being charmed' is, and in this case it is the causal power of the music to charm us on which the expressive character is based. Arousalism looks right here. But there are many other expressive descriptions of music which could not possibly be mirrored in the listener. As I write, I am listening to Mexican polyphony by Padilla. It is sublime, but it does not express sublimity; nor is my state sublime (whatever that could be). It exhilarates, but it does not express exhilaration. Davies observes that music may amaze me, but does not express amazement.[21] There is much music which does not seem to have an expressive face at all. Commentators from Hanslick to Gurney have pointed out that not all music is expressive of emotion.[22] Hanslick thinks that Bach's Forty-Eight Preludes and Fugues are examples of abstract music in which the emotions are absent. Perhaps the examples are ill chosen, but, no doubt, we could find music by Boulez or Elliott Carter which we might think it impossible or crazily inappropriate to characterize in expressive terms. When we do describe music in terms drawn from human activities, the vocabulary ranges far beyond moods and emotions. There are many predicates which we use to describe music which have no relation to mental states. The opening bars of the Haydn quartets Op. 71 and 74 frequently sound like a command to the audience to pay attention. Handel's music often has a public oratorical manner unique to him. Indeed, recent work has raised the question of the relationship between music and rhetoric, and I shall turn to this issue in the second chapter. For the time being, let me register my discontent with the terms in which the expressiveness of music has been discussed. Some music produces a matching reaction in a receptive audience; some does not; some music entitles us to conclude that the composer has the character we ascribe to the music; some does not. To the extent that arousalism is defensible, the range of expressive predicates it covers is slight.

[21] Stephen Davies, *Musical Meaning and Expression* (Ithaca, NY: Cornell University Press, 1994), 190.
[22] Edmund Gurney, *The Power of Sound* (New York: Basic Books, 1966). Eduard Hanslick, *Vom Musikalisch-Schonen*. Trans. as *On the Musically Beautiful* by G. Payzant, Indianapolis: Hackett, 1986, and as *The Beautiful in Music* by G. Cohen Indianapolis: Bobbs-Merrill, 1957.

### (iii) The Asymmetry Question

Still, the arousalist can force a concession, and the concession leads to what I shall call 'the asymmetry' problem. Again it depends upon introspective reports (though others with whom I have discussed this bear me out). I say that sad music does not make me sad, or tragic music tragic (whatever that might be). But I acknowledge that exuberant music makes me exuberant, and cheerful music cheerful. So there is an asymmetry here. The sheer life-enhancing exuberance of Benny Goodman's small group jazz from the Thirties or the unrestrained joy and gaiety of Tippett's Concerto for Double String Orchestra is a reason for valuing it. The mood it creates matches the mood of the music. But music which is grave or sad does not, *ceteris paribus*, depress me. I will need external reasons to be saddened or depressed. So whereas music which is exuberant may make me exuberant, and I may value it precisely for that, I do not value music which is sad in the same way. The arousalist, then, can point to an important concession.[23]

Why should negative expressive qualities not affect me whilst positive ones do? Whilst I may acknowledge that I do remain sober in the presence of sad music, sad music may impress me without making me sad.

One answer, I suppose, is that this is a brute fact about some human psychologies, and, in the end, this may be all that there is to be said. But I think there may be at least a partial explanation. The explanation is that there is a cognitive element in our reaction to music, a recognition that music is a human creation, composed and played. An appreciation of creativity is an intrinsic part of our response. So even in cases where arousalism seems plausible—for example, when I become exuberant listening to exuberant music—my reaction involves a judgement, and the judgement is that the music has this quality and that it is good. It is like the exhilaration I may experience in watching an outstanding game of cricket or football. The causal force is indirectly effective. It depends upon my judgement. Part, too, of that judgement is the recognition of supreme skill on the part of composer or performer. My admiration of the music and of the composer's skill in, say a Mozart piano

---

[23] Cf. Charles Avison, *An Essay on Musical Expression* (London, 1775), 4; and Daniel Webb, *Observations on the Correspondence between Music and Poetry* (London, 1769), 28, both of whom think that music arouses only the pleasurable emotions. This is, of course, not quite my position, but it is similar.

concerto, is an essential ingredient in my being moved by it. 'He is capable of this' is the thought, and, equally, when I hear Janet Baker sing Fauré, I wonder at her ability to catch just the right inflection. It would not be a very musical response if there were no awe at her artistry. My reaction is not a gut reaction caused in me by the music. There is a cognitive element which explains the exhilaration of recognizing the best.

But such an answer, although it seems to me to meet the phenomenological facts, cuts both ways. It will equally be the case that I am exhilarated by grave music in which I see the supreme accomplishment of the creative hand. And, of course, I may be. Then the arousalist has to acknowledge that the character of the music is not mirrored in our response; in this case, where the music is tragic, we are exhilarated. My sobriety at the Funeral March from the 'Eroica' is a matter of observing the proprieties; listening to it alone, without allowing associations to enter and acknowledging its mastery, I may find it exhilarating. But music's link with dance and movement renders the 'brute fact' account preferable. We are, I suspect, thrust back into the intuitively plausible position of saying that exuberance and vigour are infectious, whilst sobriety is not. Vigorous movement excites; whereas sedate movement does not make us sedate unless additional factors operate.

The arousalist faces a final problem. Levinson raises for music the time-honoured aesthetic puzzle as to why we would choose to experience those emotions which are our normal reaction to the ghastly, the terrifying, the revolting, or otherwise disturbing.[24] Why do I go to the cinema to see Cronenberg's *The Fly* when I have some inkling that I shall be disturbed and revolted? Likewise, why listen to music which is sad? Only if you think the negative emotions which are evoked in these contexts are emotions which we actually experience can there be a problem with negative emotions in music. But whatever the case as far as drama or film is concerned, there is no reason to think that negative emotions are involved in music. That the slow movement of Elgar's Second Symphony expresses grief gives me no prima-facie reason to avoid it, reasons which somehow have to be countered by more positive ones. Not only do I not think that music alone can make you grieve, but I deny that music makes us sad (save the bizarre experience of being

[24] Jerrold Levinson, *Music, Art and Metaphysics* (Ithaca, NY: Cornell University Press, 1990), 306 ff.

made sad by a bad performance, but that usually makes us irritated or angry—I take it that these cases are not at issue). If I become sad, it is because the music recalls other associations. Thus, though the first movement of Janáček's piano sonata 'i. x. 1905' expresses rage, I have never felt rage listening to it. (It commemorates the death of a carpenter in a street demonstration at the hands of Austrian troops.) In a good performance I may find the figure at bars 11–21 thrilling and exhilarating. If I think of the events which this sonata commemorates, I may feel rage. In the same way, I might feel sympathy for Janáček at the opening number of 'On an Overgrown Path', which is simply entitled 'Our evenings'. I recall that it is a remembrance of his daughter Olga. It might represent just those family evenings when each attends to his or her own concerns in an atmosphere of quiet contentment. If this was Janáček's thought, then it might have been sentimental; perhaps they were usually at loggerheads; but then again I might empathize with somebody who remembers the best of his days and glosses over the worst; it is human. What has this to do with the music? Well, as we shall see in a later chapter, music cannot be isolated as a purely formal art. These connections matter. In the same way, I may be moved by what I take to be the genuine loss and bereavement expressed in Bishop King's 'Exequy'. That the writer is sorrowing for his wife matters; it is not merely a question of the properties of the verse in isolation from the life of the writer. But such situations are those where I know or believe that the music expresses an attitude of the composer towards an actual event or experience and where my responses are marked, in part, by understanding and sharing those responses.

Levinson gives a list of ways in which having negative emotions might be thought worthwhile; the music might facilitate our grasp of these emotions, and enable us to understand our feelings, to savour them, to imagine being in such a state, to encounter vicariously the power of the composer in writing such music, and so on. I remain unconvinced. The scherzo of Walton's symphony is marked, unusually, 'con malizia', but it does not make me feel malicious or enable me to understand more fully the nature of malice. If that is what I want, I would be better off seeing *Othello*. If it is a good performance of the Walton, I find it exhilarating, not malice-forming. I see no reason to think I acquire a better understanding of malice through the pure contemplation of the music. Indeed, a better understanding of the emotional life requires understanding how the emotions are or are not directed to the proper objects. We better understand malice, jealousy, or resentment when we see whether it is or is not justified, the sorts of circumstances which lead us to have these emotions, and how we can govern them effectively, if self-control is in question. Since it is precisely the relevant beliefs and objects which are absent in expressive music, Levinson's thesis is unsupportable.

## A PURE, CONCEPTLESS EXPERIENCE OF MUSIC?

No contemporary arousalist would, I imagine, deny that there are other important and valuable features of music over and above its impact upon our passions. They need not deny that learning about chord structures may help us to appreciate what Charlie Parker was up to; nor need they deny that knowing the various devices such as canon, inversion, augmentation, and diminution which a contrapuntal master like J. S. Bach uses helps us to evaluate his music. But they do, I presume, think that the arousal of states in the listener is of peculiar and central importance for the music-lover, and that it must be central in an answer to the question as to why we love and value music.

But there is a more extreme version of this that has its defenders; it is that music is to be valued not only inasmuch as it creates a state in us which is intrinsically valuable, but, more significantly, that what ideas we have about the music are either irrelevant to or actually spoil the pure musical experience. In ending this first chapter with a discussion of such an extreme theory which minimizes the importance of our understanding of musical structure and design, I shall pave the way for my claim that our experience of music is through and through imbued with ideas about the music, ideas which vary from the uncontroversial to the highly ideological.

So, let us now consider this extreme position with respect to the knowledge we bring to music. It is that, left to itself, music will speak to us. It is a mistake to think that we need to learn about it, that background facts about the society in which it originated, or that information about its structure and the influences upon it will enhance our appreciation. They merely interfere. What we need, if we are to take pleasure in the music itself, rather than pleasure in reflecting on how knowledgeable and cultured we are, is the music untrammelled. This approach is popular. Many ordinary people would endorse it. I suspect that its origins lie in Kant's notion of free beauty; it is, I think, yet another example of how philosophical ideas permeate into the general consciousness.[25] Perhaps surprisingly, the view has recently found an advocate in Nicholas Cook.[26]

This view, a view associated, on the one hand, with the idea that aesthetic properties are always and only perceptual properties, and, on the other, with the positivist idea of a primitive experience, a pure perception which is encapsulated in an observation statement, is a myth.

Let me begin with a famous passage from Proust's *A la recherche du temps perdu*:

The year before, at an evening party, he had heard a piece of music played on the piano and violin. At first he had appreciated only the material quality of the sounds which those instruments secreted. And it had been a source of keen pleasure when, below the delicate line of the violin-part, slender but robust, compact and commanding, he had suddenly become aware of the mass of the piano-part beginning to merge in a sort of liquid rippling of sound, multiform but indivisible, smooth yet restless, like the deep blue tumult of the sea, silvered and charmed into a minor key by the moonlight. But then at a certain moment, without being able to distinguish any clear outline, or to give a name to what was pleasing him, suddenly enraptured, he had tried to grasp the phrase or harmony—he did not know which—that had just been played and that had opened and expanded his soul, as the fragrance of certain roses, wafted on the moist air of evening, has power of dilating one's nostrils. Perhaps it was owing to his ignorance of music that he had received so confused an impression, one of those that are nonetheless the only purely musical impression, limited in their extent, entirely original and irreducible to any other kind.[27]

Proust describes in this passage the experience of music which a tyro might have: the sort of experience which opens a new world to us, which makes us aware that there are undreamt-of wonders and beauties to be explored. It is the sort of experience which leads

---

[25] Utilitarianism seems to me to have deeply infected modern thinking about morality amongst ordinary people as well as philosophers.

[26] Nicholas Cook, *Music, Imagination and Culture* (Oxford: Oxford University Press, 1990). Cf. Kivy, *Music Alone*, ch. 5.

[27] Marcel Proust, *Swann's Way: Remembrance of Things Past*, trans. C. K. Scott Moncrieff and Terence Kilmartin (Harmondsworth: Penguin, 1983), 227–8.

a sensitive child to become a music-lover. Some readers might be able to remember their first such experience—a Prom, perhaps, or some great music sung at a cathedral. In the last part of this chapter I shall discuss the aetiology of a love of music. But the passage also suggests a musical ideal for the mature music-lover, particularly the last few sentences. As regards this, I have severe misgivings.

In this passage Marcel is apparently aware of melodic lines and the differences of texture in the instrumental parts. He may not be able to recognize the music if he hears it again. Certainly there is an object of his experience, and he is aware of certain features whilst being unaware of others. Like a child who is absorbed in the sound of the trumpet, there is something to which he is attending, but, lacking a vocabulary for this, Marcel cannot describe what he hears. At most he can try to indicate what catches his attention by the use of metaphors ('the piano part beginning to emerge in a liquid rippling of sounds').

Two questions arise. First, could there be a pure, concept-free experience of music which we would value? Second, is his experience enhanced by the knowledge which he might later acquire of musical forms and patterns? Does he benefit from knowing that he is listening to a canon, for example? Nicholas Cook's asides about 'the appreciation racket' suggest that he believes that the untutored experience is only tainted by such preoccupations. These he assigns to the musical culture. Typical is his observation: 'my basic argument in this book is that there is always a disparity between the experience of music and the way in which we imagine or think about it'.[28]

Other writers have taken an interest in the first topic. Diana Raffmann devotes a recent book to arguing that some of our experience of music is ineffable.[29] If, indeed, this is so, it will follow that the paraphernalia of musical culture, the inversions, *canons canzicrans*, the augmentations and diminutions beloved of musicologists, will not capture that experience. Such 'learned reactions' are, again, irrelevant to an important part of our musical experience, though on grounds different and more radical than Cook's. If there is such an ineffable knowledge of music, that knowledge is non-conceptual.

[28] Cook, *Music, Imagination and Culture*, 135.
[29] Diana Raffmann, *Music, Language and Mind* (Cambridge, Mass.: Bradford Books, MIT Press, 1993).

Whether this is so depends upon what ineffability amounts to. But we have as yet no definition of ineffability. A first stab at a definition would be that *x* is ineffable if I cannot describe it in such a way that my hearer can identify it if she has not previously experienced it. You might be tempted to say that you have to experience the sound of an oboe to know what it is like. But I am inclined to reply that it depends upon the relative skill and degree of articulateness of the describer and on the background of the hearer. If a pupil who has been playing in a wind band with clarinets, flutes, horns, and bassoons but lacking oboes asks me what an oboe sounds like, and I tell her that it is a nasal, plaintive reed instrument with a treble register, I would expect her to pick out the sounds on a first hearing (provided she is not being confused with oboes da caccia or oboes d'amore). Without a setting we cannot answer the question as to what, if anything, is ineffable. There is an interesting analogy with recognizing a human face. No description of a human face can usually be given which is good enough for its hearer to pick out an individual in a crowd, though a description might be given so that I could pick out somebody at a small party. (I suspect this might prove quite a deep truth about human beings and their interrelations, the extraordinary individuality of the human physiognomy and its undescribability.)

A second try: x is ineffable if I cannot describe it in such a way that my hearer misses nothing which she would have experienced had she been present. Cavell makes such a general observation about the arts. There is no substitute for hearing the music and seeing the painting (which gives one reason why much avant-garde 'art' cannot count as art, since we do not need to see or hear it, but only to be told about it for its full point to be registered). However, on such a definition, art is not alone; much is ineffable. Although I can describe a simple geometrical figure such as a cube so that my interlocutor knows everything I know about it, I cannot describe a curry, the taste of a wine, as well as the sound of a piece of music in such a way.

What is true is that until I hear the music, something is lacking. A test of this is the modes of metaphorical description that are open to me. Only when I hear a bassoon, can I appreciate the justice of Gordon Jacob's characterization, 'the high notes are querulous'. In the case of a metaphor I have to assess its appropriateness, its fitness. Of course, if I were given such a description before hearing the bassoon in its upper register, I might rightly take it to be true simply because the speaker knows about such things. Now whether we should describe such cases as ineffable, I do not know.

Raffman distinguishes structural ineffability, which occurs when a player just 'sees' where a phrase should end, without being able to give any further explanation, from the ineffability of the slightly delayed note, the nuance, the sharpened or flattened note which cannot be notated in existing metrical and tonal systems. It is this second which occupies most of her attention. Raffmann's difficulties arise from an inadequate and pre-Wittgensteinian view of language. Because nuances cannot be assigned to existing categories, they must be ineffable, she concludes. But of course they are described; she does it herself. 'Make that a little sharper', says the teacher. 'No, not as much as that'.

By contrast, Cook does not seem to require that the primitive musical experience is ineffable, though, as I have observed, it would entail some of his proposals. Salient amongst these is the thesis that the structure which musical theorists describe does not generally play a role in musical experience, even the experience of the musically sophisticated who are trained to recognize these things. For they often listen without paying that sort of attention.[30] These concepts belong to the culture of music, rather than to the listener's experience, and such structures can hardly be important to the pleasure of the listener if even those who can hear them do not bother.[31]

But Cook is surely too quick. To listen to music with concentration is not always easy. I put on a compact disc of a Haydn quartet. After a bit I pick up the newspaper. A favourite passage catches my attention, and I listen avidly for a few minutes, and then go on reading. Isn't this typical? It is also typical that when I finish, I am a little frustrated with myself for not paying attention. Now it may be that I know the music well, so I know, being a bit of a sophisticate, that this is one of Haydn's monothematic movements. I have studied it carefully in the past, in order to prepare a lecture on it. Now I play it for my favourite bits. Later I might listen more carefully with subdued lighting.

It is neither surprising nor regrettable that music should reward different degrees of concentration in different ways. I can read, and

---

[30] Cook, *Music, Imagination and Culture*, 3 and 53.
[31] Ibid. 46. Cook refers to some empirical research of his own.

I can read closely. In the same way, I can listen, and I can listen closely. Sometimes an early hearing of a work so grips me that I cannot let my mind wander. A great performer on stage, screen, or concert platform can seize and hold my attention. Cook certainly recognizes this, but thinks it atypical.[32] Atypical it may be, but in the arts we are constantly considering the ideal case, and if the best listening is listening in which we approach maximal awareness of the progress of the music, then, trivially, the best listening is concentrated listening. But although this pays the greatest respect to the music, we often use music for other purposes, as background or as a source of examples for a discussion like this. This is not immoral. So the fact that an awareness of structure does not play a role in all listening has no consequences of note. It does not follow that our best experience of music is not that in which we are most aware of such structure, and it certainly should not be assumed, as Cook seems to assume, that pleasure is the proper goal of listening.[33] I shall say more about this later.

I have said that Cook thinks of the formal analysis of music as belonging to a culture of music, which develops under its own steam. The form, according to Cook, is not so much something to hear as a way of hearing things.[34] His remarks suggest a kind of positivism which emerges at various points in the book. He thinks of the work of music as a sound pattern which gives pleasure to the listener in the ideal situation. To this the listener applies a set of concepts which he draws from a musical culture, a culture which, over the last century and a half, has been concerned almost exclusively with formal properties such as thematic relations, transformations, harmonic relations, and the like. Through the application of these concepts, the heard music acquires a different intentional character. Although Cook does not enlarge on this, I imagine that the intentional character is displayed in the way we think of the music as possessing tonal direction and such like. To suppose that the formal features discussed in analysis are features of the music itself is, according to Cook, to commit a fallacy, the fallacy of reification.[35]

---

[32] Cook, *Music, Imagination and Culture*, 66.

[33] A view which seems to be universally held. See Richard Taruskin, *Text and Act* (Oxford: Oxford University Press, 1995), 30, and compare with his more sensible remarks later on (p. 314).

[34] Cook, *Music, Imagination and Culture*, 48.    [35] Ibid. 225–6.

Nevertheless, despite his acknowledgement of the 'intentional', Cook's own position owes too much to positivism. Contrary to what he thinks, the work of music is not an intentional object because the musical culture chooses to view it as such (and might not). It is an intentional object because it was written by a composer who himself belonged to that musical culture and used the very formal techniques that analysis unfolds. We do not 'hear' the *Pathetique* as a sonata. It really *is* a sonata. The situation is in no way similar to Wittgenstein's duck–rabbit picture. This can be seen as a duck or seen as a rabbit, but to the question 'Which is it really?' there is no answer. But there is an answer to the question 'Is the "Pathetique" really a sonata?' and the answer is a resounding 'Yes'. For the creative intentions which are themselves inconceivable in the absence of a musical culture characterize the work *ceteris paribus*. It is not an object whose properties are merely perceptual. Cook admits this in so far as he concedes, illegitimately on his view, a distinction between a right and a wrong way of playing Schumann's 'Einsame Blumen'.[36] The assumption must be that the correct phrasing is that intended by Schumann, and that the player should observe it. But Schumann also wrote in a certain form, and that too must be respected by the player.

So what part does the knowledge that I am listening, say, to a canon play in my apprehension of the music? First of all, there is a continuum between appreciating the shape of a simple piece and following longer and more complex structures. To follow a simple unaccompanied strophic song like the beautiful unaccompanied Irish melody 'She moved through the fair' (Ex. 2) requires that we appreciate it as a tune and not as disconnected notes. Mentally we 'punctuate it'. But that requires a gestalt; we have a sense of closure as each phrase draws to an end. We notice points of rest, a stepwise

---

[36] Ibid. 26.

cadence, or an arch. Unless something like this occurs, we are not hearing a tune; we are merely hearing discrete and unconnected notes. As we begin to grasp longer melodies, so we stretch our capacity to hold a single shape in the mind.

Cook's remarks strongly suggest that he thinks that there is an experience of music which is antecedent to the concepts in terms of which we describe it. It is clear from what I have just said that it cannot be entirely antecedent, because such an experience would cease to be a musical experience. I may not choose to tell myself or anybody else that the first phrase stops here, but it is clear that recognizing this or something akin to this must be part of my experience of music. But Cook might intend something different—perhaps a distinction between the concepts (of phrase, texture, etc.) involved when I hear a tune or notice the rich orchestral panoply of Strauss or the texture of a Monteverdi accompaniment and the more complex analytic procedures which he describes as belonging to the musical culture. (I am not even sure whether 'concept', which is a term of art in philosophy, is the right vocabulary for describing the phenomenon I am trying to catch.) The obvious rejoinder must surely be that there is a continuum between paying attention to a tune, a rhythm, or a sound texture, which are matters so primitive as to be essential for the listener to be hearing music at all, and the more complex forms of canon, two-, three-, and four-part writing, fugue, sonata form, harmonic structure, and the rest. A good deal of the effect of these more complex manœuvres will not be lost on a listener, even if he or she lacks the technical vocabulary which enables their description. Thus the excitement of the Finale of Schubert's Great C major Symphony has everything to do with the enormous force of tonal 'gravity', as Casals called it, dragging the music back to C major, and the listener who knows nothing about home keys and sonata form may still be overwhelmed by its effect. She notices what she cannot describe. Equally, the interweaving of lines in the Bach Double Violin Concerto will be the focus of attention of the involved listener, even if she does not know that the writing is imitative.

Such judgements as 'that again', minimal in their content, are a *sine qua non* for the most basic and most mindless appreciation of music. As our appreciation becomes more discriminating, so the concepts involved become more sophisticated. But the closer we are to the origins of our musical experience in the child's first fascination with sound, the closer we are to pleasure at mere beauty. Such a response is a limit, albeit the lower one. The infant has no capacity to imagine how the music might go on. No question of Hanslick's 'pondering of the imagination' here. This is what Wittgenstein might have called a 'primitive response'.

Of course, to understand the musical culture is to amplify one's understanding. There is a wonderful short motet by Tallis, a seven-part *Miserere*, in which the two superius voices sing a normal canon while the discantus part is also sung by two lower voices beginning at the same time, the three respectively doubly augmented, augmented and inverted, and triply augmented and inverted versions of the same line.[37] That Tallis could compose a piece of such intricate structure which nevertheless sounds so artless is a miracle. Awe at such a gift is an important aspect of our admiration for the arts.[38] By the same token, in drawing my attention to a feature of the music I have overlooked, an analyst may modify my experience of it. A passage which I had overlooked may become highlighted in my experience, and thereby change my overall sense of the work. Cook suggests that such a change will not enhance my experience of the music. He is certainly wrong.

In discussing Cook, the concept of pleasure has been moving increasingly centre-stage. Since this will play an important part in my subsequent discussions, it needs examination sooner rather than later.

## PLEASURE

What impressed me most was just how much most of the men around me *hated*, really *hated*, being there. As far as I could tell, nobody seemed to enjoy, in the way that I understood the word, anything that happened during the entire afternoon. Within minutes of the kick-off there was real anger ('You're a DISGRACE, Gould. He's a DISGRACE! A hundred quid a week? A HUNDRED QUID A WEEK! They should give that to me for watching you'); as the game went on, the anger turned into outrage and then seemed to curdle into sullen, silent, discontent.[39]

[37] See Paul Doe, *Tallis* (Oxford: Oxford University Press, 1968,) 41. The recording is by the Tallis Scholars on Gimell, and contains a memorable performance of the celebrated *Spem in alium*. Your life, dear reader, will be greatly the poorer if you do not hear this.

[38] A point well made by Peter Kivy, 'How Music Moves', in P. Alperson (ed.), *What is Music?* (New York: Haven, 1987), 158.

[39] Nick Hornby, *Fever Pitch* (London: Gollancz, 1992), 20.

Nick Hornby's book is a brilliant exploration of the way in which
grown men spend wet, cold, Saturday afternoons watching something that they rarely enjoy, sacrificing their peace of mind to a
quite arbitrary identification with one particular team, often a team
which has never achieved much and is never likely to. Why did I
not choose to support Manchester United, a team whose achievements are likely to give me pleasure?

Hornby obviously exaggerates. The supporters did not hate being
there. But it is reasonable enough to think that they did not enjoy
it. I have spent much time following professional sport on televi-
sion, in particular watching rugby union. The question is 'Why'? For
every game such as the Barbarians versus New Zealand in 1973, I
can tick off a dozen or so which were poor, in which the only spectacle on offer was thirty grown men wrestling in the mud, display-
ing a violence that would mean instant arrest anywhere else, or, if
they were playing a decent game like soccer, an immediate sending
off. I desperately want England to win, especially if they seem likely
to, and am wretchedly disappointed when they fail. Sometimes I
enjoy it, but more often I do not get any pleasure from the game.
Yet I compulsively watch it. In a word, I am 'interested' in it.

Now philosophers still frequently speak as though the reason for
listening to music is the pleasure it arouses in us. Pleasure is evidently a state of intrinsic worth which will account for why we value
the music. Any account which stresses the causal power of music
to move us is likely to find itself saddled with pleasure as the ultimate rationale for listening to music. But now reflect on your concert-
going experience as I have on sport! I go to many concerts. Do I
enjoy them? Well, it is hard to say. Sometimes I am dissatisfied with
the performance; sometimes it is dull, sometimes wrong-headed,
and sometimes just bad. The occasions on which the music is
brought to life are relatively few, though generally one piece in a
concert takes fire. Yet I still go, just as I still buy compact discs.
Indeed, if somebody invites me to listen to some new music, I am
prepared to try it, even though I know that the likelihood is that it
will be incomprehensible or boring. I don't expect to like it, because
I realize that only a tiny proportion of music is deeply moving and
affecting, and it is highly improbable that this new piece by Birtwhistle or Glass will be in this class. Yet I will listen, as the saying
goes, 'out of interest'. The natural rejoinder from an advocate of
pleasure as the end motive will be that I listen on the off-chance

that it will give me pleasure. But when the chances are so remote, is that a reasonable account?

The fact is that I love music, and I am very interested in it. Life without music would be, I am inclined to guess, very nearly intolerable. A day does not go by without my listening to music and playing a keyboard instrument. I do not do it for an end. I do it out of love. The focus of my interest is the music. That is the object. I don't pursue it because of what I can get out of it; that would be a travesty. My interest in music is, in the proper sense, disinterested, and to suggest that music-lovers are concerned with what it can do for them is to attribute to us a sort of egoism. It is the music that counts (or the film or the poem if you are more deeply interested in another art). I may be saddened by a film. Is that a reason for not watching it, or for advising somebody else not to see it? I might avoid a disturbing film if I am depressed or unstable. But this is not usually the case. I might listen to the shrieks and howls of Maxwell Davies's *Songs for a Mad King* and be glad to have heard them. Do they give me pleasure? Well, not really. Do they interest me? Certainly. I am astounded at their power and imagination, and that is enthralling even if they are disturbing, alarming, and discomforting. Although I do not deny that much music gives us pleasure, and that the pleasure of the connoisseurs is the basis for our judgement about the value of such music, it would be sentimental philistinism to seek only pleasure in the arts. Yet such a sentimental philistinism has found its way into most philosophical accounts of the arts. Taruskin, writing about Bach's cantatas, rightly observes that 'the idea that great music can be ugly, or ugly great, is unthinkable to most music lovers'.[40] We forget the religious context of the cantatas, and forget that Bach intended to harrow his listeners.

Equally importantly, an essential feature of learning about the arts in general and music in particular is ignored in such a view; it is that we learn where and when to discount our pleasure. A piece may be enjoyable without my thinking it good. On occasions I have been angered because I am moved by something which I think is meretricious and obtains its results by cheap effects. Many feel this way about the music of Puccini, and some about the music of Richard Strauss. Part of the problem may be the fact that we feel that this music manipulates us. The composer sets out to thrill or

---

[40] Taruskin, *Text and Act*, 314.

to move us, and chooses his means very deliberately. So the music may be enjoyable; it may give us pleasure. But, none the less, we judge it harshly.

The question is, of course, how may this be done? How can we, for example, discount the pleasure we take in the music? Unquestionably, pleasure is one indicator of worth in music, arguably more central in the case of music than in the other arts. Of course, it has to be qualified as far as any judgement of the 'real' quality of the work is concerned, by insisting that it is the pleasure of the experienced or qualified that counts. However, most writers grossly overemphasize its place in motivating our interest in the arts.

According to my analysis, indicators such as pleasure can be displaced or rendered nugatory through some overarching view of what is valid. It is not hard to imagine cases where somebody misjudges the cause of his pleasure; he might think that the pleasure is caused by the work of art, when it is actually caused by something extraneous not only to the merits of the work, but perhaps to the music itself. Suppose he enjoys a concert not because of the quality of the music but because of the company of the pretty girl he is with, or because he met the chairman of the local Conservative Party during the interval, or, at Glyndebourne, was able to fix a highly lucrative deal concerning sugar futures during supper. He might be mistaken in thinking that it is the music he enjoyed; he could make the mistake because he wants to be cultured, wants to enjoy music, and would prefer not to be, or to think of himself, as merely a greedy speculator. Contrary to what is sometimes imagined, the causes of pleasure may sometimes be discovered through inductive methods. On another occasion he hears *Jenufa* and does not enjoy it, and then realizes that he misidentified the cause of his pleasure. In such cases I take the object of pleasure to be the same as the cause of the pleasure. We can say that he thought that the object of his pleasure was the opera, and it was also the opera which he thought was the cause of his pleasure, but on both counts he was mistaken.

But these are not the significant cases, of course. Much more interesting are the cases where a critic listens to some new music, say, by Finnissey or by Stockhausen. May he not find it difficult to distinguish between cases in which his pleasure is caused by the music and cases in which, whilst the music is the occasion, his pleasure is magnified by the thought of being in the same fold as the *cognoscenti*? He catches something interesting; in his anxiety to get to grips with the music, he mistakes his enthusiasm for the daybreak with pleasure owing no more to outside factors than does his pleasure in Mozart. In such a case he has got the object of his pleasure right—it is the concert; but he has misrepresented to himself the features of the object which produce the major part of the impact upon him. What is crucial is that the music is advanced and difficult. His pleasure in fact depends upon features ancillary to the qualities of the music itself.

I do not deny, incidentally, that pleasure in the classics may be enhanced by a feeling that your taste is maturing. This is quite important for the developing listener, and I do not underestimate it. There are delights in learning about the world of the arts, as there is a thrill of discovery in finding music new to you which is strange and excitingly different from what you have heard before. But the tyro is anxious to enjoy a work whose stature is beyond dispute. The problem in my example is that the critic has a rather different interest in enjoying the work; since critics cannot be eagles, they hope at least to be cuckoos. The kudos of recognizing a new talent is much prized, and the critic's pleasure may be enhanced by his anxiety to enjoy the work. Philosophers will be familiar with a parallel problem. How often has one wrestled with some mannered writing only to find that what one took to be the pleasure of illumination was not so much illumination about a philosophical issue as pleasure at having at last found out what the writer was trying to say? The thesis turns out to be a rash generalization or a triviality dressed in portentous language. It is not so far from mistaking the relief of recognizing any landmark in the music for pleasure taken in the music itself.

Terence Penelhum argues that whenever we are mistaken about the nature of the pleasure we take or about its object, the error must involve self-deception.[41] He agrees that we can be mistaken about the object and think it has properties which it does not have, but a mistake about the object itself must, he believes, be self-deceiving. My case is such an example; the visitor enjoyed the ambience and thought he was enjoying the music. I agree that it might be self-deception. That is a possibility. If the listener refused to acknowledge the real grounds of his pleasure, despite having the

---

[41] Terence Penelhum, 'Pleasure and Falsity', *American Philosophical Quarterly*, I (1964), 81–91.

evidence put in front of his nose, then we would probably judge
that he was self-deceiving. But it does not have to be self-
deception or lying. It could be just error. For it to be self-deception, the listener needs a motive for the error. He wants to enjoy
the music and wants to like it. So he refuses to admit that it is not
the music *qua* music which gives the pleasure.

So sometimes we discount pleasure. But not always. In some
cases we accept that the pleasure is genuine, but that it does not
provide grounds for valuing a work. Pleasure really occurs, is produced by a work, yet must be set aside. Why? There are various
reasons. If the reputation of the composer persuades us that this
cannot be a work of merit, we admit that the work fascinates, but
deny that the fascination will last. We think it gives no grounds for
appraising the music. So probably the most important reason for
doing so is the familiar one; we assume that the pleasures of art
ought to last. If we discount the pleasure on this occasion, then we
assume that the work will not continue to please us (unless, for
example, the grounds for pleasure on this occasion are to do with
a meretricious and loud performance which we can immediately
see is only superficially exciting but where we gauge that the work
has other qualities). An *education sentimentale* in the arts is essentially concerned with evaluating and, where necessary, discounting
pleasure, and many of the most important cases are those where
we believe that the cause of pleasure or the features which give
pleasure have been misidentified. A great work will repay many
hearings, and in listening again, we not only recapture the old experiences but acquire new ones as well. The good critic guides us
to these works. We may set down our interest in a particular work
or performance to our depraved or immature taste. More likely, we
will judge our taste to be eccentric. Where a work does not engage
us but we think it ought to, then we may conclude that we are too
unfamiliar with the idiom, that it requires rehearing, or we may
judge that we have a blind spot as far as that particular composer
or style is concerned.[42]

[42] Although I have not quoted from it directly, I have been much influenced by
Lionel Trilling's classic, *Sincerity and Authenticity* (Oxford: Oxford University Press,
1972). Some of the issues are discussed by Roger Scruton, 'Notes on the Meaning
of Music', in Michael Krausz (ed.), *The Interpretation of Music* (Oxford: Clarendon
Press, 1993), 193–202. Some of the ideas in this section received a previous airing in
R. A. Sharpe, 'Solid Joys or Fading Pleasures', in E. Schaper (ed.), *Pleasure, Preference and Value* (Cambridge: Cambridge University Press, 1983), 86–98.

To return to my earlier theme, it is now possible to reconstruct the moves which led Cook to his positivist view of music and the culture in which it is embedded. If you think that there is a context-free experience of music which is prior to learning about its methods and techniques, then it is natural to think that the experience is pleasurable. As a matter of the genealogy of an interest in the arts, this is surely right. I have watched infants, in evident pleasure, rocking to the rhythm of a street band. Such pleasure in sound and texture is presumably what Wittgenstein would have called a 'primitive reaction'. But it is the basis on which an interest in the arts grows. Now a requirement for an 'interest', as opposed to mere pleasure, is that we have ideas about music, that we can see how a piece develops, or that we can make comparisons between one work and another and one performance and another. Without such beliefs about it, we have no basis for having an interest in music as opposed to merely taking pleasure in it. The complexity, accuracy, and sophistication of these beliefs will vary, but nobody who has the slightest interest in music can be devoid of beliefs about the canon of great music, about what music is worth listening to, or about musical structure or about performers' abilities. Like many writers on aesthetics, Cook fails to distinguish between pleasure and interest. For the primitive basis for musical appreciation does not explain the nature of that appreciation in the adult. Such a conclusion commits the genetic fallacy.

It also displays the corrosive effect of utilitarianism. Just as an attempt to live one's life so as to maximize happiness is likely to be counter-productive, so any attempt to pursue the arts so as to maximize pleasure is likely to be counter-productive. The focus must always be the work, and our attention must be upon it and what it contains, not on the nature of our experience of it. When a writer like Malcolm Budd identifies artistic value with the 'intrinsic value of the experience the work offers',[43] he does us a disservice. The stress on experience seems to me to misplace the centre of our interest in the arts. I certainly would not say that I value my children or a friend for the intrinsic nature of the experience they offer; rather, I value them for what they are. Equally, it misrepresents my valuing the music of Janáček to say that I value it for the experience it gives me. I value it for what it is. This does not mean

---

[43] Budd, *Values of Art*, 13.

that I do not value my experience of the music of Janáček; I certainly do. But the valuing of the experience is not identical with valuing the work. Indeed, it is possible for me to do the former without the latter. I share with the late Dennis Potter a rural Nonconformist childhood in Gloucestershire during the Second World War. For me, like him, the effect of a hymn like 'Will there be any stars in my crown?' is quite extraordinarily powerful, yet the hymn itself is undoubtedly mawkish, trite, and false. I value the experience, and I can see no reason to deny that it is an aesthetic experience. But it does not lead me to value the hymn.

Furthermore, an approach which makes our experience central seems to give us no reason to work at a piece of music, to try hard to see what is in it, or to prepare ourselves for it by reading or listening to other works which might cast light upon it, except as a means to an end—namely, the increase of pleasure. If you believe that finding out more might dilute the experience, you will avoid it. If your current experience satisfies you, why look further? The misplacement this involves takes centre-stage in a currently fashionable aesthetics, functionalism, in which art is defined in terms of the intention to bring about certain valuable states in its public. But I dispute such an instrumentalist view.[44]

Giving primacy to the effect also seems to encourage choosing an interpretation whereby the work will come out best. If, by a judicious choice of interpretation, we can see *Meistersinger* as an onslaught on the evils of xenophobia, and thereby obtain an intrinsically valuable state thereby, there seems no reason on Budd's account not to do so. But the fact that the interpretation is unfounded, because there are good reasons to believe that Wagner's motive was racist, surely matters and, in fact, excludes such an interpretation.[45] Budd does not deny, of course, that the importance of my experience of hearing the 'Eroica' is that it is an experience *of* the 'Eroica'. He is not saying that if it is the experience that matters, anything which produces that state in us would do as well. We cannot say 'Take another minuet', observed Wittgenstein, mocking this picture of how art works. On such a view, if somebody could discover a derivative of Ecstasy which delivered

---

[44] See Robert Stecker, *Artworks* (University Park, Pa.: Pennsylvania State University Press, 1997).

[45] Marc A. Weiner, *Wagner and the Anti-Semitic Imagination* (Lincoln, Neb.: University of Nebraska Press, 1995).

the impact of Bach's B minor Mass, there would be no reason not to take it. Neither Budd nor, indeed, arousalists are guilty of this error. But Budd does misplace the prime focus of our interest. It is the work which is central.

Those of us whose life involves the arts do not pursue them for pleasure or even, as I have thought in the past, as an alternative to boredom.[46] Poetry, painting, or music is in the life you live. I want to go to the opera. I look at my watch, waiting for the curtain to go up. Once it has started, I may look at my watch to see how much longer it runs. But I don't regret going even if I don't enjoy it. Just occasionally, I wish it would go on and on, but not very often. It might seem that I always hope to see or hear something wonderful. But I am wise enough to know that it is unlikely. Sometimes I am confident that I shall, and look forward with great anticipation. If I am lucky, then I shall remember that performance for the rest of my life, and there are half a dozen such memorable productions that I can immediately recall. But I can hardly expect these very often, and much of the life of the arts is concerned with making judgements. 'Not as good as the Welsh National Opera Production!' 'But did you see the ENO?' And so on. I build up those private bench-marks with which I compare performances in the concert-hall and theatre. Great discoveries are rare, but, to paraphrase Tagore, when they occur, I count myself lucky to have heard such things.

---

[46] A view found in David Hume's essay on tragedy (*Essays Moral, Political and Literary* (London: Grant Richards, 1903), 222).

# 2

# *Language, Metaphor, Emotions, and Moods*

## I

Those attempts to account for the power and value of music which emphasize the causal connection between the music and its effect upon the hearer are open, then, to objections. None of these theories need exclude the role of ideas about musical form and structure, about fugue and sonata form, thematic development and harmonic and rhythmic structure, and all the paraphernalia of what Cook calls 'musical culture'. But they underestimate it; it seems clear that a proper account of music's significance for us requires a cognitive element.

This cognitive element is not merely the formal apparatus I have mentioned above. It also includes, as I shall show, the expressive function of music, the possibility of describing it as 'sad', 'grave', 'ebullient', 'tragic', and so on, for I shall argue that these aspects of the character of a piece of music also require a cognitive theory. The importance of these judgements lies not in the appraisal of value that they might, occasionally, entail. What is more important is that they are a necessary pre-condition of more significant judgements about musical value, the sort of judgements we make when we say of music that it is overblown or sentimental or heroic or timely.

As we saw, expressionist and arousalist theories offer an explanation of how music can be sad. Music is sad if the composer is sad when composing it, or if it makes the hearer sad, or both. In rejecting these, we have left ourselves with a problem. How can music be sad? To this I propose a solution of the kind which is generally described as 'cognitivist'. By this I mean that it is the music itself which is sad, not the composer, performer, or listener. The sadness is in the music, and we recognize it as such, much as we recognize canons or sonata-rondos in the music we hear.

It is worth while stopping for a moment and asking ourselves when we describe music as being expressive, and of what? Wittgenstein encouraged us to look for a context for a claim. But what contexts are likely for the remark 'This music is sad'? I do not think I have ever heard anybody other than a philosopher say or write, 'This music is expressive of sadness'; it needs a bit of ingenuity to find a context. If, for example, this character is surprising, given the general setting or the text, the remark might serve as a reminder. Then, to say the music is sad might not be otiose. It draws the listener's attention to other features of the context which are illuminated when we point out that the music is sad. Here is a characteristically thoughtful and suggestive observation which characterizes the music in an unexpected way. Hans Keller speaks of Mozart's sombre and tragic D minor quartet K. 421 as possessing 'a smile', but goes on to say that 'here the humour is behind the tragedy'.[1] More generally, we might say that Elgar's music expresses the spirit of imperialism, Schubert's domestic music expresses Biedermeier culture, or Bach's Cantata No. 82 'Ich habe genug', 'a heavenly homesickness' (in Schweitzer's words). All these phrases serve a critical function in judgement about the nature and merits of the music. Such judgements must have a point, and the point will rest on how they are used in critical judgement. So how could calling music 'sad' reflect or, indeed, affect our judgements of music? Offhand I can think of three ways in which it might be useful, though there may, of course, be others.

First, it is a means of drawing our attention to what we might otherwise overlook. But this function, of course, might be equally well performed by other vocabularies—'the passage at bar 18', for example. (I will discuss the question as to whether expressive predicates could be replaced by other ways of referring to the music later on.)

Second, sometimes expressive predicates draw our attention to a wider context. To see Nielsen's Fifth Symphony or Stravinsky's Symphony in Three Movements as war symphonies and, consequently, to hear certain episodes within them as 'violent', not only places them in a wider context, enabling us to see them as a response to the events of their time, but also affects how we hear certain passages. The dramatic kettledrum passages in Nielsen's

[1] Hans Keller, 'The Chamber Music', in H. C. Robbins Landon and Donald Mitchell (eds.), *The Mozart Companion* (London: Faber, 1956), 116.

symphony then become not aspects of variety within unity, but violent interruptions of the flow of the music, as war is a violent interruption of the flow of ordinary life.

Third, more broadly, suppose I describe a Shostakovich symphony as expressing an aching nihilism. How does this expressive description help me to understand the music? For a start, it makes me hear the music as a human document. It becomes expressive and representational of the devastation wrought by Stalin's tyranny. This does matter to us. It is part of the reason for our valuing Shostakovich that he shows himself to be aware and responsive to what is happening in the world around him, just as, for all the stunning beauty of Richard Strauss's late music, we convict him of blindness to the evils around him. When millions of his fellow countrymen were being gassed because they were Jews, he composed a threnody over the destruction of his beloved opera-house.

In all these cases the expressive character which I see in the music is not just the result of a causal process which results in my being put into some particular passionate state. Particularly in the last two cases, it is my knowledge of the context in which the music was composed which affects my judgement, and who can deny that this is both relevant and, by the same token, increases my understanding of the music? Furthermore, the expressive character of music is, of course, a matter of the character of the music itself. As I have said, this is the view known as 'cognitivism' amongst writers on the aesthetics of music.

So it is the music itself which is sad. Most recent writers concur, taking this to be the correct reading of 'The music expresses sadness'. This they also take to be a locution in which 'expression' has a distinct meaning. For whereas we normally conclude that it is a reasonable question what the person who expresses sadness is sad about, such a question cannot be asked of music. Hence we have an objectless form of expression in which the normal reaction to sadness, an attempt to cheer up whoever is sad, makes no sense. No doubt, the centrality of expressions like 'The music is sad' in the debates amongst philosophers is due to the feeling that these make some link between normal human preoccupations and concerns and an art that, otherwise, seems the epitome of abstraction. They are a shadowy version of the representational which links literature and the visual arts to human life. In the latter cases there is a prima-facie basis for understanding how fiction, for example, moves us; for a novel tells of the life and experiences of a character not so remote from ourselves. If, at a minimum, music expresses psychological states, then we seem to have some grasp of why it fascinates and moves us.

It will be evident from the first chapter that I do not share this view. If, in general, it was the right explanation of why music moves and fascinates us, then Malcolm Budd's claim that music is to be valued for its expressive qualities would be correct. I can concede that we value the fact that the art of music has such general connections, but I deny that, save in very special circumstances, we value a specific piece of music for its precise expressive qualities. In other words, I am prepared to allow that we find our lives richer for an apparently abstract art which has such expressive features, but I deny that, in most cases, the expressive qualities of the music are grounds for valuing or disvaluing the music (setting aside such properties as nobility, grace, pomposity, sentimentality, vulgarity, etc., which already carry an implicit grading). As I have said, if music is sad, its sadness is not a ground for admiring the work. The point becomes clearer if we think about the use of music in opera, as incidental music, and in the setting of words. Here the fact that music has a certain expressive face is crucial to the way the music fits or comments upon the drama or the text. If this were not the case, much of its power and point would be lost. It is not that the music alone, viewed in abstraction from the text, is valuable for being gloomy or optimistic; it is the fact that it has that character which is an element in the value we attach to the role of the music in this situation.

If I were to say, more plausibly, that just that combination of intimacy and wistfulness is what enchants me about Schubert's German dances, I might have indeed pointed to something which I value. But it is clear that this is not so much a reason for liking them, as though it were detachable as a statement of reasons for admiring the music, as a statement of what I like about the work. Perhaps more important is the fact, registered earlier, that there is no general connection between music moving us and its expressive character. I am not moved by music because it is grief-stricken.

I have remarked on the way in which many, perhaps most, features of sad people are absent from sad music. Music is not sad about something, has no beliefs, and so on. The temptation, then, is to suppose that its sadness is metaphorical rather than literal. My own view, as I shall shortly explain, is that if music is metaphorically sad, then it is in a fairly minimal sense of 'metaphorical'.

My decision to discuss this matter in terms of metaphor will not please some writers on aesthetics. I have said that I believe a rationale can be given for the application of expressive predicates, and in the next chapter I shall try to give one. But before I come to that, I need to deal with a fundamental objection to this programme, for not all writers believe that a rationale can be given. Two recent writers on aesthetics, Ben Tilghman and Oswald Hanfling,[2] have suggested that we ought to take 'The music is sad' as an example of the use of 'sad' in what Wittgenstein called a 'secondary sense', and of secondary usages no justification can be given. In a famous and frequently quoted passage of the *Philosophical Investigations*, Wittgenstein introduces the idea of 'secondary senses'.

Given the two ideas 'fat' and 'lean', would you be rather inclined to say that Wednesday was fat and Tuesday lean, or the other way round? (I incline to choose the former.) Now have 'fat' and 'lean' some different meaning here from their usual one?—They have a different use.—So ought I really to have used different words? Certainly not that.—I want to use *these* words (with their familiar meanings) *here*.—Now, I say nothing about the causes of this phenomenon. They *might* be associations from my childhood. But that is a hypothesis. Whatever the explanation,—the inclination is there.

Asked 'What do you really mean here by "fat" and "lean"?'—I could only explain the meanings in the usual way. I could not *point* to the examples of Tuesday and Wednesday.

Here one might speak of a 'primary' and 'secondary' sense of a word. It is only if the word has the primary sense for you that you use it in the secondary sense.

Another example Wittgenstein gives is less often quoted. 'The secondary sense is not a "metaphorical" sense. If I say "For me the vowel *e* is yellow" I do not mean: "yellow" in a metaphorical sense,—for I could not express what I want to say in any other way than by means of the idea "yellow".'[3]

[2] B. R. Tilghman, *But Is It Art?* (Oxford: Blackwell, 1984), ch. 7; Oswald Hanfling, '"I heard a plaintive melody" (*Philosophical Investigations* p. 209)', in A. P. Griffiths (ed.), *The Wittgenstein Centenary Essays* (Cambridge: Cambridge University Press, 1990), 117–33.
[3] L. Wittgenstein, *Philosophical Investigations* (Oxford: Blackwell, 1953), p. 216e.

I have always assumed that these examples are rather whimsical and of no intrinsic importance; their significance lies in the fact that they point up a more general lesson: that we might get agreement over usage where that usage is an extension of ordinary practice, without our being able to give an account or a rationale. We may incline to call Wednesday 'fat' without being able to give an explanation as to why this should be so, and without being able to give any paraphrase of what is meant.

It is this which makes them unlike metaphors, as Wittgenstein says. Even where we cannot give a 'literal' equivalent for a metaphor which completely conveys its force, nevertheless we can be helped towards an understanding by a partial paraphrase which partly accounts for its impact. This may be so even when we are dealing with those profound metaphors which only the reader with a tin ear would assume can be totally explicated.

Tilghman suggests seven 'features' which secondary senses share, some of which are clearly indicated in Wittgenstein's introduction of the concept.[4]

1. The object to which the word is applied may be altogether different from standard cases.
2. A word in a secondary sense has not changed its meaning.
3. Any causal story we can offer as to why Tuesday seems lean is 'philosophically irrelevant'.
4. We can use it in the secondary sense only if we can use it in its primary sense.
5. There are no criteria which justify secondary senses.

(The last two points, which are the most important for the subsequent discussion, I place out of the order in which Tilghman presents them.)

6. There need be nothing in common between what a word ordinarily denotes and how it is used in the secondary sense.
7. A secondary sense is not metaphorical. Tilghman quotes Wittgenstein's remark that 'I could not express what I want to say in any other way'.

It may also be true of a metaphor that I cannot say what I say by means of it in any other way. It does not follow from this that

---

[4] Tilghman, *But Is It Art?*, 160 ff.

no paraphrase or part-paraphrase can be given which would help
me to grasp the point of the metaphor. It is not because I cannot
say what I want to say in any other way that a secondary sense is
not a metaphor; it is, rather, because we cannot even begin on a
paraphrase or an explanation for the usage in such cases.

To this we must add a further condition which Tilghman does not
mention and which, as we shall see, will prove destructive for his
position. It is, however, implicit in Wittgenstein's remarks on being
'inclined'.

8. The application of a word in a secondary sense is not true or
   false.

With this in mind, Tilghman turns to a suggestion by O.
Bouswma;[5] it is that 'The music is sad' has similarities with 'Carrie
is sad'; he also acknowledges Richard Wollheim's observation concerning 'a particular look which bears a marked analogy to some
look that the human body wears'. Tilghman denies that the appropriateness of speaking of the sadness of music depends on such
similarities, and stands out against the customary view, a view which
dates back at least to the eighteenth century, that music is sad
because it imitates the rise and fall of sad speech. So Tilghman concludes that we are dealing with words used in secondary senses. 'My
own suggestion . . . is that in musical and other forms of artistic
expression we are frequently dealing with words used in secondary
senses, with what is to all purposes a whole body of language taken
over from its primary use in talking about people.'[6] We can concede
that sometimes we have cases of secondary senses in the extension
of words to discourse about art. In fact, Hanfling produces what
looks, at first sight, like a very plausible example in the application
of 'high' and 'low' and 'sharp' and 'flat' to musical tones, initially
more convincing than the sadness of music.[7] But in both cases there
seems to be a killing rejoinder to the attempt to treat these as secondary senses. It is that these statements are true or false. It is true
that Mozart's Symphony no. 40 in G minor is passionate, that the
beginning of the last movement of Mahler's Tenth Symphony
contains a flute melody whose register is high, but it is false that

[5] Bouswma, 'The Expression Theory of Art', in William Elton (ed.), *Aesthetics and Language* (Oxford: Blackwell, 1959), 73–99.
[6] Tilghman, *But Is It Art?*, 178.
[7] Hanfling, ' "I heard a plaintive melody" ', p. 124.

*Götterdammerung* is jolly, and false that Chaliapin had an unusually high voice.

This objection will be avoided if we take secondary usages as shifting what Tilghman calls 'a whole body of language' over to a new context, thus allowing cases of truth and falsity within a new way of talking. Then the thesis becomes a piece of speculative conceptual history about the origins of the way we talk about music. Thus Hanfling allows that secondary usages can be true or false, so he is not open to the objection of the last paragraph. (However, of Wittgenstein's own examples, only one favours the idea that 'whole bodies of language' are being moved about; he does speak of 'calculating in the head' in a context which suggests it is a secondary sense, and it is certain that here we have an established use which is true or false.)

So this objection will not be a problem if one can show that secondary senses display a spectrum, running from the whimsical cases which Wittgenstein introduces to important ones. 'The atom is a miniature solar system', 'Jesus is the good shepherd', or 'The music is sad' (if the latter is figurative) are examples of highly important figurative utterances, and this is intrinsically connected with the fact that we can show their point. Then some secondary usages have a truth value, and some do not. But if these all count as secondary senses, such a use of 'secondary sense' has expanded far beyond what Wittgenstein seems to have had in mind, and now includes what we usually call 'metaphors'.

Indeed, and more significantly, unless you make some sort of distinction between secondary and ordinary cases, you lose the connection between the application of expressive predicates to music and their central use in talking about human beings. In a word, the human connections of music are lost. If there is nothing more which connects the passionate in music with the passions of a human being than what connects the fatness of a Sumo wrestler and Wednesday, then you have impoverished the art. It is also no longer clear what would be the point of matching passionate music to what a dramatic situation or a text requires. If there is more to be said about the expressiveness of music (as there is), then these are not secondary senses. That a view closer to the cognitivist's would have appealed to Wittgenstein is suggested by some remarks in *Culture and Value* where, speaking of irony in music, and of the fugato in the first movement of Beethoven's Ninth Symphony in particular, he writes: 'I could have equally well said the distorted in music. In the sense in which we speak of features distorted by grief.'[8]

It is important that we make these judgements straight off in some cases, even though we do not in others. I see that the Schubert is sad straight off, and no doubt this is what encouraged Tilghman and Hanfling to use the model of secondary senses here. Generally, the more complex and interesting expressive judgements will be explained in terms of the more straightforward. It is worth concluding this part of the discussion with a few such examples, partly because they display a sort of structure in expressive predicates which cannot be found in secondary senses, and partly for their own intrinsic interest; it is the sort of thing aestheticians should get up to on occasion.

Take a composer about whom Wittgenstein was very nearly completely wrong: Mahler. (Although he showed insight into what made Mahler's symphonies different, he judged them to be worthless.[9]) If I wanted to justify the claim that Mahler was the composer of twentieth-century metropolitan life *par excellence*, how would I do it? I might maintain that he expresses alienation in his music, and to do this, I might point out the rapid transitions from point to point, which mirror the way in which opulence gives way to squalor in the course of a few streets, or perhaps the sudden appearance of banal and commonplace tunes reminiscent of the music-hall, the use of military marching themes which we associate with the constant presence and threat of the military in this century, the sense of rush and bustle—perhaps above all, the sense of a nightmarish world in which nothing is around long enough to be grasped properly, something which Mahler shares with the Ravel of *La Valse*, in which the *echt* bourgeois genre of the Viennese waltz whirls away into a spiralling, uncontrolled finale ending with an orchestral tutti which sounds hollow, as though the guts have been taken out of the orchestral texture. But above all, Mahler's melodies, bitter-sweet, have something of the potency of cheap music, because they are always on the verge of kitsch.

And with that judgement I am at the level of an expressive claim which I might find hard to justify further. These tunes are bitter-sweet—though, if a listener could not hear it, I might attempt to

---

[8] L. Wittgenstein, *Culture and Value*, trans. Peter Winch (Oxford: Blackwell, 1980), p. 55e.  [9] Ibid., pp. 20e, 67e.

show that the melodic elegance is undercut by the context or by an unsettling harmonic basis. But I could do none of this if 'bitter-sweet' were applied to music in the way that 'fat' is applied to Wednesday.

I have focused on the way in which we talk of music as sad. In doing this I have suggested that such locutions are metaphorical. The problem is not that this precludes our saying what we need to say, that sometimes 'The music is sad' is simply true. It is rather that looking at music this way encourages a positivist tendency by which we see the sadness as something we read into the music; this suggests that the description of the music as sad is dependent on an intellectual move whereby we infer or project upon the music its expressive qualities. This seems to me a misdescription of what happens when we recognize the sadness of the music. That experience is transparent.

So more needs to be said about metaphor. Let me begin by rejecting a view which, though still widespread, is fairly obviously wrong. Many writers, especially those versed in logic and linguistics, take a metaphor to be a form of utterance which infringes linguistic rules. Thus 'Richard is a gorilla' is metaphorical. Because it draws together concepts from disparate contexts in such a way as to produce an utterance which is superficially nonsensical, it has to be reinterpreted in order to be made sense of. The example in question might also be taken as obviously false and, again, reinterpreted on that basis. The assumption is that since nobody could mean what they appear to be saying, something else is afoot.

Some metaphors are like this. But many are perfectly normal utterances which are metaphorical only because of their context. I doubt whether there is any utterance, no matter how banal, for which we could not imagine a context in which it would be metaphorical. 'Smith is always dressed in grey' might be used to express metaphorically the fact that Smith always dresses so as to avoid drawing attention to himself or his clothes. A metaphor might be obviously true taken literally ('No man is an island') as well as obviously false ('Ulysses was an old fox').[10] The point is that the literal/metaphorical divide is at best an abstraction. Literal usage

[10] Several writers have pointed this out recently. See, for an excellent discussion, Peter Lamarque and Stein Haugom Olsen, *Truth, Fiction and Literature* (Oxford: Clarendon Press, 1994). See also Claes Entzenberg, 'Metaphor, Interpretation and Contextualisation', *Danish Yearbook of Philosophy*, 31 (1996), 21–38.

shades into metaphorical, and the metaphorical into those *outré* and puzzling cases that Wittgenstein described as 'secondary'.

Some metaphors are so immediately telling, their point so easily recognized, that we find no resistance to saying that they are true (or false). If I say of a colleague 'He is in something of a sub-fusc mood today', I have spoken metaphorically; but it will be taken to be no more than a slightly fancy way of saying that he is sombre. Normally metaphors which are true or false are what Cooper calls 'received, conventional or established metaphors'. But, as this example shows, though it may usually be the case that it is stale metaphors which can be used to make a statement which is true or false, this is not always the case.[11]

Other metaphors are rich and complex, and it would be an over-simplification to take them as either true or false.

> But wherefore do you not a mightier way
> Make war upon this bloody tyrant time?
> And fortify your self in your decay
> With means more blessèd than my barren rhyme?
> Now stand you on the top of happy hours,
> And many maiden gardens yet unset,
> With virtuous wish would bear your living flowers,
> Much liker than your painted counterfeit:
> So should the lines of life that life repair
> Which this (Times pencil or my pupil pen)
> Neither in inward worth nor outward fair
> Can make you live your self in eyes of men,
> To give away your self, keeps your self still,
> And you must live drawn by your own sweet skill
>
> Shakespeare, Sonnet xvi

William Empson says that 'lines of life' refers to the form of a personal appearance, the young man's face, the face as it appears in his descendants, of time's wrinkles, the family lineage, a portrait in pencil, a pen-portrait, destiny, the line of life on the palm—and more.[12] Many literary figures are like this, of course. So are some others: 'The brain is a computer' and 'Light is the darkness of God' are other metaphors which deserve pondering at length. Even to

---

[11] See David Cooper, *Metaphor* (Oxford: Blackwell for the Aristotelian Society, 1986), 216, who gets this wrong.

[12] William Empson, *Seven Types of Ambiguity* (London: Chatto and Windus, 1970), 54.

contemplate truth or falsity where the process of interpretation is so open-ended is to coarsen, and this, of course, relates to the fact that such metaphors cannot be exhaustively paraphrased. Of course, they can be paraphrased to an extent, and this is what Empson does when he shows how a metaphor 'works'. But when the context indicates that this is a rich metaphor, we assume that the task cannot be satisfactorily completed.[13] Where a metaphor can be exhaustively paraphrased, then, if it entails a statement, that statement can be true or false. (Bear in mind that a metaphor could be a question or some other form of utterance!) To some extent this connects with the intentions of the speaker. If the speaker intends his metaphor as a fancy way of making a statement, then it will be an assertion which can be true or false. However, we also need to remember that sometimes writing which began life as factual may be taken under its wing by the literary establishment, and may continue its life as a work of literary artifice to be interpreted in a variety of ways. So speaker's intention may be overruled.

But a metaphor might be true or false without its being exhaustively paraphrasable. To see this, let us return to our starting-point, the banal remark 'The music is sad'. I do not think that this is paraphrasable. This does not mean that there is no account which can be given as to why we use the word 'sad' about music, a story which might begin with the central usages of 'sad' to apply to people. There might be a rationale behind the extended use, and in the next chapter I shall suggest such an account, a philosophical disquisition on why and how language is extended. But when I say the music is sad, I do so 'straight off', and my hearers will not embark on a complex round of interpretation of the sort Empson produces for the line by Shakespeare. They will simply judge whether I am right or not. They will almost certainly agree that the little Allegretto in C minor by Schubert is sad, and will agree that that judgement is true. Indeed, as Leo Treitler points out,[14] it would be odd for me to add 'only in a metaphorical sense' to the remark 'Schubert's Allegretto is sad', much as it would be odd for me for me to say 'What a gloomy day (in a metaphorical sense, of course)'.

---

[13] Cooper, *Metaphor*, 70–1, makes the valuable point that paraphrasability and indeterminacy are not the same thing, since a metaphor could be indeterminate between a limited number of disjuncts, the sum of which constitutes a paraphrase.

[14] Leo Treitler, 'Language and the Interpretation of Music', in Jenefer Robinson (ed.), *Music and Meaning* (Ithaca, NY: Cornell University Press, 1997), 39.

Does this amount to any more than saying that it is a dead metaphor to say of sad music that it is sad? It is hard to say when a metaphor is dead and when not. As must be clear from my remarks earlier, context rules, and it would be possible to think of a context in which a 'dead' metaphor is revivified. We might very well point to aspects of the music which justify the claim that it is sad, and, if the metaphor is dead, this would not be an appropriate move.[15]

## II

Now you might accept everything I have said and think that such descriptions of music are only for novices, sentimentalists, or the confused. So, from paraphrasability to eliminability! Could we change our ways of talking about music so as to drop all references to its sobriety, sombreness, gravity, exuberance, or vitality, and merely talk about the music as notated? So are these expressive predicates eliminable? If they are not exhaustively paraphrasable, then presumably they are not eliminable without loss. The variety of exhaustive paraphrasability popular in some musical circles should, perhaps, be described as 'reductionism', for that gives it its proper philosophical location. For reduction to occur, it would be necessary to show that the statement that a musical phrase is sad says no more than to say what specific notes it contains; to say that a piece of music is grief-laden, will, according to the reductionist, be to say no more than that it is in a minor key, and has a slow accented pulse. To say that a cadence is banal will be reducible to the assertion that it is a simple dominant–tonic cadence. But it is now easy to see why such reductionism is implausible. The properties of music are not just the properties of its notation. They depend also on when and where it was composed. A phrase that expresses ardent longing in Schubert can sound trite in Lehár. What is disturbing in Mozart might be restful in Schoenberg. A simple

---

[15] Fowler distinguishes between stone-dead, dead, three-quarters dead, and half-dead or dormant metaphors (discussed by Cooper, *Metaphor*, 119), a little reminiscent of the language in which somebody who is seriously ill is said to be 'dead', terminally ill 'seriously dead', and what we call 'dead', 'fully and finally dead'. I pass over the difficulties of translation in this case.

dominant–tonic cadence may well be banal in John Adams; it may equally be profound in Monteverdi, and context has everything to do with this. Ergo, a description of the expressive content of the music cannot be equivalent to a description of the notes.

A plausible case for eliminability, then, must be a programme for conceptual change such as the programme of those musicologists who wish to turn musical analysis into a form of science. By substituting a description of the notes for the expressive predicates, we replace one vocabulary by another more austere alternative. For these analysts pukka musical criticism concerns itself, they think, with formal relationships only. They examine thematic transformations, contrapuntal devices, harmonic structure, and the like, in a largely technical vocabulary.[16]

When philosophers make a case for elimination, they usually do so on the grounds that the concepts they propose to eliminate are unsatisfactory in one way or another. Some philosophers argue that our ordinary conceptions of mind are confused or inconsistent or unable to explain such matters as madness, memory, or creativity. They advocate their replacement by a vocabulary of neurones and synapses or the apparatus of cognitive psychology, which uses concepts drawn from computers. Alternatively, the grounds for elimination may be economy; it may be argued that an application of Occam's razor makes our theoretical apparatus more spare and more elegant by excising unnecessary complications.[17] Whatever the reason for elimination, we are committed to the supposition that the new conceptual vocabulary explains the relevant issues more successfully than the old. Scientistic musicologists will argue that the austere vocabulary is to be preferred on explanatory grounds. Whilst those who favour a 'scientific' model for musical analysis do not generally argue that expressive terms are confused, they do maintain that modern 'scientific' musicology, such as the

---

[16] The debate between 'scientific' and 'humanist' critics has a longer history than is sometimes imagined. Shaw parodied formal analyses, and commended Grove for seeking 'always for the mood': *Shaw's Music*, ed. Dan H. Laurence, vol. 3: *1893–1950* (London: Bodley Head, 1981), 384–7. See R. A. Sharpe, 'What is the Object of Musical Analysis?', *Music Review*, 54/1 (1993), 63–72.

[17] See Peter Smith and O. R. Jones, *The Philosophy of Mind* (Cambridge: Cambridge University Press, 1986), 181–3, for a lucid discussion of eliminativism in philosophy of mind. Also R. A. Sharpe, 'The Very Idea of a Folk Psychology', *Inquiry*, 30 (1987), 381–93.

techniques of Schenker, Reti, Forte, and Boretz, offers better explanations of music.[18] In this case, whilst allowing that expressive predicates are unparaphrasable, they maintain that they are eliminable.

I think that this approach is the heir of the classic case against expressive predicates made by Hanslick. Admittedly, what Hanslick seems to have in his sights is not expressive predicates *per se*, but an expressionist account of expressive predicates. Nevertheless, there is a distinct suggestion in *The Beautiful in Music* that expressive predicates are a rather inadequate tool for describing music. Hanslick argues that no definite feeling is represented by music;[19] so the objection to describing music this way is its inadequacy as a precise characterization. Indeed, most of his arguments aim to show the poverty of characterizing music expressively, and in this way his arguments offer a basis for eliminativism. (Hanslick, incidentally, allows that music sometimes arouses feelings, but he denies that this is necessary. For him, music aims at the creation of beautiful forms of sound.)

Hanslick's position depends upon the belief[20] that emotions are distinguished one from another through the thoughts that they contain. Music does not articulate thoughts, therefore music can neither express nor represent the emotions proper. Like Hanslick, I am sceptical of the suggestion that we can individuate emotions in terms of a 'feeling-tone' alone, dispensing with the object of the emotion, because, like many philosophers, I doubt whether a different 'feeling-tone' can be found for each different emotion. Jealousy and anxiety do not seem to me, introspectively, to differ much in how they feel. What differentiates one emotion or mood from another is a complex of beliefs, objects, causes, and behaviour, and these are generally absent when we ascribe an expressive characteristic to music. So far, so good! Unfortunately, as Budd observes, one of Hanslick's main examples, 'cheerfulness', is a mental state which does not have an object. Many descriptions of music are like this in using expressive terms which do not require objects. Kivy remarks that music can be pompous, and it is by no

---

[18] See Douglas Dempster and Matthew Brown, 'Evaluating Musical Analyses and Theories: Five Perspectives', *Journal of Music Theory*, 34/2 (1990), esp. 247 ff., and Nicholas Cook, *A Guide to Musical Analysis* (Oxford: Oxford University Press, 1987).
[19] Eduard Hanslick, *On the Musically Beautiful*, trans. Payzant (Indianapolis: Hackett, 1986), 10.                    [20] Ibid. 9.

means clear that an object is required for pomposity.[21] Indeed, Hanslick's case against expressivist predicates is more properly a case against the use of predicates which normally ascribe emotions to people and animals, and not against those many predicates which we use to describe music which, in other contexts, do not have associated objects and beliefs. He has a point, but it is a rather limited one.

Hanslick's main target was the thesis that beauty in music depends upon the exact expression of feelings. *A fortiori* he must oppose the view of expressionists like Deryck Cooke who believe that music is beautiful in so far as the deep emotions the composer feels are reproduced in the listener. Hanslick believed that music cannot express more than the dynamic properties of feelings, their intensity, their waxing and waning, hastening and lingering, and the like; that is its limit. He gives two principal reasons for advocating this view; first, there is music with which no feeling can be associated, such as some of the Bach Preludes and Fugues, and, second, there is disagreement, even amongst experts who agree about the quality of the music, on what the music expresses.[22]

Neither of these last two arguments has been found quite persuasive. Budd points out that such counter-examples will not rule out the possibility that the beauty of at least some music depends upon the expression of feeling. A single counter-example does not rule out the possibility that some such music exists. The objection is well founded, of course; but Hanslick does seem to be concerned with the general thesis that beauty in music relies on the accurate expression of feelings, and against this a counter-example is telling. As far as the second argument is concerned, once we recognize that the view he attacks maintains that music must accurately represent or express feelings (he does not clearly distinguish between representing and expressing), the argument seems prima facie telling. For accuracy suggests publicly accessible standards of assessment. If Hanslick is right about the facts, these are absent.

But is he right about the facts? Do musicians differ so much about the character of music? I think not. As I have already argued,

---

[21] Peter Kivy, *Music Alone* (Ithaca, NY: Cornell University Press, 1990), 178. For discussions, see Malcolm Budd, *Music and the Emotions* (London: Routledge and Kegan Paul, 1985), 24–5; Stephen Davies, *Musical Meaning and Expression* (Ithaca, NY: Cornell University Press, 1994), 205, 214, 216, 217.

[22] Hanslick, *On the Musically Beautiful*, 14.

if the level of description is broad, you will find agreement without that agreement being trivial. There is much unanimity about the broad characterization of music. As I said earlier, the description of music in such terms is often straightforwardly true or false. The more precise the predicates, the more the experts disagree. But that is unsurprising. The more specific or the more elaborate the characterization, the more highly metaphorical it is likely to be, and, in consequence, the less it is a matter for straight agreement rather than interpretation and controversy. If I describe a piece by Mahler as *faux-naif*, I may not describe so much as open a debate. The sense that I have *le mot juste* here may itself be due to the aesthetic merits of the description.

The form of eliminativism with which I began is not the only possibility. We might also maintain what philosophers would call an 'error theory' about expressive predicates. An error theory would maintain that it is a mistake on a very large scale to suppose that music can be described by expressive predicates at all. It is not that it has a certain rough applicability, by comparison with which other vocabularies do the job much better; nor are these predicates reducible without residue to some other terminology. Rather, our description of music as poignant is as unjustifiable as astrologers' talk of starry influences. There is no such thing. Perhaps the most famous statement of an error theory is by Stravinsky: 'For I consider that music is, by its very nature, essentially powerless to *express* anything at all, whether a feeling, an attitude of mind, a psychological mood, a phenomenon of nature etc.'[23]

If music cannot express in this way, then the expressive predicates we attach to it are the result of a massive error on our part. (Stravinsky immediately qualifies this by speaking of the 'conventional' connection of expressive characteristics with music, and indeed, later, in *Expositions and Developments*, he allows that music is an expression of the composer's feelings.[24] But by now his formalism looks virtually indistinguishable from one form of classical expressionism. Its distinctiveness merely amounts to the rider that there is no exact correlation between feeling and music.)

So hostility to expressive predicates is compatible either with an eliminativist approach to expressive predicates, where it is assumed

---

[23] Igor Stravinsky, *Autobiography* (London: Calder and Boyars, 1975), 53–4.
[24] Igor Stravinsky and Robert Craft, *Expositions and Developments* (London: Faber and Faber, 1962), 101.

that they provide a theoretically inferior vocabulary, or with exhaustive paraphrasability, or, finally, with an error theory. To end this part of the argument, I give an example which offers positive grounds for the importance of expressive predicates. It tells against all three attacks on expressive predicates.

Consider the judgement that the ending of Mozart's G minor string quintet is too light-hearted for the previous three movements. This highly significant criticism has no equivalent formulation which refers merely to the notes. Admittedly, it is the configuration of the notes which makes the music have the property of light-heartedness, so the expressive features are less primitive than the notes. Some might describe them as supervenient on those notes. But since there are many configurations of notes for which 'light-hearted' might be an apt description, it follows that in characterizing it so, we characterize it generically. Any competent musician could, of course, deduce that the music has whatever quality it has by looking at the score, but what we wish to say about the mismatch of moods could not be said in any other way. Or take Hans Keller's description of the minuet of Mozart's Clarinet Quintet as 'mock drama'. It is a bit hard to understand; it does suggest listening with the operas in mind; that way certain features, such as the dialogue between the instruments, become more evident. It also suggests ways in which the music might be played. But the thought is not captured by talk of the notation alone. This objection tells against both eliminativism and reductionism. We have here an important criticism of music which can neither be reduced to, nor supplanted by, a notational description.

Another example: somebody recently described on radio the finale of Schubert's Sonata D. 894 as 'The Gods at play'. Something like this might be an ineliminable weapon in the armoury of the teacher who is trying to get a pupil 'to see how it should go'. Formalism—and eliminativism is a sort of formalism—is distant from musical practice. It is a matter of fact that we decide on the overall character of a piece—sentimental, detached, sardonic, or whatever—and determine how the detail should be played in the light of this. And to miss the general character of a piece is a grave charge against an interpreter. It is, I think, very significant that so much of the reaction against formalism has come from thinkers who are deeply interested in the interpretation of music.

Normally the predicates used by philosophers as examples are

too generalized to give reasons for valuing the music. Both
mediocre and great music can be light-hearted. The music needs
other qualities before we rate it highly. But consider a critical
judgement using expressive predicates like Keller's. Is music which
is 'mock drama' prima facie good? A fine critic may be able to
describe music in words so well chosen as to be illuminating and
which, simultaneously, offer prima-facie grounds for thinking the
work good, though I have to say that the achievement is exceptional. Not even Tovey's *Essays in Musical Analysis* succeed, to my
mind.

As I shall argue later, not only are expressive predicates a
requirement in developing an understanding of music; they are also
a logical requirement of certain more important critical judgements
we make, such as judgements that music is authentic or inauthentic, sincere or insincere, sentimental or unsentimental. Expressive
predicates are important, then, for some of the most controversial
and important critical judgements we make about music.

Admittedly, expressive predicates are, largely even if not entirely,
the predicates of the tyro. It is unlikely that an experienced musician or anybody knowledgeable about music should say of a piece
'What sad music' and think that anything useful is being communicated. It's all too obvious, and, as I showed earlier, we have to
think of fairly exceptional circumstances in which it is helpful. Such
a person is more likely to speak of the inexpert handling of the
transition to the recapitulation. But for the beginner these predicates, or some surrogates, are essential. Teaching people to love and
understand the arts is probably as salutary for the aesthetician as
Wittgenstein's experiences in teaching young children was for his,
and our, philosophy of language. Anybody who has tried to teach
musical appreciation knows that the initial step in getting familiar
with a piece of music is grasping the themes; this is a pre-condition
for grasping the structure in classical music. It is necessary to recognize the themes as they recur. Perhaps it is less important elsewhere, but in jazz, for example, it is often important to know the
'standard' being used, as well as to have a sense of where the climax
lies. Calling a theme 'joyful' labels the theme, and the competent
teacher will help the listener to recognize the theme when it
appears in an altered form in the development section. A quick
look at many concert programmes confirms this. The writers,
because they cannot assume their readers' familiarity with staff

notation or with the music, use expressive predicates. Tovey's analyses are the classic examples. When modern analysts disdain Tovey's flowery descriptions of music, as they sometimes do, they forget that he was not writing for an audience of musicologists.

Still, as I have indicated, such predicates tend to drop out of critical consideration. Once we have the necessary vocabulary, 'that passage in G minor' is more reliable as a means of identifying a passage than 'the sad bit'. The last is a ladder to be thrown away. Yet these predicates cannot be dispensed with entirely, as we have seen, and they will always have a role in musical education. Lest this seem too dismissive, let me say that music would be a very different sort of art were these judgements not to be made. We have seen how expressive predicates have a role in drawing our attention to salient points; a consequence is that they are a means whereby new listeners may be drawn into the company of music-lovers. The implications are wide, and many writers who advocate a humanistic musical criticism are, I think, aware of the way in which the arts are convivial. Certainly, without friendship there will not be a life of the arts; but art, in turn, also nurtures friendship. A fragment of what philosophers like Danto and Dickie call 'the art world' is needed for the beginner to make distinctions in terms of which art becomes both intelligible and available. Expressive predicates are a pre-condition for the existence of an individual's development of her taste, because they enable her to come to terms with the work. Indeed, to the extent that existing music influences the next generation of composers, it will do so only through the creation of a listening public of which the young composer is a member. Each member of that public developed his or her taste, in turn, and for each there is an individual history.

## III

As I remarked earlier, most writers think that the vocabulary of emotions is the starting-point for our expressive description of music. We are now poised to throw a little more light on this assumption. Robert Nozick[25] follows recent writers in distinguishing within emotion a belief component, a feeling, and an

[25] Robert Nozick, *The Examined Life* (New York: Simon and Schuster, 1989), 87–98.

evaluation, features of emotions which, as we have just seen, Hanslick in part recognized. Thus, if I am angry with a colleague, the object of my emotion will be that colleague; standardly there will be a belief that she has done something and, further, that it is something I believe she should not have done. Other recent writers distinguish cause and emotion.[26] Thus, my fear of death has death as its object, but death is not the cause, since it has not, at the time of writing at least, occurred.

Nozick's original contribution to the debate is a sketch of what he calls an 'analogue theory'. In his earlier *Philosophical Explanations*,[27] he suggested that I know *p* if my knowing 'tracks' the facts in such a way that my beliefs are sensitive to a change in those facts. He models this on a digital relationship. Beliefs are discrete. Emotions, Nozick now suggests, have an analogue relationship to value. If I am proud of my garden, and it visibly deteriorates, standardly my pride will decrease in intensity (not Nozick's example).

Now connect this with hearing music. Allowing the doubtful assumption that music is essentially correlated with emotions, there might be an analogue relationship between the flow of the music and the natural history of the emotion.[28] It might even allow us to give some sense to Hanslick's idea that music represents the dynamics of feeling or Langer's talk of parallels in form.[29] Take a non-musical example: my spirits rise as a noted wit approaches me at a party, remain at a high level whilst I enjoy his wisecracks, and subside once he has moved on. My emotional state of exhilaration, amusement, and interest corresponds with my valuing of the state I am in (listening to a wit), and declines as that state changes. An adequate account of emotion, as well as recognizing that emotions have objects, will allow that emotions have a narrative shape, a dynamic rise and fall, and that different emotions will differ in these respects. Emotions have a natural life. They may develop slowly or attack us suddenly; in either case we may be left with the aftermath once the conditions that brought them into being disappear. My

---

[26] Though this distinction is widely acknowledged, there are dissenting voices. See Robert Gordon, *The Structure of the Emotions* (Cambridge: Cambridge University Press, 1991).

[27] Robert Nozick, *Philosophical Explanations* (Cambridge, Mass.: Belknap Press, Harvard University Press, 1981).

[28] See Davies, *Musical Meaning and Expression*, 262.

[29] See also Kendall Walton, 'What is Abstract about the Art of Music?, *Journal of Aesthetics and Art Criticism*, 46 (1988), 358.

anger is assuaged, but I remain anxious. The frightening object goes away, but I remain disturbed and shaken. Such analogies lie at the root of the new humanistic musicology to which I referred earlier, and which stresses the dramatic and narrative structure of music.

The parallel transitions in art can be very sudden, and this has led Hindemith,[30] for one, to object that no emotions could, in life, succeed one another with the rapidity with which they do in music. It spurs him to reject any form of expressionism in which the emotions, say of the composer, are represented in the music. Although I am inclined to agree with his conclusion, the premiss might seem ill judged. Art is not life, and we do not object that in fiction events follow one another with a precipitation not possible in life. As Samuel Johnson remarked, in objecting to the three unities of time, place, and action in drama, he that has imagined this much can imagine more. But Hindemith has something in his favour; the 'emotional life' which is 'represented' in music might be comparatively aetiolated. In life, emotions hang together. I feel grief when a friend dies, because I loved him. Jealousy is only possible where there is first of all love. As a matter of fact, these are emotions which cannot be represented in music save where there is an action or a text, and their rapid succession in music might in any case be a flaw. Where transitions are very abrupt, our uncertainty about their intelligibility might be explained in just this way. So the finale of Schubert's C major quintet could, in some performances, lack the troubled undercurrent which makes it an appropriate conclusion to a profound work. In other contexts, rapid contrasts are not an occasion for criticism. A contemporary work in which mood follows mood kaleidoscopically might seem convincing just to the extent that it reflects modern metropolitan life. (I have some of Mahler's middle-period symphonies in mind.)

Most writers have assumed that emotions provide the most likely raw material for a vocabulary with which to describe the character of music. (Stephen Davies says, obscurely, 'it presents emotional characteristics in appearances'.[31]) We have already seen some grounds to doubt this presumption, but these grounds have been inductive. We merely noted that many of the words we use to

---

[30] Paul Hindemith, *A Composer's World: Horizons and Limitations* (New York: Doubleday Anchor, 1961), 45.

[31] Davies, *Musical Meaning and Expression*, 261.

describe music are not ordinarily used to ascribe emotions to people. But perhaps even where the vocabulary of emotions has been used, it has been a mistake. There are some stronger considerations which suggest that, in those cases where we seem to characterize music in terms of emotions, we might be on safer grounds speaking of moods, not emotions.[32] The role played by objects in emotion talk is now familiar. When I attribute an emotion to somebody, I take it that the emotion has an object. If Jane loves, then there is somebody she loves; if she is fearful, then there is something about which she is fearful; or if she hates, then there is something or somebody she hates. We may be able to tell by her behaviour and by the context just what emotion she is suffering in any particular case. But music has no context, no correlated behaviour, and no object. The music is not sad about anything. Once all the arguments are absorbed, the position which remains most plausible is the cognitivist one that it is the music itself which is sad or gay, calm or tempestuous, ferocious or exuberant, and that these are words which in non-musical contexts more typically ascribe moods, not emotions. A rapid survey of the way in which we ascribe moods suggests that moods do not necessarily have objects. If I am in a depressed mood, then the world looks black, but there is not a particular object which is necessarily the object of my depression. Of course, there may be. I may be depressed because my team has lost, and that loss is both cause and object of my depression. I might say that I am sad at their defeat. But on occasion I am depressed because I am tired or ill, or just because I 'got out of the wrong side of the bed'. The tiredness need not be the object of my depression, though it is the cause. Of course, whether we attribute emotions, on the one hand, or moods, on the other, to music, we are doing so with some restriction on the conceptual content. My position here is merely that moods are the best bet as a vocabulary for this sort of expressive content in music. They are less likely, by a short head, to lead us in the direction of philosophical expressionism, because they do not invite us to supply an object of the mental state.

I have expressed scepticism as to whether the proper vocabulary to describe music consists generally of words which in their usual context ascribe emotions. Philosophers who, like Levinson, believe

---

[32] The recent, much discussed debate between Kivy and Radford on arousalism, to which I referred earlier, is largely, and mistakenly, couched in terms of emotions.

that there is a strong relationship between music and the emotions, do so on the basis that emotions are complex states, some elements of which may be paralleled in music even if others, such as the possession of an intensional object, are lacking. Recent work on the concept of an emotion has tended to stress the variety of conditions which are present in paradigm cases of an emotion. Some of these conditions are not to be found when we move towards the periphery of our usage of words; the content of expressive predicates when applied to music is slimmed down. Furthermore—and this is extremely important—the application of these predicates to music has a history, and it is that history I shall explore in the next chapter.

A way of summarizing the arguments of these first two chapters is by means of a little taxonomy.

1. Some expressive predicates entail that the composer exhibits the features whereby we characterize the music. If the music is ironic then the composer was ironic in writing it. His wit, irony, or sarcasm expresses itself in the music, and causes the music to have the qualities it has. Note, however, that what we infer about the composer is not an affective or expressive state. The composer does not *feel* ironic, for there is no such thing. Could he feel sarcastic? I don't know. But again, there is no general pattern here, and no grounds for deducing that the composer is in a certain frame of mind.

2. Contrast these with epithets which describe causally powerful aspects of the music. If the music is exciting, moving, or exhilarating, then, providing the listener is in 'a standardly receptive condition', he will be excited, exhilarated, or moved by the music. Again, this is an entailment. Of course, his state may be countermanded by other considerations. If he has just lost his winning lottery ticket, he will be less exhilarated. ('Standardly receptive condition' cannot be usefully defined, because it is too open-ended; but the condition is not circular or regressive for all that.)[33]

3. Finally, there are predicates which entail nothing about the composer or the listener. I suggest 'sad' and 'optimistic' as

---

[33] My views on these topics are rather more complex than they used to be. They have changed somewhat from the positions attacked by Davies (ibid.).

examples. It does not follow that listeners will be saddened by Elgar's Cello Concerto just because the music is sad, nor is there any special reason to suppose, from the character of the music alone, that Elgar was sad when he wrote it. The assumption that he was comes from biographical data which have become available.

4. I have said that if music is high-spirited, then it tends to make a sensitive listener high-spirited. That it is exuberant is a reason for valuing it, whereas the fact that music is sad is not a reason for disvaluing it, because sad music does not, *ceteris paribus*, make us sad. Budd's claim that music is to be valued for its expressive qualities is a half-truth.[34]

As I have intimated, these expressive predicates, though often by themselves boring and hardly explanatory, are a pre-condition for other judgements. I say little if I describe a Haydn finale as feline. But I may go on to show how this is just the proper character for that movement. Composing is an action, and in part we understand the music when we understand what reason the composer has for putting that particular passage there or for composing a passage with that particular character.

Briefly, then, the use of expressive predicates to describe music is neither eliminable, nor can it be reduced; and there is no general answer to the questions 'Does music express the mental states of the composer?' or 'Does music arouse, in the hearer, the expressive states which, "metaphorically", describe it?' It is said that we see sadness in music as we see sadness in the face of a woman or in a cityscape or a landscape. We can say that the expression in the face is appropriate to sadness even when we know that the owner is not sad. Certain breeds of dog have sad faces, or indeed a dog may have a quizzical face without it even making sense to say that the dog is quizzical. For a child, a page of musical notation full of black notes, of semiquavers and demisemiquavers, looks cross, forbidding, and bad-tempered, but the music itself is not bad-tempered or expressive of bad temper. But, as I shall argue in the next part, these are not the best of analogies. We hear sadness in music as we hear sadness in a voice, and this, I suggest later, is a primitive or natural response. Whether these are, as Kivy suggests,

---

[34] A point made frequently by Budd and endorsed and discussed by Davies, ibid. 269–72.

hard-wired in the brain, I have no idea, and no idea how it could be shown.[35] Certainly the proper response to sadness in music is sobriety, though, rather than showing that sadness is aroused, this may show merely that the proprieties are being observed. A more interesting question, which does belong to the philosophy of mind or to empirical psychology, is why beautiful music moves us to tears. When it does, the tears are not tears of sadness. This power of music to move us is mysterious and wonderful, but it has nothing to do with the mirroring in us of the expressive qualities the music contains. It is even questionable as to whether 'emotion' is the right word to describe my being moved by music. For a start, my emotional relationship to a piece of music may not require my being moved by it. Love is an emotion, I suppose, but I may love music without necessarily being moved by it. And what beliefs are relevant? It is easy to see that a feared object must be believed to be dangerous (at some level), but what parallel beliefs do I have when music moves me? Secondly, is excitement an emotion, or is ecstasy an emotion? I am not sure; but if these describe our being moved by music, but do not ascribe emotions to us, then it is clear that being moved does not necessarily amount to being under the sway of an emotion. It is certainly not necessary that if I suffer an emotion, then I am moved, and it is not clear that if I am moved, I am in an emotional state.

We should remember, as well, that though these are the most salient of reactions to music, more frequently music offers rewards which are less dramatic and will not be accounted for in these terms. I follow the music, I am engrossed in it, I acknowledge the imagination and inventiveness of the composer, and I am delighted by the individuality of the music. None of this has much to do with emotion or mood. It is difficult to describe what absorbs one about music and what one feels deeply satisfying when one is not actually moved. For this we need to pay more painstaking attention to the phenomena than most philosophers attempt. I shall return to this, but first I want to examine the application of expressive predicates and their roots. Why are these metaphors, if metaphors they are, powerful and important? In what follows I shall show why.

---

[35] See ibid. 257–9 for a discussion.

# 3

## Music, Rhetoric, and Oratory

> Remember how it was said of Labor's playing: 'He is speak-
> ing'. How curious! What was it about this playing that was so
> strongly reminiscent of speech? And how remarkable that we
> do not find the similarity with speech incidental, but some-
> thing important, big!
>
> Wittgenstein, *Culture and Value*

I began the first chapter by imagining aliens trying to understand
the human practices of making and listening to music. I now ask
you to focus on one particular time in the history of Western music.
In the sixteenth-century, composers began to develop substantial
pieces of instrumental music which could take five or more minutes
to perform. Sixteenth-century keyboard composers provide the
earliest familiar examples of such music. How could they organize
a piece in a way which would both hold the listener's interest
and impose a unity on the music? The answer to this question has
a double significance. I shall suggest that the formal models for
musical structure were, in part, drawn from classical discussions
of rhetoric. But, as we shall see, rhetorical models have a pro-
founder significance, for they provide the basis for a solution to the
problem which has occupied us till now, the question of musical
expression.

But I will begin with some alternative models for musical structure. In his recent book *The Fine Art of Repetition*, Peter Kivy distinguishes three models which have played a role in thinking about
music: they are the literary, the organic, and what he calls, in a
manner reminiscent of Kant, the 'wallpaper model'.[1] It is the last
model which, rather surprisingly, he regards as giving the most
accurate picture. To take the literary model first of all, Kivy distinguishes three variants: first, there is the discourse model, which sees

[1] In Peter Kivy, *The Fine Art of Repetition: Essays in the Philosophy of Music*
(Cambridge: Cambridge University Press, 1993), 330.

music as a kind of argument; then there is the dramatic model, which views music as a kind of stage play; and finally, there is the narrative model, which views music as a kind of 'emotive story'. On his view, all three versions of the literary model founder on the role of repetition in music (hence the title!). It is the role of repetition which makes a figured carpet or wallpaper a better model for music, though, unlike other patterns, music can be both deeply expressive and deeply moving.[2] (I suspect that Kivy has Proust or Thomas Hardy in mind as literary models, rather than, say, 'The Three Bears'; in folk and nursery tales, repetition can be very important.)

We can, for reasons that Kivy does not give, dismiss the first alternative. Music does not present an argument. The idea that music is some sort of logical process is most often encountered in musical analysis. Schenkerian analysis, by stripping down a musical work to essentials, claims to uncover a basic form which explains the unity of the music. David Epstein is one writer who claims to be able to isolate a substructure in music which offers musical premises on which musical reasoning proceeds.[3] But reasoning is normative, and if there is such a thing as reasoning in music, then some reasoning will be valid, and some not. Central to logic is the understanding that valid inference is truth-preserving. If you put true premises in, you get true conclusions out. Since the concept of truth cannot be applied to a phrase in music, it follows that we cannot extend to music the notion of reasoning. We can never say of music that, having heard it, we know something about the world, independently of the music, which we did not know before. Neither can we say 'How true' or That's false' of a passage.

What is meant by 'musical logic' is more the sense that the music seems to have a direction, a conclusion towards which it is leading. I shall later discuss the way this is connected with understanding music. The consequence is that there is a sort of phenomenology of musical experience which invites the illusion of inference. Because this can be explained in terms of cadence, tonality, and chordal progression, there is a sense in which, in music of the classical era, the appearance of inference is justified, as opposed to much of Stravinsky's and Debussy's music, where we have an

---

[2] Ibid. 358. Hanslick uses the word 'arabesque' to convey a similar point.
[3] David Epstein, *Beyond Orpheus* (Cambridge, Mass.: MIT Press, 1979), 12 and 161.

appearance of logical progress without such substance. Analyse a
good deal of middle-period Stravinsky, and you will not be able to
find a tonal basis for the sense of development. It is in this sense
that Stravinsky's music is properly described as 'synthetic'.[4]

The second and third variants of the literary model that Kivy
describes seem to me to be sufficiently similar to merit treating
them together. After all, a narrative naturally incorporates a drama
of the emotions. One character may respond with pride, anger, or
jealousy to the actions of another. *Othello* is both a story and a
study of emotional reactions—of envy, jealousy, remorse, and grief,
as well as of *naïveté* and innocence. We cannot make a clear distinction between literary works which are narratives and literary
works which are emotional dramas; of course, it has seemed plausible to many writers to take music to present the dynamics of
feeling in abstraction from a plot. But such an approach, it might
be thought, abstracts the literary model to the point where it no
longer seems an analogy of the art of music.

However, there is a case for treating the kinds of thematic
development which we find, *par excellence*, in Haydn, Mozart,
Beethoven, and Brahms, as shadowing the thematic structure which
we find in the human personality.[5] Consider, as an example, the way
the character of a person or his or her deeper religious or ideological commitments surface from time to time. They are not
perpetually on view in the human personality. They appear and
reappear on occasions on which people may be said to 'act in character'. Such traits are not a Humean thread conferring identity on
the individual. Rather, they are like 'deep idiosyncrasies' which are
not clear to sight; in the same way, a motif may appear and reappear through a work, or a theme may turn up transformed in different ways in different parts of a play, a novel, or an opera. The
art of critical interpretation is to show just this, the way that a leit-
motif like the contrast between youth and age is shown in different ways by different characters in *Der Rosenkavalier*. Contrast
the relationships of Sophie to her father, to the baron, and to the
marschallin! More particularly, the character of the marschallin

---

    [4] See Stephen Walsh, *The Music of Stravinsky* (London: Routledge, 1988), 119–28.
    [5] See Norman Holland, *The Dynamics of Literary Response* (New York:
Columbia University Press, 1989), pp. xiv–xv. Holland cites some work by the psy-
choanalyst Heinz Lichtenstein. Also Ernst Bloch, *Essays on the Philosophy of
Music*, trans. Peter Palmer (Cambridge: Cambridge University Press, 1985).

emerges in different ways in her reaction to the various characters. Of course, there are differences between art and life; art is at once more orderly and more concentrated. The contradictions which are familiar to us in a real person might not show in a play, and, indeed, if they did, might be grounds for criticism. Henry James remarked on 'the fatal futility of fact' and 'clumsy life'. Nevertheless, differences aside, there are what are nowadays called 'homologies' here.[6]

So far, then, I have suggested that one form of the literary model, the narrative, can be illuminating in the task of trying to establish links between this quintessentially formal art and those human interests which might seem to be indispensable if an art is to move us as music does. But any parallels between music and life will have roots. There needs to be a historical account which will provide a foundation for parallels which, otherwise, will be adventitious. I shall try to elaborate, but before I do so, let me return to Kivy.

Kivy proposes what he calls a 'wallpaper model', a model which, he claims, is required to explain the central role of repetition in music. There might seem to be a natural reply to Kivy. Repetition is just the means whereby we grasp the thematic material which is then 'developed' in sonata form (that is, varied in various ways, by being inverted, or shortened, or lengthened, or fragmented) or ornamented in variation form. A master will show us the possibilities of even the most unpromising material, but repetition is required to familiarize us with the material before development begins; otherwise we will miss the point. Consequently, repetition is a necessary means to a further and more important end: recognizable thematic development of the music. (Note, too, that this is a central aspect of music through its 'classical' period.) Certainly, if we take this argument seriously, and some interpreters do, then when music is familiar to its hearers, it is right to omit the repetition. But the persuasive counter-argument we hear so often nowadays is that to omit the repeats in the opening of a sonata form movement is to disrupt the balance. So far, then, the evidence seems to favour Kivy. As he argues, the repetition just *is* the pattern.

Kivy offers what he calls 'models'. I have talked about the

---

[6] See David Drew's introduction to Bloch, *Essays*. Also John Neubauer, *The Emancipation of Music from Language* (New Haven: Yale University Press, 1986), cites Vicenzo Galilei as proposing that we can characterize people in music by imitating, in the music, their typical intonations (p. 27).

possibilities of a literary model. His second model is the organic. Now a model is a model, not a theory. Different models suit different kinds of music. The organic model, surely, particularly suits the symphonic music of Sibelius, where themes frequently grow out of fragments without there being much actual repetition. (The minimizing or even the absence of repetition is, of course, what makes modern music, and especially atonal music, 'difficult'.) The dramatic model, which I have tended to underplay, also characterizes some music, music aptly described as involving a struggle between thematic groups of key systems. Perhaps this is the most apt description of some of Neilsen's symphonic works. In all these cases, as Philip Alperson observes, we 'follow' the music in a way in which we do not follow the pattern on wallpaper or on a figured carpet.[7] But perhaps 'wallpaper' is the most suitable epithet for minimalism, and for much minimalism, such as the music of Adams or Górecki, I would not wish to suppress the pejorative connotations; we might make exceptions for, say, Steve Reich.

That we 'follow' music is deeply important to us. It is one of the reasons why we value music, and it is one of the features of music which underpins the ideal of music as a kind of language, something central to our culture, as I try to explain in the last chapter of this book. Significantly, the organization of a speech, a lecture, an essay, or a book is important precisely to the extent that it enables the listener or reader to follow it. No teacher or author needs to be reminded of this. So what organization should music have if it is to be sound which can be followed? Now the model which is most relevant to the music which Kivy draws on for examples in his various books is one which he does not mention, and one which, very probably, was actually used as a model—namely, rhetoric. Recent scholarship suggests that musical construction during the great period of classical music, roughly 1500 to the Second World War, is largely based on the structures studied in rhetoric. When Quintilian's treatise *Institutio Oratio* became available once again in 1416, rhetoric became a central feature of Renaissance culture. The principles for designing a sermon, a speech, or a treatise in such a way as to hold interest and create variety were widely appreciated, and repetition is central among them. In my student days, aspiring preachers were told that their

---

[7] Philip Alperson, 'The Arts of Music', *Journal of Aesthetics and Art Criticism*, 50/3 (1992), 217–30.

sermons should be divided into three parts; the old tag, which I often repeat to students, 'Say what you are going to say, say it, and then say you've said it', represents a sort of bastardized rhetoric.[8] The repetition that Kivy stresses in music is commonly found in any form of explanation and description, as teachers, writers, and lecturers know very well, and this feature links rhetoric and music in an important way.

Rhetoric is a branch of study that has largely been lost to view, but for centuries it was a basic part of education. We can see how widespread it was by the number of editions of a standard treatise like Erasmus's *De ultraque verborum ac rerum copia*, eighty-five editions of which were published in the sixteenth century, mainly in the Low Countries, France, and Germany, but also in England. The translation of 'copia' is not easy; it is variously rendered as

---

[8] The most accessible general account of the relation of rhetoric to Renaissance music is found in the entry 'Music and rhetoric' in the *New Grove* (London: Macmillan, 1980). George J. Buelow, the author, suggests that there was no settled vocabulary or any settled set of correspondences between musical elaboration and the rhetorical figures. It suggests, rather, that the techniques were passed from musician to musician in a fairly *ad hoc* way. For general discussions of rhetoric, see George Kennedy, *The Art of Persuasion in Greece* (Princeton: Princeton University Press, 1963); *idem, The Art of Persuasion in the Roman World* (Princeton: Princeton University Press, 1972). A useful short discussion of rhetorical forms is found in the introduction to Lucan, *De bello civili*, i, ed. R. J. Getty (2nd edn. with corrections) (Cambridge: Cambridge University Press, 1955, pp. xliv ff.). Damon R. Leader, in *A History of the University of Cambridge*, i (Cambridge: Cambridge University Press, 1988), 117–21, indicates the ubiquity of rhetoric in Renaissance education. A standard text of the period, much reprinted, is Erasmus, *On Copia of Words and Ideas*, trans. and introduced by King and Rix (Milwaukee: Marquette University Press, 1963). A philosophical discussion is found in Paul Thom, 'The Corded Shell Strikes Back', *Grazer Philosophische Studien*, 19 (1983), 93–108. A glance through recent journals suggests that there is an increasing interest in the relationship between rhetoric and music. Richard Greene, 'A Music-Rhetorical Analysis of Holst's Egdon Heath', *Music and Letters*, 73 (1992), 244–67, contains an introduction to recent work together with a bibliography. There is, however, little awareness amongst many of these writers of the vocabulary of rhetoric in classical and Renaissance times. 'Rhetoric' is used in the rather loose way that 'discourse' is used amongst the trendier intellectuals. Without a historical basis, the work strikes me as slender. Buelow is right to insist on the great importance of rhetoric for an understanding of classical music. A helpful general discussion is John Stevens, 'Music, Number and Rhetoric in the Early Middle Ages', in Paynter *et al.* (eds.), *Routledge Companion to Contemporary Musical Thought* (London: Routledge, 1992), ii. 885–910. One philosopher worth consulting on this is Thomas Carson Mark, 'The Philosophy of Piano Playing: Reflections on the Concept of Performance', *Philosophy and Phenomenological Research*, 41 (1980–1), 299–324, who draws an analogy between quoted phrase in music and assertion, though without alluding to rhetoric.

'abundance' and 'eloquence', but principally as 'variety'. Essentially Erasmus is concerned with the methods of varying and enlarging on a topic. The importance of rhetoric for a humanist education can be seen not only from the number of textbooks available, but from the number of abstracts, which usually incorporate a commentary. So, unlike ours, Renaissance education involved a training in eloquence. We can imagine that what seems to us to be verbal extravagance was appreciated, discussed, and analysed by its hearers. There is more than a hint of this in the 'fustian' both indulged in and mocked by Shakespeare.

During these years the principal changes in rhetorical theory were taxonomic. Thus the Ramist revision of Ciceronian rhetoric reduced the five parts of classical rhetoric (invention, arrangement, style, memory, and delivery) to just two (style and delivery).[9] Eventually the famous reaction against high-flown verbiage to be found in Glanvill, Sprat, Boyle, and Fénelon[10] in the mid-seventeenth century seems to have ended, to all intents and purposes, a tradition which had flowered for centuries, a tradition in which rhetorical speech was thought to transcend ordinary talk, just as it, in its turn, was transcended by poetry.[11] The rhetorical movement survived into eighteenth-century Britain in a debased form as the elocution movement, which, as the name implies, emphasizes delivery rather than questions of structure. One of the best-known writers of this movement, Thomas Sheridan, father of the playwright, explicitly emphasizes the relation to music,[12] and this is a connection I shall be developing.

The historical point I have adumbrated. The natural forms of organization available to any composer with a humanist education are to be found in rhetoric. Its application to music was both

---

[9] What recent work there has been on rhetoric has largely been taxonomic. Group mu in Liège make three devices fundamental: suppression, addition and permutation (*General Rhetoric*, trans. Paul B. Burrell and Edgar M. Slotkin (Baltimore: Johns Hopkins University Press, 1981). But the latest redactions of rhetoric bear a curious air. Rhetoric is no longer a live part of our culture, and this arrangement is a purely academic exercise, a sort of tidying of the desks, whereas the classification of tropes at the time when rhetoric was studied widely did have some significance.

[10] W. S. Howell, *Eighteenth Century British Logic and Rhetoric* (Princeton: Princeton University Press, 1971), 516.

[11] W. S. Howell, *Logic and Rhetoric in England 1500–1700* (Princeton: Princeton University Press, 1956), *passim*.

[12] Ibid. 226.

general and particular. A speech is divided into an exordium or introduction, a narrative or statement of facts, followed by a second more elaborate narrative, and concluded by a peroration, the latter customarily divided into two parts. The structure is paralleled in some of Handel's constructions, and seems to have been adapted in sonata form, with its dramatic use of key contrasts. There are obvious analogies between exordium, narrative, second narrative, and peroration, and the exposition, development, and recapitulation of classical sonata form. Add a slow introduction, which you often find in Haydn and Beethoven, and a coda, and the parallels are complete.

More specifically, and at the level of the particular, the Renaissance theorists Burmeister and Nucius developed a theory of musical figures explicitly analogous to the rhetorical figures; examples are *repetitio*, *exclamatio*, and *interrogatio*. Repetition includes techniques such as the removal of a note or a musical idea on repetition in a setting of words, in order to emphasize part of the text, and anaphora, where the same phrase is repeated on different tones in different parts, and ellipsis, the omission of an otherwise essential consonance to give a new direction. Some of these techniques of variation are parents of the forms of thematic development codified in our century by Reti, amongst others. (Indeed, a subsidiary consequence of my proposals is that Reti's type of thematic analysis is closer to the roots of the classical styles than Schenker's essentially cadential analysis.) The parallels between rhetoric and thematic transformation are not exact. How could they be? But the parallels are close enough. Most scholars suggest that the shaping of musical ideas was inspired by rhetoric, and I have concurred, principally because rhetoric was widely studied before these musical forms were developed. It is conceivable, of course, that all we have here are parallels and not a causal connection,[13] and that is a possibility which cannot be ruled out, though, in this context, it smacks too much of a generalized scepticism.

Let us now turn to matters of aesthetics. An immediately plausible analogue for the expressive power of music is that of the power of a speaker in a language we do not understand. The rise and fall of the voice, the changes in volume, the dramatic vocal

[13] The view of Professor Peter Williams.

and physical gestures, and the sense of a rhetorical structure reveal eloquence even if we do not understand the words.[14] Vibrato or tremolo is particularly important. Nowadays you are unlikely to hear it much in the West outside the Welsh chapel and, I am told, amongst some Gaelic preachers. (It is interesting that in music, we are constantly being reminded that it is a mistake to lay it on with a trowel and that it should be used primarily as a heightening, expressive device.) As I wrote in *Contemporary Aesthetics*, 'music says nothing but its manner of saying it speaks volumes'.[15]

There is, then, a pretty strong case for saying that large-scale organization in music borrows its structures from rhetoric. It is as strong as any case is likely to be in the rather dubious field of intellectual history. We cannot be sure that musical structures did not develop independently; nor can we be sure that the humanist education a composer received affected his compositional practice. But the latter does seem highly likely. After all, the very word 'composition' was borrowed from rhetoric.[16] Burmeister and Nucius were, to be sure, provincial figures,[17] but this does not rule out their reflecting something quite widely recognized amongst musicians. And there are major writers who endorse the connection, such as Bacon, Morley, Peacham, and Mattheson.[18] It might be countered that since there are no other ways of organizing music, the forms of classical Western music are necessary, and that therefore no explanation of why they came to dominate is needed. But this argument does not wash. The premiss is false. Even within Western music there are other forms, such as the fugue, which have less obvious parallels with rhetorical forms (though some scholars

[14] See Vicenzo Galilei's recommendation that madrigalists return to a more natural way of matching words to music (*Dialoga della musica antica e della moderna* (1582)). It is cited by one of the 'new musicologists' much influenced by hermeneutics, Gary Tomlinson, *Music in Renaissance Magic* (Chicago: University of Chicago Press, 1993), 141.

[15] R. A. Sharpe, *Contemporary Aesthetics* (Brighton: Harvester Press, 1983; Aldershot: Gregg Revivals, 1991), 109.

[16] See Mark Evans Bonds, *Wordless Rhetoric: Musical Form and the Metaphor of the Oration* (Cambridge, Mass.: Harvard University Press, 1991), 80, an invaluable survey of this territory.

[17] As Peter Williams has pointed out to me.

[18] See Gregory C. Butler, 'Fugue and Rhetoric', *Journal of Music Theory*, 21 (1977), 49–109.

demur[19]). Sonata form, variation form, and the rest are not the only forms of musical structure and design, and it is reasonable to ask why they developed as they did.

These connections were well understood by some earlier theorists. Mattheson is perhaps the most familiar name, and his use of rhetorical imagery in the description of music must not be thought of as mere ornament. It is something more than a metaphor, and the rhetorical basis of the vocabulary he uses leads to the central question as to whether, and in what sense, music is a language, an issue which, as I argue in the final chapter of this book, lies at the heart of our conception of music. As the role of rhetoric in education declined, and as its use as a model in music fell into desuetude, modern formal analyses became central, and obscured the role which rhetoric had played. Yet, because of the ubiquity of the model of language, its traces can be seen in E. T. A. Hoffman and Hanslick, and even as late as Schoenberg.[20]

It is also highly plausible to suppose that the expressiveness of the single vocal phrase—what we describe as sad or gracious—is expressive precisely because it mimics the shape and movement of the rhetorical gesture. At a primitive level, these are the musical features to which we respond and which move us, and to which we apply expressive predicates. The musical structures which have enabled composers to create massive unified works lasting up to an hour are structures taken from rhetorical models. But, equally, our response to the individual phrase is pretty close to what Wittgenstein would have described as a 'primitive reaction'. It owes its power to our natural responses to rhetorical shapes. (Note, *pace* recent discussions, that it is vocal rather than physical gesture which matters here. The account I give does not need a separate treatment of musical gesture and musical motion.[21]) Although there may be parallels between hearing sadness in music and seeing

[19] See Warren Kirkendale, 'Ciceronians versus Aristotelians on the Ricercar as Exordium, from Bembo to Bach', *Journal of the American Musicological Society*, 32 (1979), 1–44; Ursula Kirkendale, 'The Source for Bach's Musical Offering', *Journal of the American Musicological Society*, 33 (1980), 81–141.

[20] Bonds, *Wordless Rhetoric, passim*. Amongst earlier writers on the connection between music and rhetoric, Bonds cites Schubak (1755), Marpurg (1761), Vogler (1793), Arnold (1810), and Carpani (1812), as well as the more familiar figures of Forkel and Mattheson.

[21] Cf. e.g. Aaron Ridley, *Music, Value and the Passions* (Ithaca, NY: Cornell University Press, 1995).

sadness in a weeping willow, in the face of a hound or in a landscape, the more primitive basis for the expressive properties of
music is in the character of speech, and we hear sadness in a
woman's vocal manner as we see sadness in her face. It is not infer-
ential. (Bear in mind, too, that a great deal of music has no marked
expressive character, a point discussed in the previous chapter.)
These responses are not mediated through convention. It is this
that ensures that music is expressive without ever developing as a
language or developing other than fitful means of representation.
Such responses are evident, too, in our response to folk music and
to demotic music of the early Renaissance. Our 'primitive reactions' to the rise and fall, the hesitations and accelerations, of a
human voice in a passionate response will be the basis on which
the larger expressive character of an entire movement in music
is constructed and in which varied expressive features appear. In
a parallel way, the primitive aesthetic pleasure which we take in
word rhythms, patterns, and sounds is incorporated in verse which
is capable of so much more. Just as the primitive response to a
glowing patch of colour is incorporated in great visual art, so
rhetoric allowed the creation of a musical culture which allows us
to place the primitive pleasure in melody, timbre, and rhythm
within a work of larger scale. (Talk of primitive reaction does
not commit me to the dubious idea that there is a universal language of music which anybody from any culture immediately
understands. But it does mean that the melodic gesture in Indian
music might readily affect me without my understanding the flow
and direction of the music on a larger span. The idea is not particularly new. Thus J.-J. Batteux thought that music and gesture
transcend conventional languages and lie 'closer to the heart';
he proposed three ways of expressing feeling—word, tone, and
gesture—and suggested that the last two are universal.[22] I do not
have an opinion on whether these responses to vocal shapes are
antecedent to music or not; music might have developed simultaneously along with speech; there is no special reason to give prior-
ity to language here.)

I used the phrase 'primitive reaction'. Wittgenstein employed the
term 'primitive reaction' rather variously.[23] What is primitive might

[22] Bonds, *Wordless Rhetoric*, 60–7.
[23] This is well discussed by Simo Saatela, 'Aesthetics as Grammar'. (Uppsala
University, Department of Aesthetics, 1998).

be a sense of puzzlement over a dream, or the impulse to tend an injured person, or the gesture of pointing. What the cases have in common is that it is in our nature to react this way, and that no further justification is available. The notion of a primitive reaction becomes an argument-stopper, and it is in this spirit that I think of our reaction to music as primitive. To hear the sadness of a piece of music is primitive. I recognize it straight off, and not as the result of a process of argument. But this does not preclude explaining why they are analogous. As I have intimated, the sadness of the music lies in the fact that sad music, like the speech of a sad man, is slowish, does not display leaps in pitch, is probably dynamically restricted, and so on. Music which is properly described as 'passionate' is music which displays energy, wide leaps in range and dynamics, just as the speech of an impassioned man does. The general principles lying behind the analogies are straightforward and fairly obvious, and the reader can easily match the range of conventional musical expressions, 'lugubre', 'appassionato', 'vivace', or 'energico', with the appropriate vocal manner of a person who is lugubrious, vivacious, and so forth.

Much ink has been spilt over whether sad music resembles the behaviour of a sad man, or whether the listener hears the music as if it were a human utterance, or whether it is merely music which would be thought appropriate for the expression of sadness.[24] Regarding the last two alternatives, sometimes I might listen to music as though I were hearing 'a plaintive voice', and sometimes I might recognize that this piece is apt as an expression of sadness. But although either can occur, neither need be the case. They are not general features of our reaction to music, and they certainly will not explain why we call it 'plaintive'. They merely register the sort of imaginative process which may accompany hearing it. To the objection sometimes made to the first, that there is not much in common between a sad person and sad music, the answer is that there is enough to support the extension of language. Remember that instrumental music is a Johnny-come-lately. Music was centrally vocal and dramatic. So if you were setting a text with a certain expressive character, what melodic shape would you use? The answer to that question is obvious.

Now a text has to be performed; this leads us to oratory. For

[24] See Derek Matravers, *Art and Emotion* (Oxford: Oxford University Press, 1998), 118.

oratory stands to a text as a musical performance does to a score. We need to hear, or hear in imagination, the spoken words to get the full effect. So rhetoric provides a structure which is realized in oratory, in the rise and fall of the voice, and in the quasi-musical use of the voice for expressive purposes. As I say, this is something to which there is a natural, not a conventional, response, just as some of our gestures, covering the face in horror or grief perhaps, are natural and not conventional; equally, the gestures of a conductor or a dancer or a performer are often natural. Evidence for the way the connection was seen in the later seventeenth century comes from Pomey's *Dictionnaire royale* of *c.*1671, a useful source for late Renaissance ideas; he advises the orator on how to deliver the various parts of a speech; the exordium requires a low vocal pitch and modest and restrained gestures, which should not be introduced until he has uttered several sentences. The *narratio* requires a new speech rhythm and tone of voice to add emphasis, and at this point the orator should move his hands more expressively. Phrase lengths are increased, and the speed becomes faster. The *confirmatio* requires the most powerful rhetorical figures and a vehement tone of voice, the orator miming with his hands the while. The *peroratio* involves an abrupt change of voice, increasingly hasty words, with a rapid and forceful movement of the entire body. The performance conventions for rhetoric do not entirely carry over to music, but that it is a model is plausible. Lamey, a contemporary of Pomey, suggests that figures of speech are analogous to the postures the body adopts when under the influence of emotion. Contemporary sources advise the singer to use a variety of gestures during the first part of an aria, but, on the repeat, to hold one suitable posture, for here the ornaments which are introduced replace physical gesture.[25]

Many philosophers have subscribed to a version of this thesis, and have supposed that hearing expressiveness in music is like hearing expressiveness in utterance. The thesis has a long and distinguished history. Stephen Davies, who is himself sceptical about the similarity, cites Hutcheson, Reid, and Schopenhauer.[26]

---

[25] Peter Seymour, 'Oratory and Performance', in Paynter *et al.* (eds.), *Routledge Companion*, ii. 913–19. P. Ranum, 'Audible Rhetoric and Mute Rhetoric: The 17th Century French Sarabande', *Early Music*, 14/1 (1986), 22–34, a brilliant paper to which I am deeply indebted.

[26] Stephen Davies, *Musical Meaning and Expression* (Ithaca, NY: Cornell University Press, 1994), 206–7.

Rousseau wrote that melody, 'in imitating the inflection of the voice, expresses laments, cries of pain or joy, threats or groans'.[27] The counter-argument of Hanslick, mentioned by Davies, that it is recitative which most closely imitates the human voice, and that it is this which is the least expressive of musical devices, has no force. It is not true to say *tout court* that recitative most closely imitates the human voice; it most closely imitates human speech when the speaker is in no way impassioned. It does not imitate the voice of somebody who is moved. (Hanslick presumably had in mind *recitativo secco*, rather than accompanied recitative or the recitative of, say, Monteverdi's operas.) Not all human speech is expressive in the way music is; nor is all music expressive; it is oratory which cultivates the expressive possibilities of the human voice, and it is that sub species of rhetoric, elocution, which categorizes the ways we use the voice for expressive purposes.

Obsessed as they are with the statement-making function of language, philosophers forget not only the innumerable other ways of talking which do not have informing as their main aim, but also the innumerable ways in which intonation affects the impact of what is said, inviting us to take it as teasing, as unserious, as a witticism, as an expression of invitation or anger, as cajoling, as inviting, as encouraging, or whatever. It is this wide range of oratorical devices, so very, very important in human communication, which music mimics.

Once instrumental music became accepted as the pinnacle of musical achievement, and, more or less contemporaneously, rhetoric ceased to be a staple feature of education, the roots of musical expressiveness became obscured. Music continued to possess the expressive predicates established through rhetoric, and it continued to develop until the resources of tonal language were exhausted. But for a century, since the loss of rhetoric, it has been a major philosophical preoccupation to explain the application of 'expressive predicates' like 'sad', 'joyous', and the rest, and Hanslick's treatment became the *fons et origo* of modern musical aesthetics.

Of course, it might be argued that the historical thesis does not establish the philosophical thesis about the role of rhetoric in understanding how music is expressive. For it is possible that the

---

[27] J.-J. Rousseau, *Essai sur l'origine des langues* (1779).

expressiveness of music might have the origins I suggest and have developed away from it, much as the etymology of a word does not determine what that word now means. It is possible, for example, that music was once very closely tied to rhetorical intentions, and has since developed into a formal art. However, I do not think so. The situation does not seem to be analogous and, indeed, could not be, given what I have said about primitive responses. The connection with rhetoric, I believe, remains; we need to be 'reminded' as Wittgenstein might have said.

No silver lining is without its cloud. The account I have given seems to work very well for monody. Though the period in which expressive character came to the fore is, essentially, a period in which monody was dominant, we still have to consider the question of harmonization. The effect of a melodic gesture can be enhanced or subverted by its harmonization. One easy way out would be to accept Kivy's early distinction, and take the effect of harmony as conventional, but I do not find this intuitively appealing. The difference between the musical character of a theme supported by minor chords and the same theme supported by major chords can hardly be purely conventional. Now one answer here might be to think of harmony contrapuntally, so to speak, and to take the force of harmony in altering the expressive character as the addition of lines which have their own expressive character, which may either modify or endorse the overall character. Or we might think of the model of conversation here. The lines compare with the contributions to a discussion; such a picture certainly makes clear the role of the various voices in a string quartet, for example.

The truth, I suspect, is that there is, in a sense, no such thing as monody. An unsupported melody is not devoid of harmony; it merely implies rather than expressly provides it. This becomes obvious if one listens, say, to Bach's unaccompanied cello suites. We might also reflect on the fact that to harmonize a monody such as 'She moved through the fair' comes close to an act of desecration, and that the result is likely to be banal simply because it states the obvious.[28]

One upshot of my argument is that there is a difference in the way expressive predicates are applied to music. Those which also

---

[28]  A point I owe to Peter Williams.

apply to rhetorical fashions in speech are literally true of music, or, if metaphorical, metaphorical in the most minimal way. These are likely to be those which are used as directions in a score: vivacious, impassioned, energetic, and so on. Elsewhere the expressive predicates become richer, and their application to music progressively more interesting and puzzling. They become a matter for interpretation, which requires us to respond in a questioning vein. When Hans Keller described a movement of Mozart's Clarinet Quintet as 'mock drama', he set off trains of thought and imagination.

A last example: Listen to the opening of Bach's Cantata BWV170, 'Vergnugte Ruh'e, beliebte seelenlust'. Its initial halting phrases expand into a full melodic line. Why does this move us, and why do we think it connects with human responses? In part, of course, the text tells us; it speaks of peace, which cannot be earned through sin. But Bach adds to this by the way he sets the words; his music speaks of initial hesitancy followed by confidence, and thus involves the idea of a spiritual journey. It is so much like the woman who, under the pressure of some powerful emotion, gradually finds her tongue and eventually speaks eloquently. Indeed the eloquence of this music, *pace* my discussion above, is hardly metaphorical.[29] It is natural, too, to think of this music as

[29] This holds good despite the fact that Bach is here using and adapting a convention of the Italian aria, opening with a phrase which is then extended and developed at length. Mattheson gives textbook demonstrations of it. I owe this observation to Peter Williams.

accompanied by gesture. It might even be hard for a singer not to gesticulate as she sings. The recitative of Monteverdi, unaccompanied by gesture or mime, is like a monochrome reproduction of a Titian.[30] As Mizler remarked, 'music is an oration in notes'.[31]

In the first chapter, I suggested that our experience of music involves ideas about music, about form and structure and shape. In the second chapter I allied myself with those cognitivists, using 'cognitivist' in a different sense, who claim that the expressive qualities of music are something we recognize in the music rather than states the music creates in us. This chapter has drawn the two strands together. On my account, substantial elements of the two major cognitive aspects of music are both explained by rhetoric or, better, by rhetoric actualized in oratory. The recognition of a theme on its return, the identification of a canon, the realization that a movement is approaching its peroration are, I argue, ingredients in our appreciation which are essentially connected with its value for us. The basis in music for these lies in those forms of melodic shaping and large-scale organization which music has taken from rhetoric. These cognitive elements in our appreciation of music are borrowed from language. The elegance of this solution to the problem of musical expression does not, of course, show the conclusion to be correct. Too much depends upon the essentially messy business of the history of ideas. Beyond its evident plausibility and explanatory power, there is not much to be said. Even the *obiter dicta* of composers, if it existed, would prove little.

But there are concepts and concepts. Amongst the concepts that have a formative influence on our musical experience are concepts which are altogether broader. These are what are now sometimes described as 'ideological concepts': concepts like 'progress', 'authenticity', and 'the autonomy of art' which infiltrate our musical responses. It is in so far as a philosophical understanding of our experience of music can be clarified by seeing the role played by ideology that these more general ideas are of interest here. This is not intellectual history, and I shall not attempt a systematic account

---

[30] This is discussed with his usual insight by L. B. Meyer in the Postlude written for the new edition of *Music, the Arts and Ideas* (Chicago: University of Chicago Press, 1994), 319–20. Music listened to at home through speakers involves, he remarks, a sort of sensory deprivation.

[31] Bonds, *Wordless Rhetoric*, 89.

of the way in which these ideas affect the writing of musical history. That has been done by others.[32] As I said at the outset, I am concerned with the way that some philosophical problems can be better understood by an understanding of ideology and what it does. So in Part II I widen my brief, arguing that such ideas are more influential and pervasive than is generally thought. This leads to the discussion of the final part, in which I endeavour to show how music can be thought of as a humanist art.

[32] By, *inter alia*, Joseph Kerman, *Contemplating Music* (Cambridge, Mass.: Harvard University Press, 1985); Lydia Goehr, *The Imaginary Museum of Musical Works* (Oxford: Clarendon Press, 1992); and Meyer, *Music, the Arts and Ideas*.

# PART II

*Playing Off Old Scores*

# 4

# The Motivations for Musical Ontology:
## A German Ideology

### I

As I have already hinted, in the rest of this book I shall argue that
quite general ideas about music, its history and its performance,
infiltrate our musical experience. So, from arguing that a causal
account of how we describe music fails to take into account the
roles played by form and structure, and that concepts drawn from
rhetoric explain the structures we find in music and are the vocabulary in terms of which we describe its expressive power, I move
to the role played by ideas like progress, authenticity, and formalism in the judgements we make about music. These are general, in
that they apply across the board to a wide variety of music, but particular in being part of what musicologists have latterly begun to
call 'ideology'.

But first things first! There are some more basic matters which
require our attention. Let me begin with two general principles: the
first is that concepts have histories, and the second that natural languages are not fully determinate. Consider the first principle. Concepts change over time, and they change through fairly large-scale
movements within a language or a community of speakers. The Old
Testament registers, amongst other things, the changes in a society's
conception of God. Such changes are gradual, and rarely depend
upon a single individual. It would be hard, even for a conceptual
dictator, to control such changes. More often, such changes are
inadvertent consequences of other things we do. A series of
small changes brings about some larger-scale changes; perhaps,
very occasionally, a particularly powerful teacher might change language, but such changes would be hard to ensure.

I talk of 'concepts', but what is it to possess a concept? To possess
a concept such as the concept of a 'performance' is to be able to

use the word 'performance' in its central cases (or 'Auffuhrung' or 'execution'). We possess the concept of a performance when we correctly use it to describe Brendel's playing of the 'Appassionata' or Olivier's rendering of Hamlet. But possession of a concept is a matter of degree. Somebody who has a rather inadequate grasp of this concept might describe Art Tatum's variations on 'Tea for Two' as a performance of 'Tea for Two', a usage with which those of us who have a good grasp of the concept would be uncomfortable. We will say that Ray Charles performs 'Yesterday' because he sings it pretty straight. But if we are asked whether the MJQ performs 'Round Midnight', we might shilly-shally, because they, quite literally, add too many notes for it to be a clear case of performance.

So the second principle is that concepts may be rough-edged; consequently, it may not be the case that we can say, in advance of a particular case, whether or not a particular concept would apply. To take an example familiar from recent philosophical discussion: if, by surgery, my brain and body were divided in half, and half placed with one prosthesis and half with another, we would be hard put to say which is the 'real me'. The difficulty is not that there is a fact of the matter and that we have not found out what it is. It is, rather, that the concept of personal identity is not articulated to cover such outlandish cases. Consequently, there is no answer to the question 'Which is me?' Our concepts are not so defined. I do not think we should conclude from this that all our concepts are 'open' in this sense. Rather, concepts tend to be open unless we arrange for them to be closed, and we may do this in various ways. The most obvious situation in which a concept may have a precise boundary is where a formal definition is possible; certain technical terms, or some concepts in logic and mathematics, may be examples. The thesis that the concept of a work of music is open is familiar, inasmuch as 'work of art' is supposed by many thinkers to be an 'open' concept; works of music are, then, *a fortiori* open inasmuch as works of music are works of art. If a concept is open, its boundaries are fluid or undefined, and vice versa.[1]

So we may ask in a particular case whether the concept of a work of music or, more generally, that of a work of art applies. Is this suc-

---

[1] See Morris Weitz, 'The Role of Theory in Aesthetics', *Journal of Aesthetics and Art Criticism*, 15 (1956), 27–35, and for recent reflections on this classic paper, Richard Kamber, 'Weitz Reconsidered: A Clearer View of Why Theories of Art Fail', *British Journal of Aesthetics*, 38/1 (1998), 33–46.

cession of sounds a work of music? To this question we might find that there is no pre-existing answer; the concept simply has not been articulated for these cases. Is John Cage's famous *Silent Music*, a work in which the performer makes no intentional sound for 4 minutes, 33 seconds, a work of music? More generally, is any artefact in which aleatory techniques are central, a work of art? To answer one way or the other may well be arbitrary. What answer one gives is very unlikely either to reflect the consensus of opinion amongst those who use the concept with proficiency, or to be binding on the rest of the musical community; finally, it is hardly enlightening, save as reflecting, perhaps, a certain evaluation by the proposer. Some other questions of this type are whether a transcription is a version of a work or not, and at what point a performance with lots of mistakes ceases to be a performance of the work it sets out to render. Is a performance of *Carmen Jones* a performance of *Carmen* or a performance of a version? Are some of the more imaginative realizations of *Orfeo* performances of Monteverdi's opera at all? Until I heard Philip Pickett on the radio talking about the material he had to go on in constructing the music for *The Journey to Santiago*, I had not realized just how much of the music was based on informed speculation. Given that the original was, in some cases, a single melodic line, how much credit is due to Pickett, and how much to the Spanish 'composer'? Suppose I unwittingly improvise in such a way that my improvisation is identical with the 'Moonlight' Sonata, have I performed the 'Moonlight' Sonata, albeit inadvertently? If you search through recent literature on aesthetics, you can find earnest discussions of such matters. The philosophers concerned apparently assume that our concepts are articulated to cover such cases, and that it is up to us to provide arguments which will show which answer is the correct one, or, failing that, to provide reasons why we should make one decision or another. The first assumption is, as I have suggested, a mistake, and the project of finding reasons to decide one way or another is not very interesting. As I have observed, any single writer is unlikely to affect the final outcome. If music whose content is largely a matter of chance comes to play an important role in our lives, then an answer, one way or another, will be imposed through changes in our culture. This might happen if aleatory music were widely used in commercials or in films, and thereby attracted so much attention that listeners to radio programmes began to request it; then it might become part of concert programmes. This kind of history is a necessary condition if a borderline case is to be accepted as a pukka work of music. The scenario I describe is but one amongst a number of possibilities. The point is that something like this, rather than the say-so of an analytical philosopher, is required to produce the requisite conceptual change.

It is sometimes argued that we cannot have an analysis of art, because any such analysis would foreclose that creativity which is exactly what we value in art. I do not find this argument telling. We might have a satisfactory definition of, say, 'crime', without foreclosing the creativity of villains who may find, within that definition, new and imaginative ways of law breaking.

Finally, in this prefatory discussion, I should make it clear that I do not claim here that 'work of art' or 'work of music' is, in Gallie's sense,[2] an 'essentially contested concept'. (An 'essentially contested concept' is one whose boundaries are drawn by different people in different places; for their users are engaged in 'endless disputes about their proper uses'.) We might all, including Cage himself, be puzzled in the same way by *Silent Music*, so that, though the borderlines are vague, different experts do not draw them in different places. We agree that the boundaries are uncertain, and agree that the border lies somewhere between here and there, without any of us having a view on the precise demarcation. And if we do make a demarcation, we must accept that it will be a ruling, not a straightforward application of the criterion for 'work of music'.

For one recent theory in aesthetics the question of whether or not a sequence of sounds is a work of music is indeed dependent on what musicians say. This is, of course, the much debated 'institutional theory'. It is not much of a parody of this to say that it claims that whether a sound sequence is a work of music depends on whether members of the 'music world' say it is. It is, I imagine, pretty clear from what I have said that, whilst we cannot deny that there are cases when an artefact is declared or 'baptized' a work of art by experts, they are exceptional. Of course, we can point to cases such as those in which Picasso and his confrères declared Black sculpture to be art rather than ethnographical exemplars, but our normal procedure is not like that. We have a set of stereotypical 'works of music' and composers who are trained in traditional

---

[2] W. B. Gallie, *Philosophy and the Historical Understanding* (London: Chatto and Windus, 1964), ch. 8, esp. p. 158.

skills. What they produce is music. Whether or not it is good music is, of course, another matter.[3]

## II

Now recent work on the metaphysics of music recapitulates old distinctions. It is easy to spot familiar metaphysical positions. We may contrast Platonist theories such as those of Wolterstorff, Levinson, and Kivy with nominalist theories such as those of Goodman.[4] On the one hand, we have those thinkers for whom the work of music is a sound pattern which exists independently of the performance and the notation; indeed, Wolterstorff is enough of a Platonist to think that all possible works of music pre-exist their notation. For him, all that a composer does is to recognize a work. The composer does not create. This extreme Platonism is distinctly at odds with commonly made distinctions, and would, of course, apply quite generally. Nobody ever creates anything. The gifted poet, scientist, or philosopher is merely good at recognizing propositions whose existence is prior and independent. For the nominalist, on the other hand, the music is essentially a matter of a notation with which a performance complies.

The strict Platonist programme allows for a plethora of sound patterns. Every possible pattern will have a Platonic existence. It might be tempting to suppose that amongst these will be the good, the bad, and the mediocre. Platonism is traditionally ambiguous about this. As well as the Form of the Good, is there also the Form of the Callous, the Envious, or the Mean-spirited? Two thoughts occur to me about this. The first is that Platonism can be seen to enshrine an important intuition, though one that can also be accounted for by non-Platonism. The second is that Platonism fails to connect with questions about real music.

The composer who creates a work may have the experience often described by writers, that of being taken over by the work. It may

---

[3] The literature on this topic is immense. I recommend G. L. Hagberg, *Art as Language* (Ithaca, NY: Cornell University Press, 1995).

[4] N. Wolterstorff, *Works and Worlds of Art* (Oxford: Clarendon Press, 1980); Peter Kivy, *The Fine Art of Repetition* (Cambridge: Cambridge University Press, 1993); Jerrold Levinson, *Music, Art and Metaphysics* (Ithaca, NY: Cornell University Press, 1990); Nelson Goodman, *Languages of Art* (Oxford: Oxford University Press, 1969).

be begun by the writer (this equally applies to other artists), but then a certain remorseless logic continues the work. To create a pattern is to recognize a pattern. It is not a matter of no importance that musicians think this way, and, of course, it favours that partial Platonism which sees the Platonic heavens as inhabited only by Forms of what is valuable. Because music which has quality also has unity and integrity such that alterations damage it, it follows that a work, once begun, can develop only in a limited number of ways. In the greatest cases we may feel that a single change will be deleterious. Not any pattern of sounds can qualify for the Platonic heaven, only those which have the beauty of integrity.

Suppose, then, that Mozart announces that he has 'discovered' the theme for the Overture to *The Marriage of Figaro*. What justifies him in saying this is that he has found the solution to a problem, the problem of composing something which fits with the character of the rest of the opera, and is superbly appropriate as an overture.

Now in what sense does this show that a previously existing sound pattern has been discovered by Mozart? To discover a solution to a problem does not require the previous existence of the solution in the way that to discover Antarctica assumes that Antarctica previously existed. Any sort of existence this music has is the sort of existence that a proof has before it is discovered; that sort of existence is Platonic in the way mathematical entities have often appeared to be Platonic; so the Platonism suggested does not have to be too realist. The problem is that whatever advantages Platonism might seem to have here are enjoyed equally by non-Platonism. The apparent necessity and independent existence of the theme for the *overture* to *The Marriage of Figaro* is accounted for by the fact that it is so appropriate to the rest of the work. Its seeming inevitability derives from the way that it and the rest of the opera form a unity.

The second consideration militates against Platonism. The sound pattern as such has no musical significance. Until the hearer hears it as an ordered sequence, as a pattern which either repeats or develops, we have nothing which we can experience as we experience music. It is merely a dead pattern. It is the fact that we hear music as a pattern with a foregrounding, an order, which makes it music and not mere sound. Music is composed, and this means that it is heard in a tradition which makes it possible for us to understand a sequence of notes as a melody, as rising to a climax and coming to a close, or as a harmonic sequence, as leading to resolution. An uncomposed 'music of the spheres' will not be music except in the derivative way that we project a pattern on to it, much as we may 'see' a landscape as a Turner or a Constable.

I do not imply by this that the form possessed by music is 'imposed' upon it by the listener. As we saw in the first chapter, this sort of positivism has its adherents. The idea is that there are musical facts, the sounds, upon which the hearer imposes a form, and thereby renders it intelligible to himself. As I have already intimated, if the music is simply a sound pattern, a bare fact, which can be heard in different ways, an aural analogue of Wittgenstein's famous duck–rabbit, then there is no right or wrong way of hearing it. Rather, each way of hearing it would correspond to yet another Platonic Form. My argument is that sound patterns uncomposed would have that minimal quality. In such an abstract sound pattern there is no right phrasing. But, of course, there is in real music. Any piano teacher will set you right if you phrase a melody in such a way that it is not apparent as a single span. What he shows you is how musicians phrase the passage. Such phrasings belong to a tradition of performing in which the composer himself worked.

I have hinted that a frequently aired criticism of such Platonism in music is that it denies creativity. If a work of music is an abstract entity, a sound pattern that exists independently of the composer, then, instead of creating it, he merely selects it. The customary reply is that there are two sorts of selectivity, and that one of these is creative. The composer who grasps a Platonic pattern is creative in a way in which another composer, who merely quotes the first, perhaps for the purpose of composing a set of variations is not, at least at that point. But on the face of it this is an evasion unless the Platonist has a theory about what it is to recognize a pattern *ab initio* and, moreover, an account of how the abstract entity enters into a relationship with the composing mind. It is as much a problem for a Platonist ontology of music as it is for a Platonist philosophy of mathematics, which has to show how mathematical discoveries are made. We need an epistemology.[5]

Let me raise two further problems. First of all, it is a fact that

---

[5] The problems look similar to that of how there can be a causal relationship between mind and body on a dualist theory, a problem that has bedevilled Cartesianism.

music is composed in a certain historical setting. Beethoven's music is, *inter alia*, an expression of Romanticism, and no abstract pattern pre-dating the foundation of the world can have this expressive character. There are, then, features of the music which the sound pattern alone does not possess. Indeed, if, *mirabile dictu*, that exact sound pattern were repeated at another time, it would not have the same properties. We can see this in a small way through quotation. When Tippett quotes Beethoven's Ninth in his Third Symphony, the music he quotes acquires new characteristics. The passage is puzzling, rather than questioning. Tippett's use of the phrase raises questions about the place of the great Viennese classics in our society, and about the differences between his musical landscape and Beethoven's. But it does not have the character it does in the original.

The Platonist will dispute the force of this objection. He will observe that a given work does not become another work when attributed to J. C. Bach rather than to Haydn. Agreed, it is discovered to have new properties; what would be dull in Haydn might be remarkable in a lesser composer such as J. C. Bach; but the notes are the same. Should we not agree with the Platonist that it is the same work but newly attributed? The problem now is that we acknowledge that the sonata when attributed to J. C. Bach has different properties from when it is attributed to Haydn. But the condition of identity is that A and B are identical if and only if they have all their properties in common. These two works do not. (Of course, it is significant that nobody argues that it has been composed twice.) Having discovered that it is by J. C. Bach, we realize that it has features which we did not know about before. The important point is that you do not exhaust the characteristics of a piece of music when you list its notes. Platonism implies that you do. But the features of a work may be a consequence of the actions and the intellectual milieu in which it was composed; that is a matter distinct from the business of the notes.

Take an analogy. Two actions might both be described as a slap across the face. So described, they are the same action. But viewed, on the one hand, as an attempt to bring a hysterical child to his senses, or, on the other hand, as an assault, they obviously differ. Thus I might say both that the sonata attributed to Haydn and the sonata attributed to J. C. Bach are the same piece, and that they are different pieces. This is not inconsistent. The question of identity ultimately depends upon how we describe it, and is, to that extent, a triviality. Platonist and non-Platonist agree that A is identical with B only if they have all their properties in common; the problem remains that the characterization of an abstract object is in our gift. We decide what will count as defining properties. So the principle of identity offers us no solutions. If you, a Platonist, wish to restrict the idea of the identity of a piece of music to only those properties which can be identified with the features of a sound pattern, I cannot stop you. But I will point out that many of the features which interest us about music, features which matter to the interpreter, and which connect with the way we understand and criticize the work, will not belong to the work on this understanding. (For example, discovering it is by J. C. Bach may incline us to perform it on an English fortepiano.) And the consequence is that we are forced towards an unhelpful ontology which sees such features as features which we 'project' on to the work. (Curiously, at this point Kivy's Platonism converges on Cook's positivism.)

Platonists and non-Platonists alike agree that a distinction between what is essential to the identity of a piece and what is contingent is required. But to say that this distinction can be settled is to place more trust in intuitions than I share. The more we have to do with problem cases, the less likely it is that we shall agree in intuitions. Indeed, the assumption that an appeal to intuitions is the right move here is already a Platonic prejudice. It forgets that our concepts are our creations, and that there is no reason to think that they will be articulated for imaginary borderline cases; it is very probable that they will not be if nothing turns on such a decision about the boundaries of our concepts. A Platonist like Kivy certainly should be concerned about conceding, as he does, that no intuitive answer exists to outrageous problem cases, for the Platonic case must be that the boundaries of these concepts pre-date our enquiries.[6] Kivy, after all, thinks that there is an answer to the question 'Is this the same work as . . . ?' But he presumably thinks that intuition will not find an answer to it. Of course, the concession may not be fatal. Arguments may provide what intuition cannot, or we may be destined to remain ignorant. Nevertheless, the concession is disturbing, partly because Platonism is not traditionally sceptical about the possibility of such knowledge.

[6] Kivy, *Fine Art*, 65.

Another issue: What makes Mozart use an Alberti bass in his Piano Sonata K. 545? This won't be *explained* in terms of Mozart's apprehension of a Platonic sound pattern. It is, rather, that this was part of the lingua franca of music at that time. Music is written the way it is because the composer is guided by the available models. Brahms uses the St Anthony chorale in his variations not because he apprehended a Platonic pattern, but because he came across a likely theme in somebody else's work. The very vocabulary of music is an accumulation of inherited devices; the figurations, trills, turns, the standard early Renaissance form of the 'In nomine', and the available chordal progressions are gradually added to and modified. A composer cannot write just anything. Gombrich raised the question as to why Leonardo did not paint Impressionist pictures. The simple and obvious answer is that style is a human historical product, and the style in question was not available to Leonardo. Exactly the same question can be raised for music, and the answer is the same. Specific music cannot be written at any time. When Levinson says that the notes of the Tristan chord could have been sounded together before, and that Brahms or Mozart must have been aware that they could, two points occur to me. Both suggest that there is a sense of 'impossible' in which it was impossible for either to have used such a chord, certainly in the way Wagner used it (it would have had to be resolved): first, it was neither in their vocabulary nor in a plausible extension of that vocabulary; second, and possibly consequently, it would not have counted for them as music (given that context). Had they thought of it, they would have dismissed it as a curiosity. Indeed, even when music seems to be plucked out of the air, or occurs to a composer in a dream as 'In dulci jubilo' was supposed to have occurred to Isaac, it is noteworthy that the composer writes in the style of the day. My point is that both creative and non-creative composition fall within the second category, which, on a rigorously Platonic pattern, will be non-creative selectivity.

Levinson differs from his fellow Platonists in taking the music not to be just the abstract pattern, but to involve the means of performance.[7] Well, there are variations in the extent to which a particular instrumentation is called for. Bach's *Art of Fugue* has been played on the organ or with various combinations of instruments.

---

[7] Levinson, *Music, Art and Metaphysics*, 73.

His Forty-eight Preludes and Fugues are commonly played on the piano, without this being thought of as an 'arrangement' (I shall return to this topic in the next chapter). But, as the nineteenth century rolled on, the instrumentation of a work became more and more part of its identity. So, certainly, our concept of some classical music requires the means of performance. Berlioz remarked, when complaining about the method of deciding the Prix de Rome through piano reductions of orchestral works, 'Can anyone seriously maintain that one can judge the true quality of an orchestral work emasculated in this fashion?'[8] Of course, the *echt*-Platonist may agree. He claims only that the notes are what confers identity. The music is not precluded from having other characteristics. But if the value of the music is lost or seriously impaired, then we cannot accept the Platonist ontology with good grace. Explicitly or implicitly, Platonism presumes that the sound pattern, the notes, are what is essential, and this relegates the means of performance to a secondary role. But listen, for example, to Rameau's *La Fête d'Hébé*. Without that exact and extraordinary imaginative orchestration, what would be left? Some music loses catastrophically when the instrumentation is set aside. Other music survives better in piano reductions and arrangements. But we have no grounds for assuming that the best music is music which can be so translated. That would be to commit ourselves precipitately to a form of Platonism. As I shall argue later, questions of value are far too closely involved in the arts to be set aside lightly when considering ontology.

In the end, what is Platonism explaining? It gives us an ontology: that the work of music is a sound pattern. Such an ontology explains if it entails assumptions which are present, if unarticulated, in ordinary talk about the work of music, its interpretations and its performance. I have argued that Platonism does not square with much of the way in which we speak of music. There is a reason for this failing, to which I shall return. For the present, let me anticipate the position I shall take up. I am not persuaded that there can be an analysis of the concept of a 'work of music'. Two arguments for this conclusion occur to me immediately. First, it might be that the problem of analysis is degenerate, in that at each point so many facets of musical practice enter that we cannot give a satisfactory

---

[8] Hector Berlioz, *Memoirs*, trans. David Cairns (London: Panther, 1970), 130.

general answer; second, it may be that the open nature of the concept of a work and of what counts as an interpretation or a performance implies the impossibility of a convincing analysis; for, since in borderline cases, we have no clear criterion for whether or not a specific set of sounds is music, or whether a specific set of sounds can count as a performance of a particular work, it might be argued that no formulaic analysis of 'work of music' is possible.

I am not sure whether this second argument is sound. After all, we can demand of an analysis only that it be as sharply defined as its target concept, and there seems to be no a priori reason to doubt that a formula can be given which matches our concept of a work of music. My own reason for doubting the possibility of analysis is, rather, the conviction that ideological elements are deeply embedded in the idea of a 'work of music'.

But before developing this, there is another matter to attend to. I have mentioned nominalism, and at this point I must say a little more about it, since it is the main alternative to Platonism in the contest. Goodman, who best represents the nominalist alternative, claims that the work is the class of performances which comply with a notation. His notorious doctrine that tempo does not belong to the notation, whereas the notes do, has the consequence, as has been so often remarked, that a performance of Beethoven which took an hour over each quaver, but where each note was accurate, would be a performance, albeit not a very good one, whereas one at a more conventional speed but with a single mistake would not. (In practice, it need hardly be said, the concept of performance is never ever used this way.) One devastating question puts all this into perspective. Lydia Goehr asks what it is a theory of.[9] If the divergence between theory and practice matters so little to Goodman, what interest does his theory have? A purely formal arrangement of definitions and arguments has no independent interest at all. Such attention to the notation is a comparatively recent phenomenon, and is connected with various other strands in musical culture. Bojan Bujic remarks that musical notation was, until recently, no more than an *aide-mémoire*; its elevation to the role of arbiter of correctness would have surprised most of the

---

[9] Lydia Goehr, *The Imaginary Museum of Musical Works* (Oxford: Clarendon Press, 1992), 36.

composers whose work dominates the repertoire.[10] (What analogies there are belong to the far distant past. The notation of Gregorian chant determined the identity of the work, and departure from what it prescribed was sinful.) This is not to say that Goodman has not latched on to an aspect of modern musical thought. He certainly has. His privileging of notation is shared by all those analysts who regard the function of musicology as the analysis of a work fully defined by its notation and whose structural features owe nothing to interpretation. Like Goodman, analysts such as Boretz and Babbitt think they are engaged in a fully scientific activity. They share a positivist approach to music. But in this respect this particular ideology is in sharp conflict with another shibboleth of modern musical research, the recovery of the original sound, so there are certainly other opinions about the prime obligation of a performer.

Let us now consider a third approach, additional to Platonism and nominalism, which I shall describe as 'deflationary'. Defining the work of music in a way closer to musical practice, its existence becomes a matter neither of notation nor of prior existence in a possible world of Platonic objects. It is a matter of the possibility of performance. If a notated score is lost, or if an orally transmitted work is forgotten, it ceases to exist. In response to questions such as 'Where then is the work really?' or 'What sort of existence does it have?', we simply refer the questioners back to what we have just said about the possibility of performance. We can say no more, and to persist in such a line of questioning shows the presence of a false picture based on misleading analogies with the visual arts. Goehr shows how the performance of music in the concert-hall was explicitly compared with the assembling of sculpture and painting in a museum; in fact, the title of her book, *The Imaginary Museum*, though taken from Malraux, recalls Liszt's proposal that concert-halls should be the 'museums of music'. The fact that this model is by now so much part of our thinking about music does not render it innocuous. On the deflationary view, the model leads us astray.

The deflationary approach coheres nicely with taking the

---

[10] Bojan Bujic, 'Notation and Realization: Musical Performance in Historical Perspective', in Michael Krausz (ed.), *The Interpretation of Music* (Oxford: Clarendon Press, 1993), 134.

interpretation of a piece of music to be a type with which one or more performances comply. Thus a performer in Western classical music thinks out a view of the work from a notated original. He makes the important decisions about precise tempo and dynamics, for no notation is completely explicit. Any player knows that the greater the work, the more exigent the decisions about such matters. The placing of the climax and the relative weight assigned to different sections and movements is critical. The performance is then a token of that interpretation type, and the work provides a recipe within which the interpreter can operate. Such an interpretation may be given several performances. Some artists think out an interpretation, and then stick to it in performance after performance. Others are more 'spontaneous', and each performance may register a different interpretation. In defending this in a paper more than a decade ago, I suggested that you cannot splice together bits of different interpretations to give a single performance.[11] You cannot, as a friend once recommended, put together Horenstein's performance of the first movement of Mahler's *Das Lied von der Erde* and follow it with Walter's performance of the rest. For one thing, what is climactic in one interpretation may cease to be so when set within another. A decent interpretation has been thought through, and it is as offensive to patch together different interpretations as it would be to make up a poem using bits of Jonson, Marlowe, and Shakespeare. Like a work of art, an interpretation has its own integrity. I acknowledge that the view I propose has become more compelling now that the recording industry gives us the chance to compare different interpretations by different performers. Concepts change. There is no doubt, too, that this ontology, if appropriate for Western classical music, cannot characterize folk music or jazz where 'the original work' is less clearly defined.

An objection is that of Levinson, who, whilst allowing that the distinction between interpretation as type and performance as token is well taken, argues that a performance may be a token of two types simultaneously, one being the work and the other the interpretation. Thus the first word of this sentence is simultaneously a token of the word 'thus' and a token of 'thus' in whatever type the publishers decide upon. This criticism tells. My original thought was that works were tantamount to recipes, but, as I shall shortly

[11] R. A. Sharpe, 'Type, Token, Interpretation and Performance', *Mind*, 88 (1979), 437–40.

acknowledge, the deflationary approach succeeds at the price of neglecting important aspects of the concept of music—in particular, its function as a forum where rival ideologies may contend.

Robert L. Martin, like Paul Thom, whose proposal I shall discuss later, has recently suggested that the work be taken as a set of instructions, rather than as an abstract object. Consequently he believes that the type–token relationship applies only to that relationship between work and performance which lies within the world of the listener; the composer's world contains no works which stand as types to tokens; for the composer the work constitutes a recipe.[12] This does not seem intuitively satisfactory. We talk of works in ways which sort uneasily with this proposal. Could a mere set of instructions convey a sense of spiritual unease? Moreover, there may be a world of difference between eating a dish cooked by a famous chef and eating one cooked according to his recipe. But we regard listening to a performance of Beethoven as at least as much like the first as the second. Again, if there are two different worlds, one of the composer, the other of the listener, how do they connect? Part of the reason why we value music is because of the way we are put in touch with the creative act of the composer. Some of the important nuances in our thought about the musical work and its performance are lost in this approach.

I have been attacked for confusing questions of identity and value in performance. Peter Kivy argues that there would be no question but that a performance involving several bits of interpretations would be a single performance, though it might be unlikely to be thought a good one.[13] An evening at the Met in which three sick Isoldes, seated or prone, each sang one act is still a performance, albeit a rather bizarre one. In such a case the unity of the performance would presumably come from the conductor and the other singers. If the conductor were different, then I do not think we would speak of a single performance. My argument, as far as I can see, does not succumb to this.

In any case, I have other grounds for objecting to a sharp distinction between questions of identity and value. Since I think that metaphysics is frequently part of an ideology, and since I shall press

---

[12] R. L. Martin, 'Musical Works in the Worlds of Performers and Listeners', in Krausz (ed.), *Interpretation of Music*, 119–27. J. O. Urmson, in 'The Ethics of Musical Performance', in the same volume, subscribes to the view that scores are like recipes.

[13] Kivy, *Fine Art*, 48–51.

the case for musical ideology being heavily involved here, it will be clear that I do not think that we are dealing with purely conceptual questions, uninfluenced by interest. Our criterion of identity for art is in part ideologically motivated, and certainly cannot be independent of questions of value. So my own reason for not pursuing a deflationary approach, an approach which naturally appeals to any philosopher influenced by Wittgenstein, derives from the sense, already adumbrated, that 'ideological' factors are deeply interwoven with how we think and talk about music and, *a fortiori*, how we practice it (just as my misgivings about Wittgensteinian philosophy of religion derive from my belief that speculation and metaphysics are integral to religion). In pursuing an ontology, we create problems for ourselves which only a deflationary approach seems likely to solve. Yet, because of the function which music has in a culture, a function partly defined by the ideas we have about it, such ontological speculations are necessary and inevitable. At the same time, I have suggested, we ought not to be sanguine about the problems of coherence and consistency which they create.

## III

So far, my objections to both Platonism and nominalism have depended on mismatches between the analyses proposed and those intuitive judgements we take to be generally true of music. But what is striking, and what will occupy me for the rest of this chapter, is the way that the two alternatives privilege certain aspects of musical practice and of talk about music. It has become usual, as must now be apparent, to talk of 'ideology' in this context, and I shall continue with this usage, though, later on, I shall say more about what the term connotes. Given, then, that the concept of ideology has entered the fray, this is the place to redeem my promise to place musical experience in a broader context.

Up until now, I have been concerned with the idea of an analysis. Now consider the various ways in which an analysis could go wrong. It may be that the philosopher is simply mistaken. This is how a philosopher customarily thinks of her activity. She is trying to get an accurate picture of some 'conceptual facts' and, because of the difficulty and complexity of the case, she fails to get it quite right. Perhaps she will try to give an analysis in nominalist terms;

it does not work, and she gives it up or tries to amend it. Certainly, philosophy is sometimes like this, but, perhaps more often, is not. For few philosophers are the islands of pure rationality that they like to think they are.

First, a philosopher may have committed herself to a theory after years of hard thinking. Naturally she does not favour infanticide, and, in any case, if she has published it, she is identified with the position, so it matters that it is defensible. This is no bad thing. The ideas get a run for their money, and her antagonists enjoy the cut and thrust of argument. It is never much fun for anybody if a philosopher loses confidence in her ideas and refuses to defend them.

But the case we are interested in is different again. We need to consider the situation where an analysis takes some of its charge from the ideologically based aspects of the situation. Thus the attractions of Platonism might be twofold, and in both respects linked with what I have called the 'ideology'. First, an analogy between music and painting and sculpture, whose position amongst the fine arts was assured long before music was so classified, might thereby be underpinned. The change in our conception of music which occurred largely in the eighteenth century placed music, *ceteris paribus*, in the company of the highest forms of art, those whose prestige was secure. Such a judgement about the place and importance of music is a judgement which forms part of our general conception of music and its place in the scheme of arts and culture; it is judgements of this sort which are described as 'ideological' by specialists on the intellectual history of music and by those musicologists who belong to the humanist wing of the movement. We need to remember, extraordinary though it now seems, that through most of its known history, performed music was not regarded as a fine art in its own right. Its role was to accompany verse, liturgy, or dancing.

To place music amongst the paradigms of art like poetry or painting means separating the work from performance and interpretation. A reason for this is that works of art are thought of as long-lasting, as objects of contemplation and wonder through the ages; the performances and the interpretations they embody, by contrast, are ephemeral, and, at least until the invention of the gramophone, could not easily be studied closely or compared with other performances. Though crucial to our understanding and

enjoyment of music, the performance, once completed, was lost
except to the memory of the performer and the audience. The idea
that the work is separate from the performance consorts particularly well with Platonism. For since, on this view, a work cannot
be directly encountered but only mediately via a performance, it
becomes natural to view it as a type of which the performances are
tokens. But such a type is an abstract object.[14] Such a view is
opposed to that nominalism which, on Goodman's account, privileges the notation. For the notation is not itself a work of art,
but merely a means of producing a performance which, as I have
said, is ephemeral. The 'permanence' and 'objectivity' which the
Platonist looks for in a work of art is then absent.

Secondly, a Platonist approach might connect with the long tradition of music as concerned with abstract forms and unheard patterns, a view which effectively divides music into two: the abstract
mathematical study of harmonic relations and number associated,
*inter alia*, with the doctrine of a music of the spheres, on the one
hand, and the art of producing audible sounds, on the other. For
centuries such a distinction was commonplace, and for medieval
theorists it was a cliché. Its rival, nominalism, might seem the
natural ontology for a notated art—Goodman certainly thinks so—
but this need not be the case. The pressures for Platonism in music
have, after all, something to do with the long accepted similarities
between a notated art and mathematics. Platonism is the child of
traditions, analogies, and even educational classifications such as
the yoking together of music and mathematics in the medieval
quadrivium. So Platonism, too, might privilege a notated score,
though that score would then stand to a Platonic Form much as a
written mathematical expression stands to the mathematical truth
it expresses.

To defend a more contemporary Platonism, as part of the current
concept of music, we need to show that the notion of the work as
an abstract object which can never be more than partially realized
in a performance is deeply embedded in how musicians think about

---

[14] An interesting sidelight on this is the existence of two odd, and probably
forged, accounts of the compositional processes of Mozart and Beethoven, which
both describe the work of music as being composed in an instant, in its entirety,
in the head, before being written down. This makes the process sound like the
intuition of a Platonic object, and, I suggest, was motivated by a desire to stress
ontological analogies between music and the visual arts. See Nicholas Cook, *Music,
Imagination and Culture* (Oxford: Oxford University Press, 1990), 114–15.

their art. I shall say something about this later; but if it is true that it is part of conventional musical thought, then it would not be surprising that challenging it might be painful, and any consequent adjustments uncomfortable. Its ideological force connects with a musician's self-assessment, with his view of the place of his art in culture and society. Goehr thinks that the analogy between music and painting was an analogy which rose to prominence in the nineteenth century, and that associated with it was the doctrine of faithfulness to the work (*werktreue*), an ideal which informed musical practice. This suggests that Platonism (at least when viewed aside from its connections with mathematics) fits most naturally with a nineteenth-century conception of music.

If, then, the concept of music thus embodies Platonism, we may well feel ambivalent about challenging the analysis of 'work of music' which embodies it. Although we may think that it fails to accord with other aspects of musical practice and with the way we discuss music, we may also believe that the purpose of such a concept is to incorporate an ideal. Undermine Platonism, and you may undermine a pillar of the institutions and practices of musicmaking. Whether this is so, of course, is a matter of fact. There are analogies in the concept of a deity; it has been a common defence of belief in God that it underpins certain moral behaviour which, in its absence, might be vulnerable.

Platonism, nominalism, and a deflationary approach, it seems, share at least one characteristic: they all attempt to articulate the prevailing conception of 'the work'. Now, as far as I can see, nothing prevents such a concept from being incoherent; after all, if, as Goehr argues, such concepts are the locus of ideological pressures, then these pressures may lead to conflicts which are located within the concept of music itself. Just as a member of the Conservative Party may believe various inconsistent things about freedom, opportunity, and equality, and a Christian various inconsistent things about God, evil, and human freedom, so a musician may believe inconsistent things about the sanctity of the composer's intentions and the freedom of the interpreting performer. But it might also be true, of course, that in paying attention to the comparative recency of the concept of music and the theorizing which has gone with it, we misrepresent a practice which is not in itself inconsistent.

So there are various ways in which the concept of music might be related to practice. It might be consonant with it or dissonant with it. In the latter case, it might incorporate ideals which either are not put into practice or could not be put into practice. Of course, an inaccurate analysis of the concept of a work of music might, nevertheless, have an effect on the way musicians use the concept. Even if Platonism fails to capture how the performer relates to the work, it might still infect the thought of musicians. Or the relation between the concept of music as analysed by philosophers and the practice of musicians might be different again. The analysis may not affect practice, or practice may fail to affect the analysis. In either case, what philosophers do is independent of what musicians do and think.

If Goodman accurately captures the concept in his nominalism, what he captures is a concept which stands obliquely to musical practice. For we do not count a performance with a single mistake as no longer a performance of a work. To say instead that he represents, by implication, an ideal of musical performance as totally accurate suggests that this ideal is what the performer should aspire to. To this extent the concept is regulative. So it is not ultimately irrelevant to musical practice as Goodman perceives it. But how seriously do we take such a statement of the ideal? What do we want from analysis? Do we want an analysis which connects with performing practice, or an analysis of regulative ideals which may be remote from that practice? A related question, then, is 'What work does the concept do?', 'What interest is it serving?' There might, perhaps, be a clear answer to this question. Although it is fair to castigate analytic philosophy for a failure to understand the historical dimensions of the concept, and a consequent failure to answer these questions, nothing I have said precludes our getting a correct synchronic grasp.

*En passant*, to avoid misunderstanding, let me say that I do not think Goodman's approach is motivated by any specifically musical ideology. His motives are more general and metaphysical, and have to do with his abhorrence of abstract entities. Unlike Levinson, Goehr, and Kivy, he shows no great understanding of music. Indeed, the nub of objections to Goodman is the sheer unmusicality of his concerns. How often is it said that whereas one pianist plays all the notes, another—like, for example, Schnabel—makes mistakes aplenty, but catches the meaning of the music? What matters to us is interpretative depth. For musicians, the differences between great re-creative interpreters such as Furtwängler or Beecham, Solomon or Curzon, and the others is a matter of central concern. The former embody the re-creative forces which produce interpretative traditions.[15] But interpretation has no place in Goodman's scheme.

Lydia Goehr argues that our concept of a musical work is historically recent.[16] The concept of the work of music, Goehr suggests, derives from a number of factors: the beliefs that fine art is self-sufficient and autonomous, and that its contemplation is an end in itself. Economic and social factors played a part as well. The ideal of an imaginary museum enshrines these ideas.[17] Prior to 1800, she argues, the idea that a work of music was composed and then performed in the same way in various places at different times, and that it was the child of its creator, barely existed. Her stress on the acceptance prior to this date of what we now regard as plagiarism hardly shows that the concept of music did not exist, though it does show—and this fits well with her general thesis—that concepts have changed, sometimes radically, sometimes a bit at a time. Certainly there were changes in the concept of music at the beginning of the nineteenth century. L. B. Meyer remarks on the repudiation of convention, the rise of the cult of genius, and the ideal of organicism, amongst other changes. These elements in the Romantic movement played a part in changing the way people thought about music.[18] Goehr and Meyer have been prominent in forcing us to confront the way in which thinking about music is guided by general values and ideas—by ideology, indeed. The importance of their work is obvious. But I find myself disagreeing with Goehr on a few points of detail. For example, it does not seem that the changes she notes introduced a concept of music as performable at different places

[15] Joseph Kerman, *Contemplating Music* (Cambridge, Mass.: Harvard University Press, 1985), 199, remarks that many musicologists are uncomfortable with this element of flair which is so important to interpretation. Their preference for the notated score as opposed to the re-creation of a work in performance suggests an ontology like that of Goodman. Indeed, if anybody embodies a positivist approach to aesthetics, it is Goodman.

[16] A similar point is made by Carl Dahlhaus, *The Aesthetics of Music*, trans. William Austin (Cambridge: Cambridge University Press, 1982), 11.

[17] On the museum analogy see J. Burkholder, 'Museum Pieces: The Historicist Mainstream in the Music of the Last Hundred Years', *Journal of Musicology*, 2 (1983), 115–34.

[18] L. B. Meyer, S*tyle and Music* (Philadelphia: University of Pennsylvania Press, 1989).

and different times. That was there before. What does differ, I suppose, is the extent to which it was thought important to preserve the sameness of the work, or—what amounts to the same thing—the judgement as to what constituted the work's identity.

Tallis's great forty-part motet was possibly a response to a challenge laid down by Striggio's precedent, which, by all accounts, it eclipses; but, suggests Paul Doe, it also surely embodies a desire for personal fulfilment, a desire shared by so many composers, to create a representative example of the best of their art in their old age. (And there is a specifically technical problem about getting forty parts to modulate to the dominant when they cannot all introduce the sharpened fourth.) Remember too that Byrd and Tallis had a license to publish music, which strongly suggests that music was performed in the absence of the composer. Let us go back even further. After his death in 1521, the music of Josquin des Prez circulated 'throughout Europe in both manuscript and print, more than any other music of his generation'. The fact is—and of course the existence of the music demonstrates it—that it did survive after the composer's death. It is hard to think that he did not care about the fate of his work.

It is true that most music performed was contemporary music prior to the nineteenth century. It is true, as well, that, as a result of this, composers probably did not expect their music to survive. But in the greatest cases it was disseminated. In many respects composers behaved as if they had the concept of 'a work'. There are, of course, differences, but they are differences of degree more than kind. After his death, Tallis's motet was performed with an English text, for example. What is true is that the work has come more and more to be viewed as an aesthetic object in its own right to which the performer must, above all else, be faithful, as opposed to being but a means to a performance.


IV


I need to return to the question of ideology. We need to know what difference it makes that a concept is, as I would put it, ideologically charged, and how we would recognize it to be such. L. B. Meyer gives a fascinating account of the changing *Weltanschauung* at the end of the eighteenth century.[19] His conception of ideology is of a complex network, not only of beliefs and ideas, but also of inter-related attitudes, beliefs, and indeed metaphors, held, consciously or subconsciously, by members of a culture or subculture. He describes Western ideology as involving 'unconscious' and 'basic' categories such as social progress, originality, the dignity of labour, dualism, and the value of aesthetic experience. To this we should add an assumption which, as we shall see, is central to how we view the arts; it is that the styles or languages of art develop, even if they do not progress. But although he distinguishes between the history of ideas and ideology, it is difficult to see why we should take such central concepts as organicism or tradition and such pre-vailing oppositions as those between feeling and reason, symbol and allegory, and culture and nature as characterizing ideology rather than the history of ideas. There seems to be no clear water between ideologies and *Weltanschauungen*, or Wittgensteinian forms of life.

The concept of ideology has been much chewed over recently. It is now widely seen as bearing either a wide or a narrow sense. In the narrow, more traditionally Marxist sense, an ideology blinds; it is a means of exploitation, a means whereby one class preserves its dominance over others. In its broader or, as John B. Thompson would have it, its 'neutral' sense, it is a system of thought which in part identifies a culture or subculture. In both 'neutral' and 'criti-cal' senses, an ideology enshrines certain values; but the broader sense does not connote exploitation; in the broader sense, ideology is not primarily a weapon, and not necessarily the locus of self-deception or false consciousness; nor does it carry the implication of being 'necessarily misleading, illusory or aligned with the inter-ests of any particular group'.[20] In both senses, an ideology defines the self-image of groups and members of groups. How one thinks of oneself and how one thinks of one's society are contained within that ideology. When an American thinks of his land as the land of opportunity for all, the bastion of freedom in a benighted world, his thought reflects an ideology familiar to us all. Characteristically,

---

[19]  L. B. Meyer, ch. 6.
[20]  John B. Thompson, *Ideology and Modern Culture: Critical Social Theory in the Era of Mass Communication* (Cambridge: Polity Press, 1992), 53, and see A. de Toit, 'On Ideology, *South African Journal of Philosophy*, 13/3 (1994), 116–17.

he will react defensively if the component beliefs are challenged. He thinks of himself as an American, is proud to be one, and believes that American history enshrines certain values. Challenge his conception of his country, and you challenge part of his identity. Naturally, then, there is a dynamic which propels the believer towards either a distortion of the truth or self-deception, and this is so regardless of whether or not an ideology actually contains false beliefs. There are beliefs which it is important to us that we do not surrender. We defend them, and the price of the defence is likely to be self-deception or false consciousness. In this broad sense, ideologies look to be an inevitable part of human existence. Like the poor, they are always with us. We might even define man as the 'ideological animal'.

For the Marxist, of course, whose sense of 'ideology' is the narrow or 'critical' one, an ideology-free view of society and its history is a possibility. Those minds which have been liberated from false consciousness can see the economic forces which determine history *en clair*. The scales have fallen from their eyes. They see things as they are. They can pick out the class which dominates, and see that it consistently acts in its own interests. Liberation from ideology is thus an important political weapon on the Marxist account, and it is the role it plays in political development which distinguishes it from concepts which are superficially similar, such as *Weltanschauung* or 'form of life'. I do not think that these latter concepts suggest false consciousness or self-deception to the same extent; nor are they so deeply implicated in the self-image. In a word, ideology is much more closely tied to complex matters of philosophical psychology and is more deeply implicated in irrationality, and this remains true even when we depart from the narrower Marxist conception in favour of a broader or neutral theory.

The advocate of ideological analysis has a problem, a problem which is essentially that of relativism. If he thinks, as I do, that ideological commitment is universal, and that there is always an impetus towards self-deception ingrained in it, then he must acknowledge that this holds of himself as much as those whom he criticizes for their ideological involvement. But then, inasmuch as the self-deception is 'realized', it undercuts the validity of his claims. It never was plausible for Marx to suggest that he and his disciples alone saw how interests determined the structure of society, whilst everybody else was blinded by the mists and myths of ideology. However, the critic might, as I do, allow that some of the claims which belong to his ideology, and which he vehemently defends, might be both defensible and true—inasmuch as they are claims capable of being true (which might arguably not be the case for judgements of value, for instance). Such claims we may defend both because they connect with our self-image, our nationality and social group, our profession and our values, and because we believe they are true. Now in the case of self-deception, of course, we may have an inkling that they are not supportable. But we might think they are true because we are blind to the case against them rather than self-deceiving. We have no 'inkling' that they can be undermined.

What is crucial for my approach is that all this can coexist with their actually being true. What I write here is conditioned, certainly, but that does not prevent it from being true. Even if to charge somebody with 'ideology' is almost invariably a criticism, it is not inevitably so. I might, with insouciance, agree that my animus is ideological, but claim, as well, that my beliefs are both true and justified.

This, I think, goes nicely with the piecemeal approach to philosophical problems that I favour. I do not think that there is any single key which unlocks the aesthetic problems of music. In particular, I do not think that the account which I give of how the debate over the concepts of work and performance is ideologically permeated can be generalized, inasmuch as I do not think that a similar approach will reveal contradictions between rival views on the analysis of expressive predicates which we apply to music, predicates such as 'heavy-hearted' or 'feline'. Sometimes an analysis can be given which is internally consistent and accords with the restricted, consistent range of usages of a concept within a culture. But then sometimes it cannot. What interest me are philosophical problems; the answers which we give to these problems sometimes demand ideological analysis, and sometimes do not. Probably ideology always hovers in the background, but it may not be relevant to philosophical inquiry; then its teasing out is a matter for intellectual historians, and not philosophers *qua* philosophers.

Given the importance we attach to ideological beliefs and our readiness to defend them, what we have so far is what we might call a 'Quinean view' of ideology. The emphasis is on the centrality of certain beliefs in a system, and on the way in which we protect them against challenge. We might describe them as belonging to our central core of beliefs.

But ideology cannot be characterized quite so simply. My belief that I am now writing at a word processor is not a belief which I am prepared to discard, yet nobody will say this is ideological. What seems also true of ideological and religious beliefs is that they are pervasive; they infiltrate our lives. They determine our role models, whom we respect, what we revere, and what are our authorities. They affect all sorts of other matters. They reverberate. Meyer was right to allude to attitudes, beliefs, and metaphors. My belief that I am working at a word processor carries no such implications. It is not central in the same way.

What gives ideology its power? Why are there beliefs and attitudes which matter so much to us that they are used to define who we are? This pervasiveness of ideology suggests an answer. It is because a Christian's belief in God, if he is a religious man, affects his attitudes, his responses to other people, his awe at certain events, and his estimate of the importance of certain events, that it plays so important a part in what we might broadly call his identity. The same is true, *pari passu*, of a Marxist's belief in political dynamics and the flow of history (just supposing there are any Marxists left).

Suppose, then, that the concept of a work of music is, as has been claimed, part of the ideology of the arts in general and of music in particular, we can still ask whether we need the concept. Could we not jettison it? We might think that the concept is so confused that nothing could be signified by it. To give up using the concept of a work of music is, we might think, much easier than giving up using the idea of God (though if the concept ceases to have a role, it is hardly a choice that we make). We would still use the concept of God in speaking of the beliefs and practices of religious people, of course; but we cease to use it inasmuch as we cease to address him, explain things in term of his will, and so on. To lose a concept like the concept of a deity, whose associated beliefs have had a central directing role in conduct and reflection, requires all sorts of other adjustments. The believer prays and goes to church. Much of his time is concerned with such matters. To put it mildly, it is a good deal of bother to change.

Now I do not imagine that losing the concept of a work of music would be similarly problematic. After all, we would still go to concerts, play music, buy compact discs, and the like. What would be different is that attention would switch away from the work and its composer to the performance. The conceptual framework of jazz indicates how things might be. The composer produces a score which is but the basis for a performance, and our interest lies really in its potential for the gifted performer, much as a good jazz tune tends to be the sort of tune which a gifted player can make much of. Its chordal progressions, its melodic shapes, and so on can be used by the inventive improviser. In the classical period the expectations about ornamentation and, in cadenzas, improvisation were such that almost certainly a classical concerto was a half-way house between a Beethoven concerto as viewed by a modern pianist— that is, as virtually sacrosanct and where the range of interpretative decision is limited—and the jazz musician's attitude to 'Round Midnight'.

But ideology in the context of music works in two rather different ways. It is not just the concept of music which is at issue; there is also the matter of the canon, that list of the 'Great Composers' which we learn when we first experience music, and which has such a formative influence on our taste. If we gave up the concept of music in the way I have just described, would we not also have to give up the ideal of the canon, that list of the great and the good? For the claim of these works and these composers to greatness would go if their role was not much more than that of the provider of raw material for the performer. No matter how marvellous and subtle a tune 'These Foolish Things' is, its composer has none of the kudos accorded to Charlie Parker or Lester Young. We ought not to underestimate the seismic change that this would bring. For here the role that ideology plays in music matches an aspect of ideology as ordinarily conceived. For the canon involves what Marx once called 'a tradition of the dead', a list of those composers and their accomplishments which are supreme amongst human achievements. Marx goes on to speak of 'ancient and venerable prejudices'. Of course, our valuing of Bach and Beethoven are not prejudices. Rather, the respect they receive is proper and a partial definition of what it is for a culture to be civilized.

Think again about the concept of God. Many people, not merely the recently retired bishop of Durham, are apparently able to continue as members of the Christian Church whilst, in private, dissenting from its salient doctrines. Amongst my friends who are

Roman Catholics, I cannot think of one who defends the papal view on birth control. How, then, do they remain in the Church? The answer is that the Church is that in which they were raised. It is their community. They feel they owe loyalty to that community of believers. Sometimes, I suppose, they might think of friends and relations and reflect 'What would they say if they knew what I really thought?' If they were to announce these views, it would be to injure simpler friends. Few people care to go through a fundamental reassessment of the ideas on which their lives are based. Some of us do, but this is not a burden which we necessarily want to place upon others. In order to avoid a scene, I am sometimes evasive when asked about my religious and political beliefs. Again, loyalty is crucial. Class loyalty, nationalism, and xenophobia all play on these. Take a case which seems somewhat parallel. From a distance there seems no reason to be proud of being English, Welsh, French, or American. First, I have nothing to do with the historical merits of my country, and second, for any merits there are demerits. Other countries and societies have complementary failings and strengths. Yet, I find that if I denounce my country, I feel I am failing my friends. And if a foreigner bewails the wretched amoralism of the British government, I may bridle, even though I may privately agree. Though I may complain about my relatives, I do not want others to do so. The fact is that I, my friends, and relatives are products of this culture. There are things which I do not want to believe about my country and its culture. In the end, I want to think that it is a reasonably good place. The slide into self-deception at this point may be rapid. My attitude to my religion or my political allegiance is not strikingly different. In both cases I may be defensive whilst seeing, clearly or dimly, the irrationality of this.

We can see now that ideological beliefs have a causal influence on other beliefs. It might be replied that all beliefs have such causal powers. Faced with contradictory beliefs, we may choose to resolve the conflict by jettisoning one or the other. And the holism of beliefs, the way in which one belief commits you to a number of others, is a cliché in contemporary philosophy. Certainly, but ideological beliefs are privileged; we reject them at some cost, and other beliefs will normally be discarded first.

The question is whether there is anything like this in music. I have already given some reasons why the concept of a work of music might be protected. It is important that there is, in music, something analogous to paintings and statuary, or to poetry, fiction, and drama, where a text can be provided. But what about the canon? What about the music of specific composers who are regarded as *hors concours*? Setting aside the case of Wagner, exceptional for several reasons,[21] there is surely no reason at all why I should not blithely set aside the music of Mozart as of no interest to me.

Well, of course there are reasons. In my subculture, to love classical music is to be worthy of respect. I might, like Ryle, dismiss 'tunes', but I would be expected to have some compensating interests for this more or less amiable philistinism such as a love of the novels of Jane Austen (though classical music is now central to our culture in the way that poetry and fiction once were). A lack of musicality is regrettable. But one cannot love music and not care for Mozart or Schubert; they are bench-marks in a way that even Beethoven is not; and a distaste for Mahler, Wagner, Brahms, or Tchaikovsky is permissible where a lack of interest in Haydn, Mozart, Bach, or Schubert is not.

At least one important locus of ideology is the written history of the art. There is no doubt that we still have a history of music based on a canon dominated by German composers, the last vestige of that German cultural and intellectual domination which the Nazis destroyed.[22] It is highly relevant that the history of music which has come to express such an ideology is one in which the central characters all belong to this canon. (As recently as the Sixties, the critic R. W. S. Mendl listed the eight supremely great composers; they were all Austrian or German; no Des Prez, Monteverdi, Purcell, Palestrina, Verdi, Tchaikovsky, Elgar, or Stravinsky.)[23]

---

[21] See R. A. Sharpe and Bryn Browne, 'The Problem of Wagner', *Cogito*, 8 (1994), 45–52.

[22] See, on the German domination of musical culture and on the social history of music in the twentieth century generally, Joseph Horowitz, *Understanding Toscanini* (London: Faber and Faber, 1994).

[23] R. W. S. Mendl, *Adventure in Music* (London: Neville Spearman, 1964), ch. 2. Kerman, *Contemplating Music*, 33–5, is excellent on nationalist ideology and the way in which musicological study has concentrated on composers who share the nationality of the musicologist. Spitta, for example, speaks of the torso of Cantata BWV 50 as 'an imperishable monument of German art' (*J. S. Bach: His Work and Influence in the Music of Germany 1685–1750*, trans. C. Bell and J. A. Fuller-Maitland (New York: Dover, 1951), iii. 382). Such triumphalism is common in Spitta, but other, more apparently self-confident nations are not immune. Perhaps it is just more noticeable in German musicology because of the dominance of German music in the repertoire.

Why do I think a canon ideological? Clearly the ideology implicit in the canon is not an ideology in the fully fledged sense (there being no account of economics, jurisprudence, or politics). However, the canon expresses the dominance of certain figures in the received history of music, just as standard ideologies are typically a means of endorsing the hegemony of one class over another. Likewise, then, the canon of music, which still has considerable force, expresses and preserves the dominance of the Austro-German tradition. L. B. Meyer, who has been largely responsible for extending the concept of ideology to the arts, does not emphasize this 'dominance'.[24] This strikes me as an oversight; Giddens, for example, makes it central, detaching ideology from questions of truth and falsity and taking it instead to be deeply connected with theories of power and domination.[25] Indeed, the thought that high culture enshrines social superiority in those who enjoy and understand it is a cliché of radical writing on the arts; it is possibly the central theme in most discussions of ideology and the arts, and, of course, it makes 'dominance' central.[26]

There is a second link with the way ideologies normally function, for there is a strong case for saying that, like standard ideologies, the canon possesses means by which potentially disruptive facts are not allowed to falsify it. There are important, original, and fertile composers who get short shrift because they lie outside the canon. Berwald, Alkan, and, to an extent, even Berlioz, leap to mind. It is because, consciously or unconsciously, we think of the development of music between 1700 and 1900 as almost entirely a German phenomenon that so much Telemann is played and broadcast in Britain and a much greater and more interesting contemporary, Rameau, is comparatively neglected. Joseph Horowitz shows how composers like Stravinsky, Elgar, and Sibelius were sidelined in American concert programming in the inter-war years.[27] Neglect is not the only consequence; there are composers whose music is played, but is not valued as highly as it should be. We are the poorer for their downgrading. The canon, by excluding or marginalizing certain

---

[24] See L. B. Meyer, *Music, the Arts and Ideas*, 2nd edn. (Chicago: University of Chicago Press, 1994), 129 ff.

[25] Anthony Giddens, 'Four Theses on Ideology', in A. Kroker and M. Kroker (eds.), *Ideology and Power* (New York: St Martin's Press, 1991), 21–4.

[26] See Thompson, *Ideology and Modern Culture*, 159–61.

[27] Horowitz, *Understanding Toscanini*. See e.g. appendix A, which quotes from the correspondence between Arthur Judson and Barbirolli on programming.

musical influences, may not be to the advantage of a musical culture. Compare the Berwald symphonies with those of Schumann, or consider whether Mendelssohn's piano concertos should be played instead of those of Hummel! The doctrine of 'the genius' with its implication that all the works of a master hang together with the sort of unity we value in a single work may lead us to privilege some of Brahms's music at the cost of better music by less well-known composers. It is not my contention that there are many such misjudgements, if misjudgements they are. (For we must remember the indispensability of the canon and the inevitability of the filtering it implies. It is hard, as well, to distinguish such errors from personal likes and dislikes.) Be that as it may, it is because of the radical consequences for our listening of the idea of a canon that it has such importance.

The canon tends to be self-preserving. We hear less non-canonic music; we take less seriously its impact upon us, and rate our experience of it less highly. We may think that its impact will be less lasting. As a result, revision of the canon is made more difficult. This is brought out nicely in Fintan O'Toole's discussion of Miroslav Horub's poem 'Brief thoughts on time'.[28] A cannon is perched on the walls of a castle over looking a city, and is fired at precisely 1 p.m. each day; the orderliness of the city has much to do with this ritual. A stranger, impressed by this efficiency, asks a soldier how he can be sure that it is exactly the right time to fire. The soldier describes how he times it by reference to a jeweller's shop which advertises 'the world's most accurate chronometer'. When the stranger visits the shop, he asks the jeweller how he can be sure of its accuracy. The jeweller's assurance comes, says the jeweller, from his setting the time against the firing of the cannon, and 'it is always right'. For 'cannon' read 'canon'! The works which are in the canon are placed there because they are great; they are also the stereotypical works of art against which we judge whether a newcomer is worthy. This will hardly be news to any reader.

Thirdly, the canon can distort our experiences of music. In this way it shares one more feature with paradigmatic ideologies. It is both inevitable and damaging. It is inevitable, in that we cannot do without a history, and a history in this ideal sense embodies a canon. It is necessary to make possible our experience of art. It is

[28] *The Guardian*, 21 Nov. 1991.

necessary because, without a history of art, we cannot make sense of the originality of a great figure. For it is a condition of understanding that we endeavour to appreciate its originality, its place in a tradition, as well as its place in an *œuvre*. Is this particular form conventional, or original, or pastiche? Knowing this materially affects our understanding. Our net impression of the work—what Ingarden calls our 'concretion'—depends upon such things.[29] But since we also need to relate the music to what we hear, it becomes evident that real causal influences are bypassed in favour of those relationships we build between the works which are in the repertoire. Whatever listings the canon incorporates, it does not merely record the real causal relationships on the composers; the sequence does not necessarily reflect the influences on each succeeding member of the canon; Chopin was influenced as much by Field, who is not canonic, as by Beethoven or Mozart, who are. Rather, our conception of the tradition is constructed in order to relate the music which is in the repertoire. Such a history has the purpose of helping us better to understand the music. This deeply affects the way we hear music, for if seeing the music as a product of a tradition has the effect of highlighting different features of the music, its face will depend upon the background against which it is viewed. Whereas Haydnesque features in Beethoven will leap to the fore, the extent to which his language is shared with Hummel and Dussek will not strike us.

As I have hinted, there is a constructivism here. Although Beethoven was influenced by composers like Neefe, Salieri, and Fischer, their names appear only in biographies. In critical studies we read of Mozart and Haydn, because it is their music we hear in the concert-hall. We 'understand' Beethoven with respect to the classical tradition. But do not suppose that this mirrors a historically accurate truth! It is a construction demanded by our particular requirements as listeners, critics, and performers.

Such a 'constructed history' surfaces in the way in which certain features of a work appear as foreground and others as background. Because works in the canon influenced later works, and because they set the norms which give point to departures from those norms, we need the canon in order to understand. But, by the same token, the ideology distorts, because it devalues our experience of

---

[29] Roman Ingarden, *The Literary Work of Art*, trans. G. G. Grabowicz (Evanston, Ill.: Northwestern University Press, 1973), 331–55.

figures from outside the canon, and inflates the experience we have of those inside. It is my thesis that the presence of the canon acts like an ideology in privileging certain responses to certain figures whilst marginalizing others (much as Marxist ideology focuses attention on economic and class factors in history at the expense of others). What is not so clear is that it serves anybody's interests that we should believe in the league table which the canon implies. Implicitly we do believe in it, even though, when challenged, we may agree that it could be wrong. It is very hard for us to reject the prejudice that the centre of music is occupied by the Austro-German tradition. It is an assumption constantly reinforced by what we hear and what we read. I suppose that, to the extent that, for music, it is an 'Austro-German ideology', it represents Austro-German cultural interests. (A parallel case could easily be made for English literature. What I say here reflects a peculiarly Anglo-Saxon background; the French or Italian musician or music-lover has a different understanding of what is central.)

Incidentally, if thinkers like Meyer are correct, and we no longer have a unitary tradition in Western music, then one function of the canon, the provision of a constructed and partly artificial history of music which connects the single work with the repertoire in ways which enhance its intelligibility, will presumably fall into desuetude. Because, where the works we hear are too disparate in their origins to throw light upon each other, that function of the canon will disappear. In its place we may have several canons, of course. But the prime reason for having a canon or canons will remain, and that is because we need to record, primarily for the sake of musical tyros, those works which have 'passed the test of time' and which are generally accepted as supreme human achievements. They must be works which offer a reasonable expectation of return for the listener who is prepared to spend time with them. Consequently, and again parenthetically, the canon cannot be entirely separated from the taste of ordinary music-lovers. It cannot be entirely in the hands of the professional and the connoisseur.


V


So what do we gain from having an ontology in which the concept of a 'work of music' looms large? Since I think that the canon gets matters broadly right, the obvious gain, as we have just seen, is that inasmuch as the notion of a work of music goes with the conception of the canon, the concept of a work of music gives us a way of marking out and thus preserving the best. If our diet, like that of eighteenth-century listeners, consisted mainly of contemporary music, think what we would lose! Most of the music composed at any time is mediocre and ephemeral. To apply the concept of 'the work' to such bland and boring works offers us very little. For listeners whose life is short and whose attention is the object of clamorous rivals, it matters that we listen to the best. The best—and this comes close to being as plain a matter of fact as we can have—will include Beethoven's sonatas, but not Lydia Goehr's imaginary case of a performer improvising on a theme from the first movement of one of them. Value is a central concern, and 'work of music' is a handy way of labelling the outstanding (as opposed to mere entertainment or 'easy listening').

That we have a concept of the work of music is, I think, no accident. The conceptual scheme we have probably has some advantages over its rivals, though, to the extent that we see the world in its terms, it may be difficult for us to evaluate the merits of others. But, of course, the important task for philosophical criticism is to pin-point its weaknesses. Paradigms of this kind of philosophical criticism are, say, Hume's criticisms of natural theology, contemporary criticism of utilitarianism, or Wittgenstein's critique of Cartesianism. It is as important as anything philosophers do. It may be that the concept of a work of music is ripe for reform or some sort of adjustment, and it will then be the task of philosophical criticism to motivate such changes; but, as I have suggested, we shall need to preserve some of the practices it enshrines.

How might such philosophical criticism proceed? Well, there is no reason why the concept of music should be a coherent concept. There are ideological pressures brought to bear upon the concept which may lead to incoherence, and if it is incoherent, a consistent analysis of the concept will not be possible. A second reason for doubting whether a consistent analysis can be given is inductive. Like the concept of knowledge, the concepts of 'art' and of 'work of music' have not been successfully analysed to date. No sooner does a plausible-looking candidate arrive than somebody finds counter-examples.

My own view is that an analysis is impossible, because there is

no agreement on which salient features of music should be preserved in an analysis. There is disagreement over whether fidelity
to the score is paramount and on the place of improvisation. For
we face two alternative views of what it might be for something to
be a work of music. On the one view, the work exists independently
of us, and performance is seen as a means of grasping, albeit imper-
fectly and partially, its nature. This view is reflected in the idea that
no single performance is adequate to communicate the nature of a
great work of art. The work of music is a product, not an activity.
In a similar vein, Schnabel used to remark that Beethoven's music
is greater than it can ever be played, thereby implying a distinction
between work and performance. Such a view of music is also largely
dependent on the music being notated, and in this respect the possibility of a precise notation is a condition both of the privileging
of music (at least in the Western tradition) and of the way it is
studied. The work then has a text as poetry, fiction, and drama have
texts. It is the existence of a notation which allows the comparison
with mathematics that makes a Platonic conception of the primacy
and superiority of the abstract structure so persuasive. Admittedly,
it is conceivable that a work should exist in the memories of musicians and be realized in performances which differ from each other
no more than do the interpretations of, say, a Beethoven sonata
today. But such a possibility is plausible only in an oral culture. We
are far removed from that. Finally, the existence of a notation
makes it possible to study the work without playing it, and such
studies are able, far more easily, to detect the organic structure
which is valued in all the arts. Treitler remarks on the way the
ideal of completeness of form which we find in Vasari has been
applied to music.[30] Musical analysis and Platonism are bedfellows.
As Levinson observes, Schenkerism, with its attention to the
tonal structure, fits with a Platonic view of the work as a sound
structure.[31]

On the other view, the score may be taken as a recipe for a
performance which, of its nature, is evanescent. Art is a matter of
making. Curzon used to object to recording because it preserved
what should be fleeting, and he was not alone in this; many musicians dislike recording. On this view, music is essentially a perfor-

---

[30] Leo Treitler, *Music and the Historical Imagination* (Cambridge, Mass.: Harvard
University Press, 1989), 67.
[31] Levinson, *Music, Art and Metaphysics*, 249.

mance art. There may be still other views which will come into contention, for the concept of music may change again; but for the
moment these approaches seem irreconcilable. Consequently, not
even an analysis which is an internally consistent one will do. There
is no unanimity in the musical community on certain fundamental
ideological issues. Some commentators are Platonists in their
approach, others nominalists. For an ideology privileges certain features of the work and certain performing practices. A 'neutral' or
deflationary analysis would merely bypass these points of conflict,
and would be no more faithful to the concept at issue than would
Platonism or nominalism or a deflationary approach.

Now I might have seemed to suggest that Platonism determines
one kind of approach to performance and nominalism another. The
first suggests realization, and the second re-creation. Things are not
quite that simple. Obviously, performing artists are not usually very
interested in metaphysics, and they rarely have a metaphysical axe
to grind. That they think of themselves as putting us in touch with
Beethoven does not imply that they think of Beethoven's thoughts
as created tokens of an abstract sound pattern or in any other way
(though I would be surprised to find a musician who subscribes to
the more extreme views of Wolterstorff and Kivy). More to the
point, you can think of yourself as communicating Beethoven to an
audience in terms of Levinson's modified Platonism, of yourself as
but a vessel through which the music passes to the audience, and
still, at the same time, take more liberties than somebody who
thinks of himself as a performer who creates a transitory work from
a notation. You may, as a nominalist, think that the notation defines
the work, and believe that it ties your hands; many do. But
interpretative freedom is possible in either case, and quite similar
degrees of license may be displayed. Mine is the slighter claim that
nominalists are more often associated with fidelity to the letter,
whilst Platonists may be expected to be more concerned with faithfulness to the spirit of the work of the composer. This might require
adjustments, so that the work speaks more directly to contemporary listeners. If a modern music-lover is to receive the work as the
original audience did, a Platonist might think it necessary to change
the instrumentation. Larger forces might be needed to create the
impact of Haydn's 'Military' Symphony in a large modern concert-
hall, for example. (Indeed, Kivy's views on authenticity are, to some
extent, what one would predict from his Platonism, as we shall see

when I come to discuss these matters in the next chapter.) A Platonist, too, might be less inclined to allow for the variability of interpretation. He is more likely to believe that there is a single correct interpretation, and that it is one which recovers the composer's initial conception.[32]

One last possible objection. A Quinean approach to concepts will suggest that as we approach the centre of our universe of concepts, their content is given by more or less broadly accepted generalizations. So the broad truths about music of which I have been speaking are generalizations which need not be true in order to capture the content of the concept of a work of music. Their seeming necessity is more a matter of how reluctant we are to discard them; the more reluctant we are, the more they approach what we intuitively think of as necessity. I am enough of a Quinean to find this persuasive, so I shall not be moved by the criticism that the claims which have led me to suppose that the concept of music is unanalysable confuse contingent truths about music with what properly belongs to the 'central core' of the concept (which is composed of what non-Quineans view as 'necessary' truths). Indeed, I would argue that these conflicting claims about the nature of music are differences over its heart, and that musical practice and performing styles reveal that these differences are real. In this way ideology enters practice. What is 'essentially contested' here is not the extension of the concept of music, which is how Gallie thought of essentially contested concepts.[33] Combatants may agree on that. Differences of view on the canon might be minor or non-existent. What is being contested is the content of the concept of music.

## VI

It is difficult to provide irrefragable proof for the position I have proposed in this chapter: that the concept of music is a battlefield for opposing ideas about the nature and standing of the art, and that the conflict makes a codified analysis impossible. Philosophers who are predisposed towards the ideal of analysis will always argue that our failure to date to find one does not show that it is a mission

---

[32] The twentieth-century history of opposing ideals in performance is well illustrated in Horowitz, *Understanding Toscanini*.

[33] Gallie, *Philosophy and the Historical Understanding*, 171.

impossible. My final defence will be no more than the one I offered for the argument of the last chapter, that my account is plausible and explanatory.[34] But, as a final throw, the unconverted might consider the old question: How would the world be different if I am wrong? This is a good way of checking the content of a claim, if not invariably illuminating. In a case dependent upon certain practices and certain historical judgements it may be valuable. For my thesis to be wrong, it would have to be the case either that music in the seventeenth and early eighteenth centuries was regarded as one of the fine arts, or that questions of status and of the relative standing of their art did not matter to musicians. Secondly, it would have to be the case that a particular analysis of the concept of a work of music can now find general acceptance amongst musicians and music-lovers.

Neither of these claims seems to me to be true. Indeed, as far as the second is concerned, the search for analyses in philosophy has largely been given up. It was, of course, part of a programme in philosophy which began with Russell; his theory of descriptions served as a paradigm of what philosophical analysis should be. Perhaps the criticisms of the Ayer–Chisholm analysis of knowledge by Gettier were salutary in loosening the grip of that particular model. But that was just one amongst many changes in philosophy in the Sixties. It is an interesting general question why analysis should fail so frequently.

One answer would be that philosophy just is concerned with what is contestable. As I remarked earlier, the ideal of analysis is associated with an ideal of philosophy as a sort of scientific discipline, an objective recording of conceptual facts. But, as I have argued here, interesting concepts are far too deeply interwoven with those general ideas which may best be characterized as 'ideological' for an analysis ever to be uncontroversial. When talking about these matters to philosophical audiences, I have been asked whether a concept like that of personal identity might also be so infected as to be unanalysable. I don't know of any general arguments which would show this. It will depend upon the particular belief structures of particular societies. I can only say that I would not be surprised to find it true.

---

[34] A suggestion that I am not alone in thinking that art involves the ideological is to be found at the end of David Novitz, 'Disputes about Art', *Journal of Aesthetics and Art Criticism*, 54/2 (1996), 162.

I have spoken, *inter alia*, of interpretation in the performing arts, arguing that it is such a central concern of musicians that it needs to be taken seriously by any philosopher interested in the nature of a musical work. We should note Kerman's strictures on musicologists who are so suspicious of interpretative flair. But, if musicologists have shown little interest in interpretation, this is not true of philosophers. The lesson of recent work on the concept of interpretation is that any work in the performing arts contains what Ingarden calls 'spots of indeterminacy'.[35] The performer has to make decisions; this does not conflict with fidelity as a regulative ideal. But it does allow that there is a class of performances which can be considered 'faithful' or 'authentic', and that some of these will be more satisfactory than others. There is no necessary conflict between the ideal of authenticity and the underdetermining of a performance by its notation. Neither party needs to see performance as approximating to a single ideal performance. Within the 'authentic Beethoven' movement there is a marked contrast between a genuine conductor like Roger Norrington and some others. For no amount of fidelity will deny scope to the gifted and imaginative interpreter. So it is to the concept of performance, and to the much debated concept of 'authenticity', that I now turn.

[35] Ingarden, *Literary Work of Art*, 246; see also *idem*, *The Work of Music and the Problem of its Identity*, trans. A. Czerniawski, ed. J. G. Harrell (London: Macmillan, 1986).

# 5

## *Performance*

### EXPRESSION

In due course I shall return to the broader 'cognitive' issues of the
last chapter, but the intervening discussion of performance and
authenticity is not entirely alien country. As we shall see, these
issues are impregnated with questions about the music's intellectual milieu.

But first, some background. Romantic aesthetics such as that
of Schumann and Schweitzer took the real work of art to be a
private mental affair which was then externalized in a publicly
accessible form as a piece of music or a painting or a poem. The
tradition is more familiar to English readers through the work of
R. G. Collingwood, who provided us with a form of expressionism:
the doctrine that art is the expression of a mental state of the
creator, which is communicated via the artefact to the audience.
Now, as I remarked earlier, expressionism has few contemporary
adherents. The objections are familiar. Where there is evidence
of the creator's mental state, it may be at odds with the character
of the work as experienced. Whether he is exuberant or troubled,
sad or serene, is only contingently connected with the character of
the work. However, to recapitulate further, expressionism was
an attempt to answer a central question in aesthetics: how we
can justify calling art serene or troubled. These are predicates
which apply in the first instance to persons, and, it is thought,
only in a secondary, metaphorical, or subsidiary way to art. The
problem is particularly acute with respect to music, for music has
no content which imparts a general character to the work. It
expresses no thoughts and no propositions; a poem on the death of
a child is, by contrast, made sad in part at least by the content; this
is so, even though a sad theme may be treated with levity, and even
though, occasionally, the banality of treatment makes a grave

subject comic. Consider McGonagall's poem on the Tay Bridge disaster.

Some of these complexities spill over at a remove into the matter of performance. Just as there may be a gap between the gravity of the topic and the lightness of the treatment, so there may be a disparity between the character of a work and the character of a performance of it. For it is possible in a performance to treat a grave work with levity or to render banal a theme which need not be so rendered. Furthermore, a performance is often characterized in terms which are different from those used to describe the work. For example, the performance may be faithful, but it makes no sense to speak of the work as faithful or not; perhaps the performance may be light-hearted and, to that extent, appropriate or inappropriate to the work itself. (We can imagine a misreading of some of Schubert's apparently uncomplicated finales.) The character of a performance is typically a joint product of the work and the creative personality of the interpreter. The performing arts are re-creative; there is a second act of creation whereby the performer breathes life into the bare score. Our appreciation of a great performance is not exhausted by our appreciation of the quality of the work; we also savour and admire the wit, intelligence, imagination, and insight of the performer. But although a performance will have its own character, and its character will reflect the creativity of the performer, his decisions about tempi, shading, and all the rest, its character will not be (or should not be) independent of the character of the work.

Significantly, many of the features we admire in an interpretation match the features we admire in a work of art. To an extent, we esteem works and interpretations for the same sorts of reasons. We admire an interpretation which presents detail in such a way that it coheres with the overall interpretation. Take a famous crux, the length of the fermata in the opening bars of Beethoven's Fifth Symphony; if a conductor opts for a long pause at this point, the signs are that his overall interpretation will be epic, rather than dramatic—that the performance will be characterized by broad tempi and a spacious overall effect, rather than by faster tempi and sharp contrasts. So the detail coheres with a general view of the work. It may prove difficult to go for a spacious view of the work if we make the fermata short, and the performance may consequently fail to 'add up'. Moreover, we value an interpretation which will make sense of all the notes. A great pianist, it is often said, 'makes all the notes count'.[1] Such 'density', as it is sometimes called, is prized in a work of art as well as in a performance. The very greatest paint-ings are paintings in which, *inter alia*, every brush stroke counts, and we cannot excise a part without damaging the whole. Finally, a Curzon, a Gilels, or a Solomon exhibits originality and creativity in the interpretation, but it is imagination which does not flaw the unity of the conception.

The performing arts are distinct because, were it not for the per-former, they would be of limited accessibility, limited in the case of music to those who can read the score. Even for those who can do so, reading a score is not comparable to reading a novel. Music needs to be heard, and to be heard, it needs performance. Since the notation is less than definitive, it demands interpretation. The nota-tion underdetermines the performance. This remains so despite the penchant of composers for increasingly precise directions as to tempo and dynamics. Indeed, it is noteworthy that even very fully notated works like the Mahler symphonies leave a great deal of scope for interpretation; consequently, successful interpretations seem to vary at least as much as do successful performances of the less fully notated Viennese classics such as Haydn and Mozart. Mahler himself remarked that the conductor must play the notes which are not written. In Kivy's telling phrase, the interpreter is neither the composer's 'fool' nor his 'tool'.

But though both performer and composer display creativity, it does not do to overstate the analogy. As will become clearer later on, I believe Peter Kivy overstresses the independence of the per-former. For he suggests that an interpretation is akin to a 'version' or an 'arrangement' of the original.[2] The corollary is that the inter-preter herself comes close to being the creator of a secondary work, a thought which has a familiar analogue in recent literary theory, where the critic is sometimes taken to be a sort of secondary creator. But this would make any edition of Beethoven's piano

---

[1] A colleague once asked me how I managed to concentrate on the music whilst at a concert. The answer I gave her is that with a fine performance one does not need to try. I heard Curzon playing Mozart shortly before his death, and one could not drag one's ears away from the music. I have never had a stronger sense that everything had been thought about. It had the concentration and depth of a great work of art.

[2] Peter Kivy, *Authenticities: Philosophical Reflections on Musical Performance* (Ithaca, NY: Cornell University Press, 1995), 131, 133, 135.

sonatas a version or an arrangement, for any edition contains edi-
torial suggestions on fingering, pedalling, and dynamics. We can
recognize the interpreter's creativity without wishing to make such
a strong claim. We do not speak this way, and there seems no great
advantage in thus changing usage. We need, I think, to preserve a
distinction between interpreting and arranging, without denying
that there are borderline cases which may not fall clearly into
one category or the other. Some musicians will claim that playing
Bach on the piano constitutes an arrangement rather than an
interpretation.[3] My intuitions are that this constitutes an arrangement only if the notes are altered as they are in Busoni's arrangements of the Bach chorale preludes or of the Violin Chaconne.
(Normally we speak of a 'transcription' when the work is played
on a different instrument with only the minimal alterations necessary to make it playable and the parts audible; the performance
of the piece is then the performance of an interpretation of a
transcription.)

At this point, we need the distinction which I introduced in the
previous chapter, the distinction between work, interpretation, and
performance. The work, recall, is presented to the hearer by an
interpreter who has to make decisions about pace, dynamics, the
placing of the climax, and so on. These decisions determine the
character of a performance. The interpretation may be given over
and over again in a succession of performances, or the interpreter
may change the character of his performance of the work each time
he plays it. Some musicians are, as they say, more 'spontaneous'
artists. As I have said, what is unique to the nature of the performing arts is the creative contribution made by the interpreter,
something familiar to any *aficionado*. Colin Davis's Sibelius always
gives me the impression that Curzon's Mozart used to, that every
note has been thought about until a mature conception of how the
work should go has evolved. Then the character of the performance
bears the stamp of the interpreter's own personality. We will
not mistake an interpretation of Mahler by Bernstein for one by
Klemperer.

As I have already intimated, the situation outside the Western
classical tradition is not really comparable. To take rock, pop, and
jazz as examples, a singer may well perform or record what is

---

[3] Peter Williams, in correspondence.

known as a 'cover' of a song associated with another singer or band. The Beatles' songs have been 'covered' by many other artists; generally 'covers' are thought to be inferior, partly because the world of jazz and popular music is much concerned with sincerity in expression, so that the song you write and sing yourself expresses, authentically, your own emotional state, and for anybody else to sing it is, inevitably, inauthentic. Particularly, songs of Black artists sung by Whites are automatically supposed to be inferior, whereas for Black singers to 'cover' White originals is not necessarily bad (presumably because Blacks have suffered more), and when the 'cover' is artistically satisfactory, it is thought of as a 'version', and not as a cover at all. Ray Charles's recording of the Beatles' 'Yesterday' is a version, not a cover; but it is not normally thought of as an interpretation of an original, perhaps because he takes more liberties with the notes than is now customary in the performance of classical music. Eighteenth-century performance practice was different, and ornamentation and the like brought performance closer to 'covering'.[4] Very occasionally a jazz classic is repeated note for note, as in Mugsy Spanier's 1938 copy of Louis Armstrong's 1927 recording of 'Big Butter and Egg Man' made with The Hot Five;[5] but this case is unusual, and again it is not thought of as an interpretation.

Enough recapitulation! What I want to propose in this chapter is, first of all, a relocating of expressionism. I re-employ expressionism in a new context in claiming that a performance lies in an expressive relationship to an interpretation of a work. This modified expressionism also gives a plausible account of the relationship between a work and an interpretation. In the relationship between music and its interpretation, humdrum expressive predicates are often of greater interest than they are when applied to the work itself. It is hardly informative to describe the 'Eroica' as grave, whereas it might not be so uninformative to describe an interpretation as grave, even though its gravity might be not unexpected.

Why should this be? One reason might be that the work is, of course, 'given'. A claim about an interpretation has a very much more precise significance in terms of how the music is played. We

---

[4] See Simon Frith, *Performing Rites* (Oxford: Oxford University Press, 1996), 69–70.     [5] Nick MacAdoo pointed this out to me.

may infer details about tempi and phrasing. By contrast, to speak of the music itself as grave is compatible with quite a variety of melodic contours. So an expressive judgement about an interpretation or a performance gives us a considerable amount of quite detailed information when compared with a parallel expressive judgement about the work.

I shall suggest that expressionism gives the truest picture of the relationship between interpreter and performance.[6] Expressionism, as I have said, has had a bad press, and it would be easy to repeat its errors when applying its essential ideas to the relationship between music and its interpretation and performance. To suggest, for example, that the emotional life of a dramatis persona is being re-created in the actor and then re-created in the audience is, on the surface of it, implausible. If the assumption is that he feels as the character feels, the assumption is probably in general mistaken (method acting notwithstanding). He might have his mind on other things. Whilst the audience is passionately involved with the fate of the king, the actor himself may be consciously controlling his movements and trying to remember what intonation to give his next words. Equally, whilst the audience holds its breath at the sublimity of the slow movement of the 'Hammerklavier', the pianist must concentrate. Samuel Johnson asked Kemble, 'Are you, Sir, one of those enthusiasts who believe yourself transformed into the very character you represent?' And, when Kemble admitted that he was not, went on: 'To be sure not, Sir, and if Garrick really believed himself to be that monster, Richard the Third, he deserved to be hanged every time he performed it.'[7] Neither is there any reason to suppose that the audience at the theatre imaginatively puts itself into the role of one character after another, or even that, in identifying with one character in particular, it feels as he does. Likewise, if the pianist, perhaps atypically, himself suffers the passions of the first movement of the 'Appassionata', there is no reason to suppose that the responsive listener shares these.

So, I do not want to defend such an unqualified expressionism. But if we adapt expressionism a bit, a more likely picture begins to emerge. Consider the following. A scientist may express a theory

---

[6] See Eduard Hanslick, *On the Musically Beautiful*, trans. Geoffrey Payzant (Indianapolis: Hackett, 1986), 49.

[7] James Boswell, *The Life of Samuel Johnson*, ed. G. B. Hill, rev. and extended by L. F. Powell (Oxford: Clarendon Press, 1934), iv. 243–4.

in different ways on different occasions, in conversation with a colleague, to himself on a walk, in a lecture, in a paper or in a reply to another speaker at a congress. Some ways may better reveal the nature of the theory; some may be eloquent, some dull. All these locutions can equally characterize the performance of a work of art. Some performances are more revealing of structure, some communicate more vividly, and in some the performer may seem detached rather than involved.[8]

The error in classical expressionism was the supposition that the work stands in a determinate dyadic relationship to some state of its creator such that the work expresses or represents that state. Such a theory encourages the wrong sort of explanation of the work of art. It underestimates the degree to which the work of art is autonomous. As readers are by now well aware, in company with most modern writers on aesthetics I reject this form of expressionism. My view is that works of art are *objects* for interpretation; they are objects which a performer, a reader, or a listener can view in various ways, finding different themes, placing some in the foreground and some in the background, and making decisions about what the work is 'about'.[9] Equally, the reader of a novel judges what features are central, what the novel is about, and what issues are being debated. The judgement he makes may or may not coincide with that of its creator (just supposing the creator consciously formulated a view), but the creator's views are not in an especially privileged position. Since music is a performing art, the actualization of a work in performance is an occurrence. The musical object is, as I have said, largely inaccessible otherwise, and the difference between musical interpretation and interpretation in the other arts stems from this. It is, as we shall see, somewhat idiosyncratic. It is also idiosyncratic inasmuch as the work of music is not often representational. Nevertheless, the interpreter will, normally, form an overall impression of the work, even if that synoptic grasp, unlike in some of the other arts, cannot always be properly described as a judgement as to what the work is 'about'.

The view of interpretation I advocate re-creates a contrast between the performer's conception and the work. The contrast

[8] See Jerrold Levinson, *Music, Art and Metaphysics* (Ithaca, NY: Cornell University Press, 1990), 88.
[9] Argued at length in my *Contemporary Aesthetics* (Brighton: Harvester Press, 1983; Aldershot: Gregg Revivals, 1991).

enables us to use concepts like 'faithfulness' and 'sincerity'. Consider, for example, Mozart's Divertimento K. 563; it has the character of an unaffected conversation between friends. To overload the expressiveness or amplify the rhetoric would be unfaithful to its character; its personality is not properly expressed in such an interpretation. Of course, interpretations can fail in other ways; the interpreter may fail to get over his own conception of the work due to technical failings or to a failure to articulate the conception in a sufficiently complete way. But the failings I am particularly interested in here are failings of imagination, failures to understand the possibilities of the work, or an inability to grasp its character. A successful and faithful interpretation, by contrast, observes the character of the work, and operates within its constraints.

The character of the work is, of course, a character its creator gives it, and it will not be easy to draw a line between a permissible interpretation which is not that envisaged by the creator and an interpretation which is impermissible because it is inconsistent, not with the creator's preferred interpretations, but with the character of the work itself. However, the fact that a line cannot be easily drawn does not entail that there is not a world of difference in many cases. What we cannot do is to take interpretation 'all the way down', so to speak, so that each different performance is, in truth, a performance of a different work. We do rule out certain performances as falsifying a work. There are arguments about this, as we shall see, but there is a general consensus that the notes have to be respected.

I have spoken of 'faithfulness to the work'. 'Faithfulness' has another application here. It is also because the interpreter, in presenting the work, expresses, simultaneously, his own conception of the work that concepts like sincerity and authenticity are apposite. As Kivy points out, there is a distinct conception of authenticity which is appropriate here, something fairly close to 'sincerity'; the performance is authentic inasmuch as it is faithful to the 'performer's own self'.[10] It is with honesty that he presents his own view of the work. On the classical expressionist theory the value of the work depends upon the accurate communication of a certain mental state by the composer to the audience. In the present

---

[10] Kivy, *Authenticities*, 6.

relocation of expressionism, value lies, largely, in the interpreter's forming a persuasive view of the work and effectively transmitting this to the listener. In both versions, the mistaken and the correct, accuracy counts.

You might object that authenticity matters little. We do not care overmuch whether the writer of a love poem suffered the anguish he describes. No more should we be concerned with whether the performer believes in the version of the work he presents. Well, I resist this objection. The writer of love poetry in particular writes in a genre where artifice is expected, and the composition does not necessarily reflect his feelings. The institution of writing love poetry is different from the institution of writing an autobiography, where questions of lying and truth telling do arise, and the performance of music is rather closer to these latter. Admittedly, there are cases where a performer might honourably present a work in a way which he believes is false. If there is a dispute between conductor and soloist over tempi or other aspects of the character of a concerto, for example, the performer might swallow his reservations. Better a unified performance than one where there is evident disagreement, and neither gives way. But such cases are rare, and the acceptability of the solution *faute de mieux*.

I suggest, then, that we view performance as expression. Thomas Carson Mark comes near to this view when he presents performance as a form of 'assertion of the work'.[11] What, of course, the performer is not doing is representing the work in the way that I represent the views of another through quotation in *oratio recta*. For that would leave no space for the contribution of the interpretative mind. However, I share with Mark a belief that faithfulness to the work is important, and I certainly place more emphasis on this than Kivy.[12] When Kivy claims that a performer may always find a better way of performing a work than its creator, I do not demur. But there comes a point at which 'improvement' departs sufficiently from the score no longer to be an accurate performance of the work. Departures from the work are permissible only to the extent that the notes as written cannot be played, or the markings

---

[11] Thomas Carson Mark, 'The Philosophy of Piano Playing: Reflections on the Concept of Performance', *Philosophy and Phenomenological Research*, 41 (1980–1), 299–324. Kivy discusses Mark's article in *Authenticities*, 114–15.
[12] Kivy, *Authenticities*, 142.

given are inconsistent (and there are many examples of these), or arguably depart from the general character of the piece. We may, as well, need a distinction that Kivy finds difficult, that between what belongs to the work and what counts as the composer's advice to the performer (advice which may be set aside). But more of all this later in the chapter.

In saying this, of course, I am distancing myself from certain current trends in criticism and performance: from the idea that a work is merely a quarry for the second-order creativity of reader, performer, or producer. 'Chaque texte une pretexte', as they say. Fortunately, the 'authenticity movement' in music, of which I shall say something in the second part of this chapter, has been a bulwark against the wilder excesses of post-structuralism seen in some literary criticism. But, invidiously, contemporary ideas have made themselves felt in operatic production. For operatic production has suffered the same fate as theatrical production. I cannot do better than echo the excoriation of John Gross:

If I call Miller's *Merchant* the key production of its period, it is not because it was necessarily the best, but because it was the one which established the principle that a director is free to do whatever he likes with the play—to bend it, twist it, advertise his boredom with it; to spice it up with anachronisms; to steam-roller the poetry; to hit the audience over the head with what ought to be subtle implications.[13]

Perhaps the avant-garde of the closing decades of the twentieth century would claim to respect the 'spirit of the work'. I shall dissent. Great works of art offer scope for the interpreter. The decisions facing the player of Beethoven who respects the notes and markings of the composer are so many, and so far-reaching, that no interpreter should ask for greater licence. And what is true of a piano sonata is true of an opera. A great opera, performed in a manner which respects the performance conventions of the time at which it was written, still leaves ample room for the interpreter. It is the unsubtle director who has to update *Rigoletto* to twentieth-century Chicago. Any valid points he wishes to make can be made within the performing traditions which operated at the time of its creation. A work assumes such conventions, and has to be understood in their terms. Take the work out of that setting, and you make your moral or political points at its expense. It is a familiar

---

[13] John Gross, *Shylock* (London: Chatto, 1992), 303–4.

claim that elaborate naturalistic settings of Shakespeare merely duplicate the verse. If in *Hamlet* we are told 'Morn, in russet mantle clad walks o'er the dew', we do not need dawn to be re-created by changing the lighting. But, more seriously, anachronistic productions can undermine the original, because they are inconsistent with it. Rodney Milnes, in a generally favourable review of Jonathan Miller's 1990s production of *Così fan tutte* at Covent Garden, points out that if Despina is an assistant in a fashion business, chocolate will hardly be a previously unexperienced luxury.[14] And as for marriage contracts! Indeed, it seems to me that less work is required for the audience to assume those eighteenth-century attitudes which Mozart and Da Ponte shared than is needed to suspend disbelief so as to swallow such anachronisms and inconsistencies as the Miller production requires.

The inconsistencies, too, may be internal. Tim Albery's 1995 production of Verdi's *Nabucco* for Welsh National Opera made a connection between the exile of the Jews and the Holocaust by means of a representation of a concentration camp train. The guards carried machine-guns; yet Nabucco was armed with a massive sword, which was in no obvious way merely ceremonial. Albery seemed unconcerned with the fact that swords and machine guns are not contemporaneous forms of arms. Of course, we can swallow these anachronisms for the duration of a performance, but what is the point in creating unnecessary obstacles to credibility? And why insult the intelligence of the audience by assuming that they will not recognize the parallel unless it is rammed down their throats?

So far, I have tried to steer a course between responsibility to the work and recognition of the importance of an interpreter's creativity. The picture I have presented of the relationship between work, interpretation, and performance raises an important question. I spoke of the relative autonomy of the work of art. It is that relative autonomy which allows differing views of the same work. Different interpreters present a work in different ways, very many of which may be perfectly valid. This is a feature of the arts which expressionism appears to play down. For, on the expressionist view, we seem to grasp a work properly when we understand what its

---

[14] *The Times*, 20 Jan. 1995.

creator is trying to express. Ambiguity may allow some play, but there is a correct interpretation, and the correct interpretation is that which recovers what the creator intended to express. In the way in which I have presented the performer as expressing a view, I, in parallel, minimize the interpretative role of the listener. His job is to grasp what the performer tries to express. So the listener is not an interpreter in the way that a reader or a performer is.

In fact, I am happy to accept this consequence of my original remarks. But not all writers agree. Paul Thom believes that the relationship between spectator and performer is similar to that between performer and work, though he allows for some differences.[15] On his view, the sorts of interpretation the audience may make include interpreting a note or notes as a mistake or a memory lapse, or taking an interpretation to be based on a particular understanding of the work by the performer. I agree that these involve important judgements by the listener. But these judgements are just where the audience's interpretation differs from other standard forms of interpretation. For the listener's 'interpretation' is either right or wrong, whereas the interpretation of the performer himself is not so constrained. The cases which favour Thom's view are those where the performance is deliberately ambiguous, allowing the listener to take more than one view of what is going on. A stronger case than Thom's own examples might be where the positioning of the climax of a movement, so important in the interpretation of Bruckner, for example, is left unclear. Wittgenstein may have had in mind such a possibility when he wrote:

Would it be imaginable, given two identical bits of a piece of music, to have directions placed above them, bidding us hear it like *this* the first time, and like *this* the second, without exerting any influence on the performance? The piece would perhaps be written for a chiming clock and the two bits would be meant to be played equally loud and in the same tempo—only *taken* differently each time.

And, even if a composer has never yet written such a direction, might not a critic write it?[16]

But if any of these cases occur, they are exceptional, and,

---

[15] Paul Thom, *For an Audience* (Philadelphia: Temple University Press, 1993), 194–8.

[16] L. Wittgenstein, *Remarks on Philosophical Psychology*, i, trans. G. E. M. Anscombe and G. H. von Wright (Oxford: Blackwell, 1980), p. 102e (§545), italics original.

speaking generally, it does not seem to be a merit in a performance that it declines a decision offered by the composer. (Wittgenstein, of course, had in mind an ambiguity which the composer introduced deliberately.)

Let us go back, for the moment, to general principles! Works of art permit a variety of interpretations; although some may be ruled out, of many it may not be possible to say which are to be preferred. They may coexist. *Hamlet* may be plausibly presented as a study of the Oedipus complex, the first study of individualism in modern literature, a brilliant and revisionary addition to the corpus of revenge tragedies, as the study of 'a man who could not make up his mind' in Olivier's notorious film redaction, or as a religious drama (though I fancy this last is harder to make out). What I don't think is possible to sustain is a recent account which presents Shakespearian tragedies as studies in management with the heroes as failed executives.[17]

In interpretation, the critic of literature or film or the performer of music, theatre, or dance offers a general view of a work which is based on certain episodes which present themselves as of particular importance or significance. I use the active voice advisedly. The 'foregrounding' of these episodes, to use the Prague structuralist jargon, is within our control, albeit only to a certain extent. These are passages which 'strike' us. They seize our interest and move us; they may give us pleasure. The literary critic then weaves these into a discursive view of the work, and, by judicious quotation and reference, simultaneously exemplifies and supports the general account he offers. Typically, he identifies pervasive themes in the work which are exemplified in the passages he cites. In the same way the performer will 'bring out' certain sections of the work he performs, and thereby both exemplify and support the general character which he thinks the work has. He might attend to one of the inner parts, voicing it in such a way as to bring to our attention a feature which other interpreters miss.

Is it then possible for a listener to make a further act of interpretation whose object is the performer's interpretation of the music? I do not count Thom's suggestions as to the way in which a listener might be said to 'interpret' as being interpretative at all.

---

[17] Jay M. Shafritz, *Shakespeare and Management: Wise Counsel and Warnings from the Bard* (Secaucus, NJ: Birch Lane Press, 1992). It is not entirely clear whether the comedy is intentional.

They do not square with the concept as we normally understand it. But are there other ways?

Certainly the listener may fail to catch on. He may not notice where the interpreter places the climax, and, through ignorance or inattention, may fail to notice or to see the point of the precise weighting of a certain cadence or a rhythm or an inner part. But could he notice things about the interpretation which the interpreter herself did not notice? Might the interpretation be better than the performer realizes? If this occurs, then it will be a case where the listener initially registers the nature of the interpretation, and then notices aspects of the performance which cohere with the interpretation in ways in which the performer herself did not recognize. In such a case the listener is still not interpreting in the full sense. For that to happen, it would be necessary that he pick out features of the interpretation and meld them into a new whole governed by an overall view of the interpretation. But in a performed work, he can be doing no more than is already done competently or incompetently by the performer, or else pointing out something the performer fails to do. In such a case the interpreting listener merely provides a recipe for a particular interpretation which could be embodied in a performance. It is not so much an interpretation of a performance as a blueprint for a different, and perhaps better, performance. So a teacher might point out to a pupil that his failure to articulate a figure makes it impossible to see the connection of that passage with a passage occurring later. The criticism of the performance is not an 'interpretation' of that performance. The criticism is the basis for putting something right.

More usually, listeners vary in their relative failure to grasp the nature of an interpretation. Whereas various readings of a Mozart piano concerto by a soloist and orchestra may represent equally valid approaches, the listener's various readings are a measure of comparative failure, not comparative richness. Through no fault of the interpreter, the listener may fail to see what the interpreter is driving at, and, indeed, may luxuriate in features of the performance which the interpreter did not intend to be at the forefront of their attention. The occasional irritation of musicians with their public, though hardly excusable, no doubt derives from this. Remember Schnabel's sour remark, 'The audience applauds even when it is good'! (Talk about 'biting the hand . . .')

So, to revert to Thom's earlier point, though it is no demerit in a work that it underdetermines interpretation, it is normally a demerit in an interpretation if it underdetermines the response of the educated and alert listener. The audience's active role lies in sizing up the nature of the interpretation and deciding whether it is a valid view of the work. Can you play Bartók's Third Piano Concerto so aggressively? Does not some of the essential poetry disappear? But this normally marks the limits of the listener's 'interpretation'. Few of us are either teachers or performers. The listener's judgement, as I have said, is right or wrong, true or false. It is not a creative act comparable with that of reading a poem or personally performing the music. And despite his speculation about a composer instructing the listener as to various ways a piece might be heard, in the end Wittgenstein seems to agree, since he concedes that his suggestion boils down to an instruction to the performer to play it that way. 'Would it make sense to ask a composer whether one should hear a figure like *this* or like *this*; if that doesn't also mean: whether one should *play* it in this way or that?'[18]

In the opening essay of the collection *On Difficulty and Other Essays*, George Steiner remarks on the fact that music has become the central art in our culture.[19] One reason for this, in his view, is that music is a participatory art, whereas reading is private. I do not see why this is peculiarly appropriate to our culture; perhaps it connects with the relative passivity of the listener. Nor does Steiner define the contrast between private and public. But if we take the privacy of reading to lie in the singularity of the reader's response, and the publicity of the performing art to lie in our sharing the insights of the performer who expresses his interpretation to us, then we may agree that the contrast between the private reader and the listening public marks a crucial difference between the listener to music and the reader of poetry or fiction.[20] The point remains even if we listen at home to a compact disc. We still share the interpreter's insights to the extent that we are alert and know the work.

[18] Wittgenstein, *Remarks*, p. 197e (§1130), italics original.
[19] George Steiner, *On Difficulty and Other Essays* (Oxford: Oxford University Press, 1978).
[20] I discuss this at length in 'The Private Reader and the Listening Public', in Jeremy Hawthorn (ed.), *Criticism and Critical Theory* (London: Edward Arnold, 1984), 15–28.

## TECHNIQUE

How much of what is going on is relevant to the intelligent listener's grasp of the nature of the interpretation and of the performance? The arts vary in the extent to which the technical means chosen by the creator or performer is a part of the overall aesthetic effect. Beardsley describes the scene-shifters in classical Chinese drama as playing no part in the overall effect of the work, whereas when, in a recent production of *Don Giovanni*, the stage-hands took away the scenery and props whilst the singers were delivering the *buffo* finale, an artistic comment was intended. We are supposed to pay attention here, whereas we are not supposed to pay attention to the corresponding business in Chinese theatre. The stage props are, of course, relevant; so, too, is the lighting, though the precise wattages deemed appropriate by the electrician are not. Certainly the brush strokes of the painter are a matter relevant for the critic's consideration, but not the chemical composition of the pigments. It matters aesthetically that the painting looks this way rather than some other way, and it may be that there was only one way available to the artist of obtaining that result. But how it is achieved is not usually part of the aesthetic plot.

The means chosen by the composer—forms, instrumentation, placing of the vocal lines—are all matters which affect the expressive power of a performance, and are aesthetically relevant. What ink or what paper he uses is not, because the notated score is distinct from the work proper, and is not itself a matter of aesthetic value *qua* music. Brahms was supposed to have needed only the presence of manuscript paper and strong coffee to begin composing, but though these were necessary conditions for the act of composition, they are not part of the composed work, of course. They may cease to exist when the work is complete, but the features I have described as part of the work are required for the work to continue to exist in its present state.

Now let us turn to performance. Take three matters: questions of fingering, of part-playing, and of balance. Consider the first. Pianists are familiar with the fact that the fingering they use determines the phrasing of a passage. Using the thumb will have the effect of setting the detached notes in slight relief, giving them an

expressive weight, as in the example from Chopin's Nouvelle Étude in F shown in Ex. 4.[21]

A pianist might have small hands and have to play a certain chord, as a broken chord, or she may have to use half-pedalling where full pedalling blots a harmonic shift. Do these matter to the listener? No! they are non-aesthetic means to an aesthetic end. The fingering may be as irrelevant to his experience of the music as the movements of the stage-hands behind the scenes at the theatre. It is not a proper part of the presentation of the music. The part-playing and the balance are, however, features of the interpretation and performance; these are not merely technical means to an end.

In his notes for the concluding Presto of Beethoven's Piano Sonata Op. 10 No. 2 in F major, Tovey writes, 'The all-important feature in this bar (*bar 8*) is the entry of a new voice on the g in r.h. It is hardly possible to make this clear unless l.h. takes over the last semiquaver'[22] (see Ex. 5). The attentive listener, though he catches the phrasing, will not know what fingering is being used unless he is very close to the pianist. (*En passant*, it is possible to achieve this effect by accenting in the right hand.)

Is there more of a story to be told? The difference between what belongs to the work and what does not is not deeply problematic. Whereas a means–end relationship exists in a practical activity like piano playing, there is no means–end relationship to the creation of an object like a poem or a piece of music. The general point is reminiscent of Collingwood's arguments in distinguishing art from craft.[23] Whereas wood is a material for the construction of a table, and sawing and chiselling the means whereby the table is created

---

[21] An example pillaged from Charles Rosen, *The Romantic Generation* (London: Harper Collins, 1996), 366.

[22] Beethoven, *Piano Sonatas*, i, Associated Board edn., 131, Tovey's italics.

[23] R. G. Collingwood, *The Principles of Art* (Oxford: Oxford University Press, 1978), ch. 2.

from the wood, there is no parallel craftsmanship in the creation
of a piece of music. The work is all that the notation prescribes.
What we mean by technical ability in a composer is rather different from the technical ability of a craftsman; it is the capacity
to handle musical form smoothly; contrapuntal technique, for
example, is in this way rather like technique in logic or mathematics. Or it is the capacity to write music which is challenging but
satisfyingly playable. In this latter sense, Rachmaninov is a technically adept composer for the piano, whilst Schubert is not.

Now performers learn contemporary music; in doing so, they are
often faced with technical problems which they find it interesting,
even fascinating, to surmount. But these are problems which,
although their solution is a matter of concern to the performer,
mean little to the listener *qua* listener. It might be a mistake to
suppose that the solutions to these difficulties never have anything
to do with aesthetic satisfaction, but they can be sufficiently distant
from it for them not to be a significant factor in a proper

understanding of the performance. But, as far as the technical issues are concerned, the pleasure in solving such problems might, as far as the performer is concerned, be mistaken for pleasure in the work. A judicious music-lover would 'discount' this as grounds for admiring a work in the way I described in the last chapter. This is an important consideration when it comes to considering why much modern music is programmed in concerts when it is clear that the audience for it is very small indeed. I shall return to this topic later, when I come to discuss what we may call 'the official history of twentieth-century music'.

I do not deny that technical virtuosity appeals to the listener, even more perhaps to the onlooker. The ability to articulate complicated series of notes rapidly and accurately can amaze and delight, much as the intricate steps of a dancer may. Patter songs or poetry with complex internal rhymes please by their accomplishment and economy. This is part of what we admire in W. S. Gilbert; rapid verbal articulation is not much different from the digital dexterity of a Horowitz. Of course, sometimes we can be misled. Some Rachmaninov looks and sounds more difficult than Mozart, whereas it is easier. This circus element may not be the highest of aesthetic considerations, but we should not deny it a role. Whilst writing this chapter, I have been listening to Janet Baker's 'live' recording of Mahler's *Das Lied von der Erde*.[24] Certainly her ability to produce a controlled diminuendo at the close, on the words 'ewig ... ewig' until her voice gradually sinks into the orchestral texture, is amazing, but it is used to profound artistic effect. The dying poet will be absorbed into Nature's round. 'The good earth grows green again ... for ever ... for ever ...'

Let me now draw a few threads together pro tem. My thesis is perhaps best stated as follows: in presenting a work to us, a performer simultaneously expresses an interpretation of the work, an interpretation which may be 'spur of the moment', may have been thought out at length, or may indeed be copied from a more distinguished musician. He may, whilst doing this, admit that other equally valid views of the work are possible. His performance expresses to his audience his view of the work (and this holds even if it has not been consciously formulated to himself). He may be

---

[24] With John Mitchinson and the BBC Northern Symphony Orchestra, conducted by Raymond Leppard on Pickwick Imp. BBCRD 9120.

sincere in thinking that the work has the character he presents it as having, and his performance may sincerely express his conception, making no concession to cheap effects or superficial glamour where those are, in his view, absent from the work. Such considerations have the serious moral charge that traditional expressionism invests in them. May he improve the work? This, I think, is a more complex matter. Performers will talk about 'doing their best for a work', and it is a fact, I think, that somebody like Beecham excelled in making second-rate music sound better than it really is. If you have followed me thus far, you will not be surprised to hear that I think there is an element of chicanery involved.

## AUTHENTICITY

Having dealt with some of the initial puzzles about the relationships of performance to work and listener to performance, we are better equipped to consider the most controversial of issues about performance, the debates about 'authenticity'. In the last chapter I suggested that the concept of a work of music is ideologically impregnated inasmuch as different views of its nature reflect different views about the importance of interpretation. The question of authenticity engages similarly broad considerations.

One of the most striking features of our experience of music over the last half-century has been the way that our taste has changed to accommodate what are called 'authentic performing practices'. Our ears have been educated, first of all to reject Bach played on the piano, even by Glenn Gould, as other than *faute de mieux*, then to accept faster slow movements, lower pitch, smaller forces, and different balances, as well as original instruments such as natural horns and valveless trumpets. Music-lovers of my generation can remember, in the decade after the war, the impact of the recordings of the Stuttgart Chamber Orchestra with Karl Munchinger. They seemed, then, to revitalize Bach's music. Nowadays, even these performances seem heavy and old-fashioned. So taste changes. We are now getting used to hearing Berlioz, and even Brahms, on instruments of the day or copies of them. A recent broadcaster remarked that this, rather than through the music composed by our own contemporaries, is how the taste of the ordinary music-lover is being expanded. When a horn player whimsically reflected on having to learn the authentic manner for Elgar, he little suspected, I fancy, how quickly the movement would catch up with him.

But the concept of authenticity is not uncontroversial. It is ripe for philosophical investigation, and it was no surprise to find the matter hotly debated in the philosophical journals. James O. Young is particularly exercised over the form that a definition of 'authenticity' might take.[25] I am less concerned with this, though it is necessary to have at least some provisional conception of what is at issue. Let me define the broad conditions for an authentic performance as those in which the music sounds as it would have done at the time of composition had it been played by competent musicians familiar with the style and performing conventions, playing on decent instruments of the sort which the composer assumed when he wrote the music. This, I admit, is vague. It does not guide us where the scoring is left to the performers, for instance. But we can hardly require a definition which answers in advance questions which are specifically left to performers. It would be an inadequate definition which rendered precise what is imprecise in practice. We need to follow Aristotle and match the degree of articulation to the subject-matter. Note that I say 'how the music sounds' but not 'how it sounds to . . .' Young, in discussing this, slips from the first to the second. But authentic reception occurs only if we can hear the music as an experienced musician or connoisseur contemporaneous with its composition would have heard it. Now obviously authentic performance and authentic reception are distinct. The performer aims primarily at the first. He cannot do much about the second *qua* performer; the task of raising consciousness is up to the educator. I do not preclude, of course, the fact that the performer also educates his audience, *inter alia*; but there are two fairly distinct functions here.[26]

It may be possible to make the music sound as it would have in,

[25] James O. Young, 'The Concept of Authentic Performance', *British Journal of Aesthetics*, 28/3 (1988), 228–38. See also Stephen Davies, 'Authenticity in Musical Performance', *British Journal of Aesthetics*, 27/1 (1987), 39–50; *idem*, 'Authenticity in Performance, A Reply to James O. Young', *British Journal of Aesthetics*, 28/4 (1988), 373–6. Other interesting contributions to the debate are Joseph Kerman, *Contemplating Music* (Cambridge, Mass.: Harvard University Press, 1985), 189 and 208 ff.; Stan Godlovitch, 'Authentic Performance', *Monist*, 71 (1988), 258–77; and Peter Kivy, 'On the Concept of the "Historically Authentic" Performance', *Monist*, 71 (1988), 278–90.

[26] See Kivy, *Authenticities*, 74–8.

say, 1700, without there being any present-day listener who hears it in the appropriate way. Thus the effect of a discord has changed, it might be argued; the clashes in the slow introduction cannot shock or puzzle us in the way they shocked or puzzled the first hearers of Mozart's String Quartet K. 465.[27] Our ears are used to Mahler and Strauss, Stravinsky and Schoenberg. And, by parity of reasoning, a listener in another 150 years might hear a recording of Britten conducting his own music, and hear an authentic performance but be excluded from authentic hearing. No more, it will be argued, can we think ourselves back into the milieu of Dittersdorff and Vanhal, who with Haydn and Mozart made up that famous original quartet party that performed Mozart's six wonderful 'Haydn' Quartets for the first time. There is an equivalent problem in literature. I can learn the significance of a metaphor in *Macbeth*, but my experience is not pristine because it depends upon propositional knowledge which the Elizabethans did not need. The significance of a metaphor now has to be learnt, whereas its impact was immediate for the original audience.

So the argument runs. But how effective is it? I can learn and then internalize. Presumably even Haydn had to switch from the expectations proper to one style to those proper to another when he switched from listening to Mozart to listening to the folk music whose influence is often evident in his own work. We can adjust.[28] Young makes much of the fact that there is no innocent ear. What he has to show is something much stronger, which is that I can only, ever, hear music in the context of my total musical experience. But why should we grant this? After all, my background also differs from that of Ligeti. He has heard and been influenced by music which I have not heard or do not know well, or where I am not struck by the passages which most influenced him. If he hears his own music authentically, which is itself a highly controversial assumption, am I excluded from doing so because my musical experience is not his? On this argument, it is unlikely that I ever hear any music authentically.

But if no music can be heard authentically, we lose the essential contrast between authentic and inauthentic hearing. For we surely need to distinguish between the listener who notices the force of the dissonance at the bridge to the recapitulation in the first

[27] Argued by Young, 'Concept of Authentic Performance'.
[28] See Davies, 'Authenticity in Performance', 375.

movement of the 'Eroica', a passage which made such a powerful impression on Beethoven's contemporaries, and the listener for whom it passes by unremarked.[29] The first we should think of as hearing more 'authentically' than the latter. (We must also grant, *en passant*, the way in which different experiences of a work interrelate and interconnect. A later hearing of the 'Eroica' can build on, or react to, the initial impression this passage makes—for example, by hearing it as an overlapping of two vast 'tectonic plates' within the overall structure of the movement.)

Now Young's objections to the possibility of authentic performance are that works might never have been performed, or have been performed on poor instruments or by incompetent performers, that the composer's intentions cannot be properly established, and that the composer himself might have been a poor interpreter. This fusillade of arguments eliminates various formulations of the requirement of authenticity without, as far as I can see, telling against the thesis I propose.

A cousin to Young's objection, but an objection of greater subtlety and interest, is that of Kivy.[30] Kivy points out that performing traditions post-date a work. There was necessarily no tradition of performing them when Bach first wrote the partitas for keyboard. When Schiff plays them, he will not play them as a contemporary might, for he has the benefit of a tradition of performing which offers ideas about them. His performance is alive in a way in which an 'archaeological' performance is not. We cannot have it both ways. We cannot have a performance which is alive in this sense, and yet is 'authentic'.

But I deny that the fork is exclusive. We need not allow that an archaeologically true performance necessarily ignores later discoveries about the way to perform a work. For if ways of performing are defensible, they are based on features of the work which, though unnoticed by contemporaries, nevertheless might have been. My criterion of authenticity is subjunctive. A valid performance has to be one which could have been produced by a contemporary of the creator. Consequently, I can allow that the discovery of some aspect of the music by a later interpreter may be used by a performer using early instruments. Thus a performance of Mozart on the fortepiano

---

[29] See Kivy, *Authenticities*, 204.
[30] Kivy, 'On the Concept of the "Historically Authentic" Performance'.

might use insights realized by Curzon in his interpretations of a Mozart piano concerto on a concert grand. Within more or less authentic performance—for authenticity is itself a matter of degree—some performances will be better than others, but different performances might be of equal value in different ways. It will be apparent from what I say elsewhere in this book that I strongly believe that it is a mistake to think that there is a single ideal performance, authentic or otherwise.

Although in this respect Kivy is close to Taruskin,[31] who also emphasizes the importance of a canonic, interpretative tradition which recognizes the centrality of, say, Furtwängler's and Klemperer's performances of Bach, in another respect Taruskin could endorse the position I advocate. For he argues at length that the so-called authentic style is merely the latest in an interpretative tradition, and happens to be the style of performance which is at home in late twentieth-century culture. It is a style which is 'not really historical', but 'completely of our own time'.[32] So he can allow that the 'authentic style', the contemporary style of performance, is the heir to an interpretative tradition. Taruskin, like Kivy, is rather dismissive of the claims of the advocates of authenticity. It is, of course, true that 'authenticity' is a contemporary movement inasmuch as the scholarship which has made us aware of how the music might have sounded is a twentieth-century phenomenon. But it certainly does not follow that authenticity is shown thereby to be a merely arbitrary exercise of fashion, which is what Taruskin suggests. That would be akin to arguing that because the physics and mathematics which made Einstein's discoveries possible were a product of the nineteenth century, Einstein's theories should be regarded as a temporary fashion, rather than as containing truths about the universe.

This is not to deny that 'authenticity' is an aspect of our musical ideology; the extreme heat that is generated by debates over it is strong evidence for its ideological force. A musician accustomed to giving 'traditional' interpretations of the Beethoven symphonies may feel that his values and his life's work are challenged by the vogue for presenting them à la Norrington. It would be hard to see why such performances would be resented were they not seen as a

---

[31] Richard Taruskin, *Text and Act* (Oxford: Oxford University Press, 1995), 106–7, e.g. [32] Ibid. 102.

challenge to beliefs deeply held, to work in which a large part of one's life has been invested, or to values which have been cherished. But to concede that the appeal to authenticity has ideological implications is not, on my 'broad' understanding of ideology, to concede that the beliefs which hover in the background are necessarily false. I believe that reasons can be given for the 'authenticity' movement, even if I admit that these would not have been available to previous generations.

By parity of reasoning, the concept of 'expression' relates so closely to matters of sincerity and authenticity which became significant in the early Romantic era, that it cannot escape being part of the ideology of music. The division between those who favour the modern style of interpretation, with its lean sound and less extreme tempi, and those who favour older, tried manners deriving, in the modern era, from Furtwängler, is a division between those who think that interpretative traditions are to be respected and not replaced by 'cleaned-up' versions, between those who see interpretative traditions as part of our heritage and those who do not, between those who think of performance as a form of expression by the interpreter which can also be honest, sincere, and authentic and those who look for an 'objective rendering' of the work. The defensive reaction to the authenticity movement shows exactly that aspect of ideology which, as I remarked earlier, differentiates it from *Weltanschauungen* and forms of life: namely, its dynamic function in our belief system.

So why should we attempt authenticity? I am going to suggest two reasons; the first might be called 'internal', the second 'external'. The internal argument is that the work of music commonly has internal relationships which can be brought out only in performances which aspire to authenticity. The external argument is that music relates to its culture of origin, and that authentic performances better reveal this. Let me consider the internal argument first. If we play the music using original instruments and practices, or as near to these as we can get, aspects of the music—the balance of parts or the precise orchestral colour—become clearer. Consider hearing Bach on a Father Willis or Cavallé-Coll with hearing him on a baroque organ. On the latter the counterpoint is lucid, and there can be no doubt that contrapuntal lines were essential to Bach's conception of what he was doing. It is as futile to ask whether Bach would have opted for a modern organ had it been available as it is to ask whether he would have preferred a modern orchestra in the B minor Mass had it been available. Perhaps he would, but then the music would have been very different. He might have wanted a larger choir and more instrumentalists playing on the instruments he knew, but, had they been available, again the music might well have been different.[33] An advocate of nineteenth-century organs might reply that she prefers an undifferentiated mass of glorious sound in which the harmonic shifts are the only audible qualities. If I then point out that my preferences are shared by the educated, she will presumably level the charge of indoctrination. We have, she will say, persuaded ourselves that this is the way to perform the music. The objection touches a nerve. No doubt taste is deeply affected by fashion and peer pressure, but the objection can be seen off. My case would fail only if musicians, after listening carefully and intelligently, did not come to prefer authenticity.

Peter Kivy describes the 'internal argument' as the 'delicate balance argument' to which he adds the 'composer knows best' argument.[34] He is sceptical about both. The first he likens to the Leibnizian argument that this is the best of all possible worlds; just as that implies that the rational and informed critic will eventually come to see that it is true, that this *is* the best of all possible worlds, so the delicate balance argument implies that musically sophisticated and unprejudiced listeners will eventually come to prefer the music played as the composer conceived. This seems unverifiable to Kivy. Providing we go on long enough we will prefer the 'original', it is said, but how long is 'long enough'? Just as long as is required, is the answer Kivy thinks they give. Now it is clear that I subscribe to the 'delicate balance' argument. But all that is required is that it is, in general, true that people come to prefer the 'original' and this is, I think, inductively supported. I also think that a form of the 'composer knows best' argument is defensible, and I remain unmoved by Kivy's objections.

So take the second, the 'composer knows best' argument. Without subscribing to the absurd view that the composer is infallible, it is none the less true that in the greatest cases we are dealing with composers who are far removed from even average talent. This is a plain matter of fact. The gulf between Bach and Telemann

---

[33] See Kivy, *Authenticities*, 38.     [34] Ibid. 162, 172 ff.

or Purcell and Lully is far greater than the gulf between Telemann or Lully and you and me. It is extremely unlikely that we will be able to improve on Bach, especially when the next three arguments are considered.

First, great works may have such a degree of formal unity that alterations will never be to the good. It is often hard to distinguish between alterations which change a well-loved piece in a way which irritates and alterations which would be seen as damaging even by the accomplished listener who is new to them. But we can certainly imagine a situation in which the first is excluded, and then we would be able to see that the parts cohere in such a way that cuts or insertions damage. It is plausible to think that Haydn's greatest quartets approach this ideal condition, as do, say, Mozart's 'Haydn' Quartets or the finest of the 'Forty-Eight'.

Secondly, it is very hard for us to get inside Bach's style in such a way as to improve on what he did. His style is an amalgam of the period and the personal. Anybody sufficiently gifted to rival Bach in musical accomplishment—say Benjamin Britten—has his own fish to fry, and the personal voice will obtrude in any revisions he makes.

Thirdly, and finally, there is an ethical matter here. We owe it to Bach to present his music, and not a mix of his and somebody else's. Kivy argues, surely wrongly, that to see this as an obligation is to suppose that music has a message which must be preserved.[35] But not all my obligations to others are obligations to transmit what they say truthfully. There are other obligations of a similar sort which have nothing to do with the communication of meanings. I might have an obligation to respect my mother's final wish to have her ashes placed at Stonehenge, but no message is involved. Nevertheless, it is still a moral obligation.

Like Kivy, Randall Dipert regards an obligation to the composer to play the music his way as having about as much weight as the obligation to unify Europe because Napoleon wanted it.[36] But the differences are obvious. Europe consists of millions of people, all of whom have objectives to be taken into consideration. Europe is not the creation of Napoleon, and its inhabitants are people with

---

[35] See Kivy, *Authenticities*, 151 ff.

[36] Randall Dipert, 'The Composer's Intentions: An Examination of their Relevance for Performance', *Musical Quarterly*, 66 (1980), 205–18. See Taruskin, *Text and Act*, 24.

their own aims and lives. But a Mozart quartet is Mozart's creation. We are not obliged to play or listen to it. But if we think that he placed a value on it, and if we take it to be as important as anything he did in his life—which is not unreasonable—then we have as much of an obligation to respect his wishes as we have to respect the terms of somebody's will. Not for nothing do we speak of a composer's 'testament'.

Kivy concludes that it may well be the case that the composer does not always know best,[37] and that 'the performing intentions of the composer . . . might turn out to be a good way of doing the business, or might not'.[38] I agree. But what does not follow is that anybody else has a better chance of 'doing the business'. For me, following the composer's intentions is not so much a dogma as proved best practice for the reasons I give.

I will end the discussion of the 'internal argument' with an instance from my own experience. There is a delightful Barcarolle by Alkan (Op. 65 No. 6) which I have played for a few decades. Ronald Smith and John White describe it aptly as the Mendelssohn that Gershwin forgot to write. The abrupt *sforzando* final chord always struck me as out of place, as indeed it did a recent reviewer of a recording. Given the latitude Kivy allows, I should have allowed the *poco calendo* to die away gradually, as any other composer might have indicated—until I realized very recently that this final bump was an application of characteristic French asepticism to German sentimentality. I need not labour the point.

But if the arguments so far fail to convince, consider the 'external' argument. The arts in general offer us an insight into cultures which differ progressively from our own, not just because they are geographically distinct, but because they belong to that other country, the past. If we interpret such art on the basis of our own culture and its assumptions, we lose something valuable, an encounter with a different way of doing things. We are as bad as those tourists who travel only to eat familiar food and practice their own customs, looking at the country they visit through coach windows without encountering it. The sound of past music can be strange and new, and it contributes to a picture of the culture from

[37] Kivy, *Authenticities*, 173.     [38] Ibid. 185.

which it stems. To update the music in the hope of making it 'relevant' does us as little service as it does the music.

Kivy draws our attention to broader issues.[39] The authenticity of the physical setting may contribute to the impact of the work. Most of us would prefer to hear Tallis or Palestrina in a great church, and that not merely for reasons of acoustics. We know, as well, that the impact of a Haydn symphony may be greater when it takes place in one of the smaller halls for which he conceived it. But is it necessary that Bach's Brandenburg Concertos be played by performers wearing wigs? Sometimes, Kivy perceptively remarks, an authentic setting can interfere. When we perform a Bach cantata in a concert-hall, the performance is inauthentic to the extent that the work was intended for a church and would have been interlarded with a sermon, Bible readings, and prayers. Now there is a temptation to think of a concert-hall as a neutral venue in which the music can be heard 'pure', removed from associations. But a little reflection shows that this is not so.[40] Certain nineteenth-century works seem at home in the concert-hall; calling for a large orchestra, they were designed for these large spaces and particular acoustics, and we are comfortable with them there. Add to this the sight of the instruments, the physical movements of the violin bow, now held high by the players, the sheen on the stringed instruments, the glow of colour from the brass, and, of course, the callisthenics of the conductor, and it becomes clear that there is a theatrical element here which is lost when I listen at home through loudspeakers or on a Walkman. Finally, of course, the sense of joining in an event with other music-lovers, the sight of the soloist taking risks in a way which will not be paralleled in a recording, all make for a spectacle. For the celebrant at mass, we now have the maestro.

Such considerations suggest that we need to return to the context in which the music was performed, in order to receive it authentically. But Kivy is surely right to be sceptical about the claim that the setting must in general be authentic as well. All we can say is that the contribution of the setting to the experience varies. It is arguable that the finest music survives transposed to new settings, just as a painting may still affect us in a gallery, even though it loses

---

[39] Kivy, *Authenticities*, 102.
[40] See Lydia Goehr, *The Imaginary Museum of Musical Works* (Oxford: Clarendon Press, 1992).

by removal from the church or private house where it was intended to be displayed.

What Kivy does point out—and this strikes me as of enormous importance—is that change will not necessarily be for the worse. We may both gain and lose from a historically authentic setting. Possibly I am more tolerant of a Lutheran liturgy than is Kivy, but it is certainly true that the presumably approximate congregational singing in a Bach cantata would have been uncomfortable. The interesting question is whether authenticity interferes with attention to the music. Kivy nicely points out that Mozart's wind serenades have details which would be lost amid the chatter, chomping, and rattle of cutlery and glasses at the dinner parties for which they were intended. A contemporary might well have argued that the music is too good to be listened to amidst such distractions.

But authenticity of setting can obviously offer rewards, and I will close with a few examples. In a Prom a few years back, Italian Renaissance music was performed with the gestures, familiar from paintings of the period, which, it is thought, originally accompanied it. The consequence was that it placed the music in a context of gesture which re-created something of the culture in which the music lived. It was revelatory, and it raised interesting questions. For one thing, it connected with a tradition of rhetoric and oratory which, as I argued earlier in this book, helps us to understand the expressive nature of music. Yet another example: Nicholas Cook remarks that Chinese zither music requires attention to be paid to the movements of the player's hands as well as to the sounds, and that in some African music the movements of the performers are part of the aesthetic effect.[41] We might feel inclined to see our own culture as stressing the sound alone, and as differing from other cultures in this respect. If we are aggressive about the superiority of Western music, we might even regard this as a sign of how 'pure' our experience of music has become. But we overlook aspects of our appreciation of music. Kivy himself remarks on the choreographic effect of the players snuffing out their candles and then leaving in the last movement of Haydn's 'Farewell' Symphony.[42] The *lieder* singer's facial expression is important, and a pianist, by his movements, may draw our attention to a climactic point in his

[41] Nicholas Cook, *Music, Imagination and Culture* (Oxford: Oxford University Press, 1990), 6–7.  [42] Kivy, *Authenticities*, 105.

interpretation. There is no doubt that seeing that a performer is moved may contribute to our feeling that the performance is not merely routine. Showmen play on this, of course, and we are rightly suspicious of histrionics. But though we can be taken in, we are also as shrewd at picking out false sentiment in the performer as we are in everyday life. A performer who is totally impassive may be unnerving. A failure to grasp the importance of gesture here may be a failure to appreciate, not a sign of a superior approach. It is a mistake to suppose that it is a mark of a superior attitude to the music to attend to its abstract qualities alone, and that the cavortings of the performer are a necessary evil; this is a mistake to which formalists are constantly prone. I conclude that there is no simple single principle governing the matter of authenticity of setting. Sometimes it distracts; sometimes it adds. So there is no alternative to a piecemeal approach here. Yes, we ought to consider the claims of 'authenticity' in setting. No, we ought not to be hidebound in observing them.

Young's proposal was that we should abandon the quest for authenticity in favour of that of 'successful performance'. In a similar vein, Kivy speaks of 'what sounds better' and of the 'test of listening'.[43] But we cannot apply such a test just like that. It is open for us to say, 'Yes, it is beautiful but it is wrong and false'. We cannot abstract from our knowledge of music history, as though this plays no part in listening. I hope that one lesson of this book is that there is no innocent ear—only ears which are to a greater or a lesser extent educated. When Young speaks of a successful performance, he begs the question in favour of the point at issue. A successful performance is one which is regarded as such by musicians of experience and judgement, and such musicians nowadays require a measure of authenticity for a successful performance. This is why the Bach of Klemperer or the Handel of Sargent are at best successful *faute de mieux*.

We have concerned ourselves largely with the ideal of authenticity in performance. I have defended it, but, in doing so, I acknowledge how deeply questions of value are involved; and when questions of value are present, ideology is not far behind. We also sometimes speak of the composer himself as 'authentic' or, perhaps more commonly, as 'sincere', which, as we have seen, is a cognate

---

[43] Kivy, *Authenticities*, 285.

concept. Sometimes we describe a composer as insincere, without implying any conscious deceit or suggesting that he was untrue to himself. It is to these issues that I now turn, and in discussing them we shall find that those questions which I have described as 'ideological' again raise their heads, if anything in an even broader and pervasive way.

# 6

## Music's Ruling Myths

### I

I closed the last chapter with the observation that 'authenticity' in music has a wider as well as a narrower sense. Not only do we debate the merits of authentic performance in playing older music, but we sometimes charge composers with inauthenticity or 'insincerity', to give it its more familiar description. Suppose we describe music as insincere. Perhaps we level this charge at Strauss's *Arabella* or Puccini's *La Bohème* or Górecki's Third Symphony. Why does the charge of 'insincerity' matter to us? Would it make so much difference if we found that the composer did 'mean' it after all? Suppose that Górecki 'believes in' his work. Would this exculpate him? I think not. The accusation that the music is insincere, inauthentic, or manipulative is independent of the composer's mental state.

I shall take 'insincerity' as symptomatic of those severer judgements which relate to a composer's failure to engage with his times and what his times demand of him. As I shall show, it is not the only form such failures may take. But it is perhaps peculiarly important in connecting with a certain prevalent, dominant ideology in music, the ideology that the language of music ought to develop or progress. It is significant that the charge of insincerity is one we level at nineteenth- and twentieth-century composers in particular, composers who wrote under the aegis of this ideology. This, in turn, paves the way for the examination of humanism in music which occupies the final part.

### II

So, to broader issues and wider contexts. As I promised, in this penultimate chapter, I shall be concerned with the notions of sincerity and authenticity in a more inclusive sense. Since these ideas have been debated more fully with respect to literature, a famous observation by a great literary critic may provide the best entrance into this nest of difficulties. T. S. Eliot warned the religious poet that it is important to record the experiences you have had, rather than those you would like to have had.[1] What is the rationale for this emphasis on sincerity and the absence of self-deception? Could you not write a perfectly good poem about the religious experiences you wished you were having or thought, mistakenly, that you were having? Indeed, the question as to whether the poet is trying to communicate a state of mind at all needs to be considered. When Milton wrote 'Lycidas', did he feel what he seems to express? If there was no specific content to his mental state, which could be either consonant with or at odds with what is expressed, then clearly whatever expressive character of regret the poetry has, it has on its own account. The question of sincerity, in its normal sense, would not even arise. Ian Robinson's *The Survival of English* places this in a wider perspective. In an acute and provoking piece on 'Religious English', he writes thus about sincerity and insincerity:

This question of sincerity, which will have to recur in these pages, is so important (connected as it is with what counts as truth everywhere outside the exact sciences) and so generally misunderstood that I must go out of my way to make it clear that I am not accusing anybody of deception or deliberate hypocrisy. But with that last word the difficulty and some of the importance of this subject may appear, for did Christ accuse the Pharisees of deception or deliberate hypocrisy? It is possible to be a whited sepulchre with one kind of sincerity, believing in one's own whitewash and unconsciously suppressing knowledge of the rottenness within. I am writing not about trickery, but the difference between the real and the sham—'sham' too, here, implying nothing for which anybody could be held responsible in a court of law (though on the day of judgement matters may be different, and it may perhaps then not count as an excuse to say we knew no better). The exploration of the idea of 'sincerity' is one of F. R. Leavis's major contributions to thought, one of the places where literary criticism may offer general illumination. Perhaps the problems become clearer if one thinks of music. With music the question of ordinary deception can hardly arise, for, even more obviously than the poet, the composer 'nothing affirms and therefore neuer lyeth'. But music may certainly be

---

[1] T. S. Eliot, *After Strange Gods* (London: Faber, 1934), 29.

sincere or insincere, real or sham, and in that way true or false. Brahms (I instance someone whose stature is real and whose talent genuine enough to invite consideration) is to my mind an insincere composer, though I wouldn't want to rebuke him for deceiving his admirers, even himself. He is, when he seems most serious, insincere because sentimental.[2]

Robinson continues:

By this argument all real insincerity is self-deceiving rather than trickery. In the fourth movement of his first symphony Brahms seems to me to be working off on himself feelings of affirmation and serenity he hadn't really got. The contrary, the sincerity that discovers the real, is what one looks for in art or religion: truth to life or to God. In that sense there could be point in saying that Mozart cannot tell a lie.

(We might recall here Nietzsche's remark that Wagner's music is never true.) Various problems arise here. We do not need to subscribe to Robinson's vagaries about truth to God to find this passage provoking. Consider the way in which Robinson qualifies 'insincerity'! 'Real' insincerity is self-deception. Now what is certainly puzzling here is that normally we think of insincerity as involving consciousness and intention on the part of the agent. If I insincerely profess affection, I show or describe feelings which I do not really have, and which I know that I do not have. Insincerity is more like lying than self-deception, though it needs to be said that 'insincerity' is broader, including, as it does, insincerity in behaviour which may not involve utterance. So, although I am not entirely confident about the nuances of the term, I would be inclined to say that somebody who is self-deceiving about his affection is not insincere. If knowing that you are insincere is a central feature of insincerity, we cannot treat the term 'insincere' as polymorphous in the way that Malcolm Budd does.[3] Budd suggests that there are various forms of insincerity, ranging from the deliberate misrepresentation of one's feelings, through the attempt to feel differently for the sake of originality, to the absence of self-examination. But the latter seem more like quasi-metaphorical extensions of the word. Such usages belong to the same family as those expressions, debated in Chapter 2, which metaphorically characterize works of art.

---

[2] Ian Robinson, *The Survival of English* (Cambridge: Cambridge University Press, 1973), 39–40.
[3] Malcolm Budd, 'Belief and Sincerity in Poetry', in Eva Schaper (ed.), *Pleasure, Preference and Value* (Cambridge: Cambridge University Press, 1983), 137–57.

So this discussion debouches into a wider and more familiar issue, and that is the basis on which we use words which normally ascribe states of persons to works of art. Once we detach 'sincerity' and 'insincerity' from the intentions of the individual as Robinson does, we find that the question as to how art can be sincere is a question which has much in common with the question of how it can be Olympian, glum, austere, impassioned, or calm. In the arts, of course, these ways of talking are so familiar that their metaphorical edge has been dulled, though the basis for these expressions remains an interesting problem, as we have seen. In an earlier chapter I tried to provide grounds for the application of such expressive predicates to music, arguing that it is based upon certain analogies with oratory. That account provides the foundation for the more complex and interesting judgements which I wish to investigate here.

John Casey eschews Croce's position, which Budd seems to share, that concepts like 'sincerity' are systematically ambiguous.[4] He does, however, raise the interesting question as to whether the way we express an emotion qualifies the emotion itself. To answer the question in the affirmative would be to commit oneself to saying that Brahms was 'objectively' insincere, because the form of expression he chose qualifies the emotion itself. What Robinson claims in the passage I quoted is that Brahms was guilty of self-deception, which I take to be a different charge. But if we assume, as Robinson does, that insincerity may be a matter of the quality of the work of art itself, does this mean that the means of expression may alter the emotion? Some examples may help. Casey quotes a passage from D. H. Lawrence's *Sons and Lovers*, where Morel's grief at his wife's death comes out in the tired, conventional clichés of the bereaved. Any 'In Memoriam' column in a local newspaper provides examples aplenty. In the latter case people seem to think that an expression of grief requires them to write their own words—as though a quotation from the Bible could not express grief more adequately than a piece of comic doggerel which has the dubious merit of having been composed by the bereaved. Something about our culture makes people think it is better or more honest to write one's own verse, no matter how bad, on the

[4] John Casey, 'The Autonomy of Art', in G. Vesey (ed.), *Philosophy and the Arts*, Royal Institute of Philosophy Lectures, vi: *1971–2* (London: Macmillan, 1973), 65–87.

grounds that it will be a more accurate portrayal of one's feelings. In fact, it is not an unfamiliar experience to find that Proust expresses obsessional love, Lawrence the tensions of family life, or Bishop King bereavement far better than you or I can. Sometimes I express myself better by quotation.

This alone might make one hesitate to take sincere expression to be the accurate representation of a prior inner state. How you feel is so often amorphous, and the difference between sadness, regret, and grief much more a matter of the difference between the objects of these states, their behavioural accompaniments and environmental setting, than a matter of a difference between how they 'feel'. It is not as though there is a prior, clearly defined 'inner state' waiting for the appropriate expression.

As far as sincere expression is concerned, then, the process classically described by Collingwood is often involved.[5] Finding the right words clarifies one's previously inchoate state to oneself. 'Getting it clear' is how Collingwood thinks of it. The idea is not so much that I only know how I feel when I have the words to describe it as that what I feel I feel when I can describe it to myself. So there is a contrast to be drawn between this more complex view and the jejune notion that I always know what I feel but sometimes cannot find the words to describe it, a view which looks indefensible as a general thesis. As has been suggested, sometimes the nature of the mental state depends upon how it is described; this has the epistemological corollary that sometimes I will not know what my state is if I cannot describe it to myself. A young person at puberty may be in love without realizing what state he or she is in. The concept of sexual love is not yet properly understood. Cherubino in *The Marriage of Figaro* is in that condition. 'Voi che sapete' expresses that mixture of pulsating urgency and mental confusion wonderfully. The young man has lost his freedom to act, and finds his new situation both alarming and exciting.[6]

We can conclude, then, that it is mistaken to suppose that every 'inner' state is perfectly defined, and that it is merely a matter of

[5] R. G. Collingwood. *The Principles of Art* (Oxford: Oxford University Press, 1978), 114.

[6] Charles Taylor has followed Croce in making much of the fact that our capacity to interpret ourselves actually changes the phenomena described. See Charles Taylor, *Human Agency and Language, Philosophical Papers*, i (Cambridge: Cambridge University Press, 1985), *passim*.

finding words to describe it. What we are considering here is a third possibility: that there are some mental states whose character depends in part on their description. I believe there are such states.

Consider again Morel in *Sons and Lovers*. Does Morel fail to express the deep grief he feels, or is the grief itself maudlin, made maudlin by the clichés in which he describes it, as I have suggested? In the end, Casey seems to favour the first, though his argument might lead us to expect the second. The grounds for the second are, of course, that we judge a person's grief by its expression, and verbal behaviour is just one form of behaviour. So, on that criterion, it is the grief itself which is maudlin.

Now as far as sincerity is concerned, we normally get the distinction we require between what is felt and what is expressed by contrasting what a man expresses on one particular occasion and what he expresses at other times. However, this will not handle all cases of insincerity. Suppose I meet a woman on one occasion only. If I am insincere in what I say, then my insincerity consists in the gap between the sentiments I express and those I would have expressed had I not suppressed them. The counterfactual contains the gist of the matter. Insincerity is a matter of the deliberate decision to behave in a way contrary to your 'natural' inclination. Left to yourself, you might wish to avoid some woman; but, for other reasons, perhaps of courtesy, you are agreeable to her. But the cases which I have been describing are obviously and importantly different. For in my cases, the question of sincerity cannot arise, because there is no gap between the inner and the outer. There is no space for insincerity. Obviously there is a pretty strong case for saying that the arts are like this, especially if you take the sort of cognitivist line on expression that I advocated in Chapter 2. It is the work which has whatever character it has. We are not interested in a mismatch between the composer's mental state and the music.

Take an example. Imagine that a composer sets out to express certain feelings about nature. As the music progresses, it develops away from the original idea, and in the end, its character seems to be different from what its genesis suggested. In his Sixth Symphony, something like this seems to have happened to Sibelius. When he was about to sketch it in 1918, he wrote that the music would be 'wild and impassioned in character. Sombre with pastoral contrasts. Probably in four movements with the end rising to a sombre roaring.'[7] The music is nothing like this. Suppose Sibelius did not update his intentions! Does this make him insincere in the music he wrote? Hardly!

Let's try again! As we have seen, Robinson faces the problem of saying of a creator that he or she is insincere and intending no such gap between what he or she expresses and what he or she would express if untrammelled. His is a notion of 'objective insincerity'. Although the idea is something of a conceptual innovation, we can find parallels. The victims of Stalinist show trials were sometimes held to be 'objectively guilty',[8] even though they intended no harm to the revolutionary cause, because their acts were, it was said, damaging to the revolution, though inadvertently. The suggestion is that equally severe standards apply in the arts. We could paraphrase Robinson as saying that Brahms is 'objectively guilty' of insincerity. Art takes no prisoners.

Consider some adjacent cases. I don't know whether 'insincere' is *le mot juste* here (and my misgivings are central to what I shall say later on), but there is something disquieting about the religiosity of the late poetry of T. S. Eliot. I say this partly because I believe that the Christian faith is not an option for modern man. But even if you do not agree with me about this, you may appreciate my misgivings about Eliot. Eliot's very title, 'The Four Quartets', hints at an aspiration to the sublimity of late Beethoven. There is, to my mind, a suggestion of intent. But a 'late style' can never be deliberate. It is achieved, not inadvertently of course, but as the inevitable outgrowth of earlier work. What is wrong in Eliot is the hint of deliberation. Necessity has to override the intentions of the creator at this lofty level, and the existence of such intentions actually undermines the achievement. Consider the diversity of late styles. We certainly find them in Shakespeare and Beethoven. They can also be found in Haydn and Titian. Mozart's late style is a bit of a moot point, as is Henry James's. In Picasso it is more defiance than acceptance. Richard Strauss, not one of the very greatest of masters, exemplifies it unequivocally. In all these cases it comes down to a deliberate simplicity, and a stripping down of language to its bare essentials. But it is not intended. It is a gift.

Now my complaints against Eliot are, of course, different in some

---

[7] Julian Herbage, 'Sibelius', in Ralph Hill (ed.), *The Symphony* (Harmondsworth: Penguin, 1949), 345.

[8] Albeit by the more humane of their inquisitors.

ways from those Robinson makes against Brahms. I am not here accusing Eliot of sentimentality (though he was sometimes prone to it). But the cases would be parallel if Eliot did not formulate to himself the intention that his poetry should begin to display the spirituality appropriate to a writer of his years and standing. This is not an implausible thesis. Then we might indict him of a lack of integrity or authenticity, or think his poetry contrived, even though there was no conscious attempt to create a late style.

Of course, we need to answer the question of how we can ascribe such features to a creative artist in the absence of the appropriate intentions on his part. There is no real problem here. A writer shows something of herself without any prior intention to do so, though, of course, she writes what she writes intentionally. At this point at least, there is nothing special about the arts. In everyday life I do what I intend to do without intending, say, to make a spectacle of myself. The latter would be an unfortunate and unintended by-product. As I put it in *Contemporary Aesthetics*, the 'intensional' features of a work of art are not exhausted by those the artist inten-tionally put into it.[9] A writer frequently expresses something of which he is, himself, unaware, and we could legitimately ascribe to his work themes which he did not intend, always providing that they are features which he, in his position in his culture, *could* have intended. This counterfactual formulation seemed to me, then, to capture pretty well the limits that critics place upon interpretation when they are not advertising some extreme theory such as decon-struction. Thus, we cannot intelligently interpret *Romeo and Juliet* as expressing contradictions between base and superstructure, for nothing remotely resembling such Marxist concepts was available in Elizabethan culture. For all I know, it might be possible to present *Volpone* as a critique of monetarist economics, but such an interpretation would be stupidly anachronistic (not that that would deter a modern producer). So a valid interpretation, though it may go beyond what an author intended, cannot go beyond what an author *could* have intended. This works negatively in the case of Robinson's criticism of Brahms. For Brahms expresses an affirmation in the last movement of his First Symphony, an af-firmation no longer right for the late Romantic culture into which

---

[9] R. A. Sharpe, *Contemporary Aesthetics* (Brighton: Harvester Press, 1983; Aldershot: Gregg Revivals, 1991). See also A. C. Danto, 'From Aesthetics to Art Criticism and Back', *Journal of Aesthetics and Art Criticism*, 54/2 (1996), 105–15.

Darwin and Nietzsche had sowed the seeds of self-doubt. So Brahms's culture allowed the possibility of a false affirmation. In parallel, Eliot's spirituality is something I find anachronistic.

Unfortunately, as we shall see, this plausible-seeming counter-factual formulation founders just on the cases in which Robinson is interested. We interpret Brahms's music as containing qualities which he could not have intended; for it is pretty certain that Brahms could not have intended a false affirmation in his music. Whatever Brahms was, he was not an ironist in the way that Mahler or Shostakovich were.

For we interpret Brahms as expressing something which he ought not to have attempted, given his times. Rather than placing limits on interpretation, as my earlier proposal did, we need to take the counterfactual clause as placing limits on achievement. What Brahms attempts could not have been achieved at the time at which he composed; its attempt reflects, at the least, a miscalculation on his part, or, if Robinson is right, a deeper failing. In so judging Brahms, we interpret his work, of course; but necessarily, our inter-pretation is not confined by a judgement of what Brahms could have intended, for he could not have intended a false affirmation. Had he known his limitations, he would not have written that music. The problem is that, on the one hand, we measure what Brahms could have intended by what could be achieved in his culture, and it is on the basis of this that we elect to interpret the work as having a given character. On the other hand, the judge-ment in question precisely depends upon a clash between culture and intention.

Since, in the rest of this chapter, I shall largely be concerned with such collisions, let me first say that there are notions of integrity or sincerity which do not require a reference to a wider cultural context. It has been suggested to me that it might not be odd to speak of a logician or a mathematician being sincere or construct-ing a proof with integrity. A mathematician who satisfies himself with a rapid, clumsy proof ('quick and dirty' in the jargon), when he could produce something more elegant, might be regarded as lacking integrity, where a less gifted mathematician who laboured to the same end might not. If Bach had taken short cuts in *The Art of Fugue*, instead of exercising his huge contrapuntal technique to its limits, we would regard him with less admiration. Part of our respect for the achievement of Beethoven's final period lies in the fact that the late quartets stretch and expand the idiom, and require all his powers and technical resources. But it is extremely significant that at this point we teeter on the edge of the idea that the role of the artist is to experiment; this reintroduces those issues germane to the criticism which Robinson makes of Brahms. There is a widespread Hegelianism in the histories and criticism of music which assumes that it is the composer's task to use up the potentialities of the existing style, and then to extend it. As Richard Crocker puts it, 'musical materials have to be "used up," their potentiality fully exploited, before style can move ahead on the long line of history'.[10] And this brings us back to ideology.

I shall have a good deal to say about this later, but for the present let us return to the problem of Brahms. What we are concerned with is what might be called 'the problem of artistic error' (analogously with the importance in epistemology of constructing a theory which allows for the existence of human error). Composers fail in various ways, and one peculiarly interesting form that failure may take is when a composer attempts what cannot be achieved, given the culture and musical language of the period in which he lives. His possibilities are limited by his times. Wölfflin summarizes the crucial premiss as that not everything is possible at all times. So far, so good; but because he thought of art as determined by immanent Hegelian forces, he does not have an account of how the artist could fail, or even be archaic, or anticipate future trends. This is a problem for any art history which minimizes the individual contribution to the extent of trying to produce an 'art history without names', as Wölfflin did. We need both the general and the particular in art history. We might accept that an entire culture may be distorted by an obsession with grandiose fantasies, as perhaps German music was in the era of Wagner, Brahms, and Mahler, and still want an analysis of the relative failure of an individual composer.

Let me return yet again to my gloss on Robinson's use of the word 'sincere'; it was that insincerity is to be thought of in terms of a mismatch between the work and its times. As it stands, this will not do. In one of the most stimulating pieces of musical criticism to be published since the war, *Opera as Drama*, Joseph Kerman reviews the case of two operas which he regards as less than total

[10] Richard Crocker, *A History of Musical Style* (New York: Dover, 1966), 525, and see the comments on this by Leo Treitler, *Music and the Historical Imagination* (Cambridge, Mass.: Harvard University Press, 1989), 102–3.

successes because, in a sense, they were composed at the wrong time.[11] The plot of *Aïda* is essentially an eighteenth-century affair, full of stiff conflicts between love and patriotism and between kings and priests. It might have made an *opera seria*, but is quite unsuitable, so Kerman argues, for Verdi. Consequently, there is an almost constant disparity between the 'glib' simplicity of the libretto and the 'alarming complexity' of the musical expression. Kerman speaks also of a 'curious falsity' in the opera.[12] His other case, perhaps surprisingly, is Mozart's *Don Giovanni*. He thinks that Mozart's whole intellectual, ethical, and metaphysical ethos is out of kilter with the Don Juan legend. His music is neither demonic nor Dionysiac,[13] and the theology of the close of the opera is alien. Mozart's terms were brotherhood, humility, and sympathy, and when contrasted with the attachment he expresses to the Enlightenment ideals of universal brotherhood in his Masonic music, the ideas of *Don Giovanni* seem to belong to another age. The twin facts that, on the one hand, it is not an easy opera to stage and, on the other, that to treat it as ironic is implausible, speak for Kerman's approach.[14]

You may not agree with Kerman's somewhat negative assessment. But, even if we reject Kerman's assessment of these two operas, nevertheless, his criticism raises a problem for the account I gave of 'insincerity': for his criticism cannot be ruled out on *a priori* grounds. On his analysis, we have precisely the discrepancy between the culture of an era and its products which made us speak of insincerity in the first place; yet nobody, I think, would believe 'insincere' to be the right criticism of either of these two operas. A criticism like Kerman's might be made, if not here, then elsewhere, and the fact that it is possible shows that I have failed to nail down the concept of 'insincerity' as it is used in this kind of artistic criticism.

The point must now be obvious. We can find much art which, placed in the context of its composition, attempts what is impossible. According to Kerman, Mozart, in *Don Giovanni*, attempts

---

[11] Joseph Kerman, *Opera as Drama* (New York: Vintage, 1956).
[12] Ibid. 165–6.    [13] Ibid. 122–3.
[14] Brigid Brophy, *Mozart the Dramatist* (New York: Da Capo, 1988), 129–30, takes the opera to be anti-Enlightenment and pro-Christianity, which does not seem to cohere with what we know of Mozart's Masonic sympathies.

themes which he cannot handle. Likewise Verdi in *Aïda*. These are works which are wrong for their time, but 'insincerity' is not *le mot juste*. In any case, a blanket use of this criterion would rule out art which anticipates future developments, or a combination of the modern and the archaic such as we find in the music of Bruckner. Last, but not least, what are we to say about primitives? They are rare in music, but perhaps some of the sturdier hymn-writers of the last century provide examples.[15] The conclusion must be that, at best, 'insincerity' characterizes but one variety of art which is out of kilter with its times. It is merely a particular shortcoming. Works of art fail in many ways.

Furthermore, what seems to be at least a necessary condition of failings such as those of Brahms, where a moral charge is made, is that there is a sort of willed or conscious reluctance to meet the demands a culture makes. This is, I think, at the heart of our misgivings about Brahms. He was a very intelligent man in a way that Bruckner, for example, was not. To continue to write in the language of Schumann argues a reluctance to engage with the problems of writing in a post-Lisztian and post-Wagnerian style. So the expressive features which encapsulate our disquiet depend upon certain broader considerations. No parallel charge can be directed at Verdi or Mozart.

The moral obloquy which Robinson denied has crept back in. For Brahms, on this story, is guilty of a kind of akrasia. The contempt which Stravinsky and some others had for Richard Strauss has the same basis: he chickened out. Note that a reference to artistic intentions has also reappeared. We began with the claim that there was a sort of objective insincerity whereby a writer or a musician might fail to be sincere without actually intending to be insincere. But our investigation has reintroduced the notion of intention, albeit in a broader way. For in many ways the creator is spokesman for his culture. Nowadays (and perhaps these ideas are Hegelian) we understand works of art in terms of more general

---

[15] Examples might be Jeremiah Ingalls, who wrote *The Christian Harmony or the Songsters Companion* (Exeter, NH, 1805); William Billings, the eighteenth-century New England choirmaster and composer; and John Foster, a Sheffield musician whose sub-Handelian version of the Christmas hymn 'While shepherds watched' has a splendid rude vigour. Examples are to be found in the Christmas compilations recorded on CD by Andrew Parrott. (The Carol Album EMI EL749809 4 (tape) 1989 and the Christmas Album EMI CDC 7 54902 2 (CD) 1992.)

features of the culture, in such a way that the artist may express what he does not realize he is expressing.[16] But he may also fail the culture by a lack of steel. However, these are only instances of a wide range of lapses, all of which involve some sort of mismatch between the artist's achievements and his times.

Now these judgements reflect a common ideology, which is that musical language evolves, and that it is part of the composer's job to push it forward.[17] The theory is that musical language develops in a linear way, progressively permitting harmonies previously thought dissonant, moving towards less prepared modulations and a denser style of argument. Any major achievement has to be an achievement made at the most advanced point of the style at the time of composition. Archaism or conservatism is not compatible with the finest accomplishment. Naturally, then, when an artistic movement, like minimalism, turns its back on this increasing complexity and 'difficulty', the reaction of some musicians has all the vehemence of those whose ideology is challenged. (I shall say more about this in the final chapter.)

Parenthetically, music here differs from literature, and perhaps from the other arts. It is inconceivable that language was developed in order to make possible the composition of Virgil's *Aeneid* or Milton's *Paradise Lost*. What writers do, in a small way, increases the resources of the language. But the transformation of musical style through the use of models from rhetoric was designed in the course of developing the expressive intentions of the composers. Of course, it would be a mistake to think of the development of a composer as an attempt to achieve expressive ends; rather, his

[16] An interestingly complex case is Evelyn Waugh's *Brideshead Revisited*, which advocates, consciously or unconsciously, a snobbery and a kind of Roman Catholicism in such a way as to make their utter absurdity and irrelevance to modern society transparent. Yet it is hard to believe that he realized this, and, no doubt, had he known his novel would have that character, he would not have published it. Much depends upon the reader, of course. The death of Lord Marchmain, a crux, is insufferable. It appears to advocate preying on the weak and the dying to a degree which is immoral. It is hard to imagine that God would happily accept an old roué whose deathbed repentance had been engineered by a persistent priest. Yet this reduced Ronald Knox to tears—and not, apparently, tears of laughter: Selina Hastings, *Evelyn Waugh* (London: Minerva, 1995), 493.

[17] See Leo Treitler, 'The Present as History', in *Music and the Historical Imagination*, 95–156. Adorno, of course, is the great apostle of this ideology. He is well discussed by Richard Middleton, *Studying Popular Music* (Milton Keynes: Open University Press, 1990), 55–63. As Middleton remarks, in Adorno's view, everything outside the Germanic tradition is either primitive or childish or a corruption.

expressive intentions cannot be separated from these means. For example, Beethoven simultaneously expanded the scale and the expressive possibilities of music. He saw the possibility of a larger scale and an extended harmonic vocabulary, as he saw what expressive purposes that expansion could serve. A great composer's development of music is incomparably vaster by comparison with what writers do for language. The contrast is that when a writer develops an individual style, he does so within a language which is always changing, quite independently. He may, by dint of his power, introduce a few neologisms or be a source of quotations or clichés, but his contribution is puny compared to the momentum of language itself. The writer swims in the sea of language. But Haydn, Beethoven, and Wagner changed the language of music in making available harmonic devices and instrumental techniques which were taken up by some of those who followed. There are some parallels with literary technique, of course, for a poet can introduce new devices as a musician like Wagner introduced the 'Tristan chord'; for example, the Symbolists made concentrated use of polysyllabic adjectives and adverbs and occasional rhyming. But then there is another difference; there is no longer a body of demotic music in which the composer swims, comparable to the demotic use of language. The contemporary composer's relation to folk music and street songs is not that of some of his predecessors.

But another problem awaits. In his *Philosophy of Modern Music*, Adorno launched a famous attack on Stravinsky, about whose music he had hardly a good word to say.[18] The attack is, in our sense, ideologically motivated. Stravinsky was not a progressive composer in the way Adorno required; he was not advanced as members of the Second Viennese School were advanced. The problem can be put this way. If intellectual elements necessarily enter into our hearing of music, then what entitles me to argue that Adorno's view of Stravinsky is distorted by a progressivist ideology? For there will not be any 'pure', concept-free judgement of music which provides the acid test of quality by comparison with which an ideologically contaminated judgement is distorted.

The solution to this problem is that I must make a distinction between those conceptual elements which are a necessary precondition of musical understanding—concepts like harmonic and

[18] T. W. Adorno, *The Philosophy of Modern Music* (London: Stagbooks, 1994), 164–5, for example.

rhythmic motion, fugal and sonata structure, and so on—and those which are more evidently distinct from the work *qua* work, such as its relationship to prevailing religious and moral ideals. One of my principal arguments in this book is that some elements of an ideology are sufficiently pervasive to distort musical experience; I think that the general assumption that music progresses may be one such. But the crucial assumption is that things go wrong when music which the experienced listener finds interesting is downgraded by that same listener under the pressure of an ideology. To put it schematically, his first-order judgement uses what conceptual resources are intrinsic to the composition of the music; it is not concept-free, but its conceptual resources are limited. The second-order judgement assesses the validity of the first, and finds it wanting. Such second-order judgements may be partly motivated by recognizing the features we have found problematic in Brahms (or Vaughan Williams, Schoenberg, Stravinsky, middle-period Verdi, minimalism, etc.). It is not my claim that a clear distinction is to be drawn between these two kinds of judgement. No doubt cases could be found which would be hard to classify. But my examples here seem to me to fall unequivocally into different groups.

I spoke earlier of it being a criticism of composers such as Richard Strauss that they failed to rise to the challenge of advancing the musical style. We cannot get away from 'intention' here. I have written that a limit on viable interpretation is given by the limits of what the author or creator could have intended in the culture of his time; rather along the same lines, Savile speaks of the 'best contemporary reading';[19] such a reading would utilize whatever concepts were available to the connoisseur in the culture of origin. Although this seems preferable to my own earlier suggestion, it does not avoid all problems. The difficulty of making judgements with hindsight remains. The extent to which Savile can handle the criticism of Brahms that we have been discussing depends upon how we read 'available'. For, if a culture may be deluded about its own vitality, then it may only be with the aid of hindsight that we can see that an individual creator, like Brahms, fails. Contemporaries would not be able to see this. Another problem which Savile's criterion might appear to face is more easily disposed of. It is one peculiar to the performing arts. A reading

---

[19] Anthony Savile, *The Test of Time* (Oxford: Clarendon Press, 1982), ch. 4.

which takes the creator to be insincere might be replaced by a reading which, by not taking certain sections at face value, is more generous. A conductor might present the Finale of Brahms's First Symphony as hollow rhetoric in the way that recent conductors of the Finale of Shostakovich's Fifth Symphony have, now that we know of the composer's hatred of Stalin. Then the charge of insincerity no longer sticks. Of course, such an interpretation of Brahms would be hard to justify. The plausibility or implausibility of such a reading depends upon what we know about the personality of the creator, and there is little reason to think that Brahms did not wish his Finale to be played at face value. Had Nietzsche, *mirabile dictu*, written Brahms's First Symphony, we certainly might take it to be ironic. Note, too, that there seems to be no reason why this information should not in principle be available to a contemporary.

Before we can say that a creator is insincere in Robinson's wide sense, we need to know that he has the requisite technical ability and is in touch with the central moves in the life of his culture—that he is neither provincial nor uneducated. Then a creator is a spokesman for his culture. The culture expresses itself through him, which is why art is so important for a theory of culture. This is his calling, and the failure of an accomplished and sophisticated composer to speak for it is ignominious even if it is not deliberate. This is at the heart of the criticism of Brahms and Richard Strauss.

A final difficulty: these criticisms might seem either circular or regressive. For I have said that the relationship between art and culture is internal. We assess a culture very largely through its art. If, then, art fails a culture, where do we get that independent assessment of the culture against which the failings of the artist can be measured? Well, there are various routes. There is other art of the period, and there are general features from which we can gauge something of the culture—its religion, its political practices, its manners, and so on. One of the arts may be more advanced than the others. This allows various mismatches between individual achievement and what the culture permits. Given such a dynamic, dialectical, or conflictual account of the relationship between art and culture, these issues fall into place.

What general conclusions can we draw at this point? Earlier in the book I made the distinction between cases where somebody expresses her own state—the state of rage, for example—in her behaviour and cases where no 'inner' state is being expressed, such as cases where the music of a composer is grave or exuberant whilst the composer himself is none of those things. In this chapter I have been concerned with what might be thought of as 'higher-order' considerations; for, when we speak of sincerity, we normally refer to the relationship between those 'inner' states and the gesture, manner, or speech of whoever is involved. So the problem of justifying the use of 'sincere' arises where nothing 'inner' is being described.

One important conclusion is that there are some highly significant forms of musical judgement which seem incompatible with formalism. Formalism has an attraction for me, and it is with reluctance that I conclude that it does not account for some of the most interesting and important critical assessments we make of music, assessments such as that the music is trivial or insincere or inauthentic or sentimental, assessments evidently central to the role of music in our culture. It does not matter that such judgements are controversial; all the cases I take are disputable. It is of the nature of such judgements that they reflect those broader concerns I have described as ideological; hence, they are almost bound to be the locus of dissension. So it has been important for me to take hard cases, cases over which there is no consensus, for only here can we see music criticism at its most significant.

### III

As this chapter has developed, I have been increasingly concerned with the widespread critical assumption that the language and style of music should develop towards increasing complexity. From the Marxist perspective, this is no more than one would expect in a capitalist economy where a progressive and dynamic economic and social structure is supposedly preferred. Inasmuch as art, being part of the superstructure, is determined by the economic base, such a homology is to be expected. It certainly mirrors economic development, though it has to be said as well that art could be determined by the base without reflecting it. The idea of a homology unites determination and mirroring. But the idea that an art like music should show such homologies with the society that produces it is open to immediate and obvious objections. One critic of a previous version of this chapter asked if he was supposed to admire

Elgar's expression of the imperialism of his time or, we might add, Richard Strauss's apparent endorsement of conservative values in *Der Rosenkavalier* or his concern with the relationship of words and music in *Capriccio*, when German culture was descending into the abyss. Where a culture seems to us corrupt or impoverished, then we admire all the more an art which stands apart. Doubt about a culture shows a deeper understanding. For art not only reflects; it criticizes. A mismatch between art and culture may not be a failing, but be admirable. We may find the optimism of Brahms objectionable not least because it connects with a sort of triumphalism in Bismarck's Germany. On the other hand, Dvorak's warmth and life-enhancing optimism are entirely lovable, and this cannot be dissociated from the fact that he was Czech. Czech culture was neither dominating nor imperialist (at least for non-Slovaks). But in German and English culture of the period we look for a disenchantment with the overweening confidence that had such tragic consequences. This is one, but only one, of the reasons why Wagner and Kipling seem objectionable. Indeed, it is obvious that the more complex and variegated a culture, the more heterogeneous it will be. There will be all sorts of currents. If we are tempted to think of Victorian society as optimistic, pious, utilitarian, and conformist, we accept its official self-image, its ideology, no less. To read Victorian critics and see how they undermine the official view is to rely on Victorian dissidents. Modern societies are deeply conflictual.

Of course, I do not dissent. My position does not preclude this feature of music or of the arts generally; my initial interests were particular. And, parenthetically, I might add that these judgements of Elgar and Strauss are a bit hasty. For example, a careful reading of *Der Rosenkavalier* shows that the settled aristocratic, thus exploitative, society of Hofmannsthal's libretto is undermined by a certain modernist fragmentation in the music. Except for the great climactic scenes of the presentation of the silver rose and the trio in the last act, lyrical lines are constantly broken off, not allowed to run their course. This feature may have a dramatic function, of course; but it may also represent the disintegration of Austrian society, adumbrated in the disintegration of the diatonic language of nineteenth-century music.

We have inherited a conception of music as a single tradition, Germanic in character, whose language developed steadily through an increasing toleration of dissonance and an increasingly oblique method of signalling changes. It was, as Wagner remarked, an art of transition. Schoenberg inherited this. He was a conservative revolutionary. Music was still to be an evolving art, and he, in a rather chilling phrase, proposed to establish the hegemony of German music for 'another hundred years'.

But what has happened in our century? The post-modernist's sense of the history of our times is accurate.[20] There are many styles which differ far more radically than those of Schumann, Brahms, and Wagner or Mozart, Dussek, Field, and Haydn. No single style now dominates. The greatest music has been written outside the serial movement. German music is neither central nor particularly important. Serial music is still in the repertoire, but that is because players put it there, rather than because many people want to listen to it. Its place is due more to the underlying ideological belief that the centre of music is Austro-German than to any other reason. We are victims of an ideology. The music that matters to us is that of Janáček, Strauss, Shostakovich, Bartók, Britten, Vaughan Williams, Walton, Messiaen, Ravel, Pärt, Tippett, and, above all, Stravinsky. I say nothing of the music of modern urban life—jazz—and its characteristic instrument, the sax. And who celebrates suburban life like Samuel Barber in 'Knoxville, Summer of 1915'?

That the problems which have occupied me in this chapter present themselves to me in the way they do is obviously a consequence of my cultural background. My preoccupation with the question of sincerity draws from a concern with music as an expressive art, a concern which itself reflects a humanist bias.[21] In the next, final, chapter, I shall enlarge on these issues.

[20] See particularly L. B. Meyer, *Music, the Arts and Ideas*, 2nd edn. (Chicago: University of Chicago Press, 1994), for the most lucid and jargon-free presentation of post-modernism (without, as I recall, ever using the word).
[21] See Peter Kivy, *The Corded Shell: Reflections on Musical Expression* (Princeton: Princeton University Press, 1980), ch. 12.

# PART III

*Humanism Founders?*

# 7

## Humanism Founders?

### I

In making a case for the ineliminability of expressive descriptions of music and for their connection with broader questions of sincerity, authenticity, and the ideology of the arts, I have made a case against treating music as a purely formal art. Music is, I believe, connected with the life humans live. The possibilities it has for expression make it possible for composers to write autobiographical music or music that expresses the conflicts of their times. Music is, to this extent, a humanist art. But what more can be said about this?

If I describe an art as 'humanist', what might be implied is that an absorbed attention in it has moral consequences. It makes us, in some oblique way, better people. Our moral judgements are finer and more imaginative through engagement with fiction or drama or film.[1] Perhaps a case can be made for saying that a fine engagement with the complexities of Henry James, George Eliot, or Proust makes us subtler moral agents—as opposed to simply self-conscious and self-absorbed—but it is hard to justify making such claims on behalf of music, opera apart. So much is clear from my remarks at the end of the first section of the first chapter. What, then, could we mean by describing music as a humanist art? Two things in the main, I suggest. First, music can be described in terms drawn from human psychology. Music is expressive. As we have seen at length, music can be described as vivacious, tumultuous, grave, calm, passionate, or dispassionate, and so on. This matters.

---

[1] Daniel Jacobson, 'Sir Philip Sidney's Dilemma: On the Ethical Justification of Narrative Art', *Journal of Aesthetics and Art Criticism*, 54/4 (1996), 327. See also, *inter alia*, the work of Martha Nussbaum, esp. *Love's Knowledge* (Oxford: Oxford University Press, 1990).

For one striking difference between art and craft lies in the fact that we ascribe such expressive predicates to the first and not the second. Indeed, it is precisely to the degree that we are unsure whether architecture sustains such expressive descriptions that we are, at the same time, unsure as to whether architecture is an art or a craft. Secondly, in our descriptions of music, we imply certain further analogies between music and language, and these analogies are central to the way in which our culture has viewed music. As somebody expresses herself through language, so she may express herself through music. Such a thesis will not, of course, do as it stands; it needs cutting to size, a task largely accomplished in earlier chapters.

For centuries music has been described as a language—often as a language of the emotions. For reasons which are now familiar, this is not a sustainable thesis; but the ease with which it succumbs to philosophical criticism should not lead us to underestimate its power as a metaphor. Like all metaphors it suggests both truths and falsehoods. What I want to suggest, in this final part of the book, is that this powerful metaphor expresses the humanist ideal in music. It is ubiquitous; indeed, it would be hard for writers about music to ply their craft without terms like 'phrase' (which is no longer very metaphorical) or 'musical sentence and paragraph' (which still are).[2] To the extent that music is language-like, it is a humanist art, and to the extent that it departs from this model, it ceases to be a humanist art.

So I begin this final chapter by distinguishing various ways in which we 'understand' music, after which I turn to the question of whether all music is music which we understand in all these relevant respects. In the last section I examine the ideology which has led us to privilege atonal music in our histories of the art.

Language is the paradigm of what is intelligible, and to say of music that it is language-like is to say, at the same time, that it can be understood. But the understanding of music is something of a viper's nest, and it is necessary to look more closely at the ways in which music can be said to be intelligible. So I shall distinguish a number of ways in which music can be said to be understood, of which two, its expressive features and the way it can be followed, are central.

---

[2]  See Leo Treitler, 'Language and the Interpretation of Music', in Jenefer Robinson (ed.), *Music and Meaning* (Ithaca, NY: Cornell University Press, 1997), 43 n.

First of all, we must set aside one general sense in which 'understanding music' is used, because it will play no role in the ensuing discussion. To say that somebody understands music may be no more than to say that she loves it, seeks it out, and has a passion for it; to say that she fails to understand music may be to say, not only that she has no overwhelming interest in it, but also that she does not understand the motives of those for whom it is a passion. That aspect of other people's lives may be a closed book. The reporter from one of our universally admired tabloid newspapers who went to Glyndebourne and reported that it was an 'expensive noise' did not, apparently, understand music in that sense. We might say that 'he could not see his way into it'. (I presume that he was not just reporting the reaction his editor required.)

Second, and more particularly, a listener exhibits her understanding of music in the choice of an exact expressive predicate to describe it. Wittgenstein describes the fugato of the first movement of Beethoven's Ninth in this way: 'There is something here analogous to the expression of bitter irony in speech.'[3] (I assume the passage in question to be bars 470 ff.). When somebody makes a precise observation like that, whether or not we agree, we grant that it shows musical understanding *ceteris paribus*. (We assume that it is not parroted, etc.) Much of the first and third movements of Brahms's Sextet in G express, to me, a sort of suppressed ecstasy. The aspiring main theme at the beginning of Schubert's B flat Trio has been described as 'ardent'. Schubert's setting of 'In stille land' finds a tune for the text which, according to Graham Johnson, is 'poised between sorrow and hope'. Understanding may also be shown in recognizing that a specific expressive character may be puzzling, given the context, and in suggesting how the puzzle can be resolved. Michael Tanner, discussing the famous opening of Mozart's 'Dissonance' Quartet, discusses the way in which this might be problematic.[4] The listener might wonder why Mozart should begin the work with an introduction of such a character, and puzzle as to how it fits with what follows. An explanation is that what follows should be thought of as uneasy, rather than confidently affirmative.

[3] L. Wittgenstein, *Culture and Value*, trans. Peter Winch (Oxford: Blackwell, 1980), p. 55e.
[4] Michael Tanner, 'Understanding Music', *Proceedings of the Aristotelian Society*, supp. vol. 59 (1985), 215–32.

Such expressive predicates are, of course, marginalized by the sterner theorists of music, who dismiss them as vague. This persistent positivist trend in musicology, of which I have spoken earlier, emphasizes the formal features of music instead. But I suspect that the paradigms of formal music-making were probably not thought of as central by their contemporaries in the way that vocal music was. Bach's 'Forty-Eight' and Domenico Scarlatti's superb sonatas were exercises first and foremost; indeed, that was the title given to the latter. I don't suppose that Bach would have been surprised to find his Preludes and Fugues admired, but he might have been surprised to find them regarded as central to the tradition.

Third, I understand music in having a sense of its progress, a sense that this chord has to be resolved, a sense that a modulation at this point is called for, or that a melodic line needs to end in just this way. Part of this may involve seeing why the composer had to do what he did just there. A listener (or player) understands the music to the extent that she 'feels' or 'senses' these exigencies, even if she lacks the technical know-how to describe them. There are patterns of tension and relaxation and of implication and realization which the listener catches. Again, when I speak of 'sensing' or 'feeling', I am not necessarily speaking of some private realm, some inner states to which the listener alone is privy. Once more, these are aspects of the understanding of music which are exhibited in certain subtle gradations of behaviour. It is possible for me to say to somebody, 'You really appreciated that piece'. 'Did I?', she says in surprise. 'Yes, I was watching you.' The rightness of my judgement lies in the way my observation of her reactions bears it out.

L. B. Meyer, in a classic series of early papers, analysed this aspect of music in terms of the mathematical theory of information.[5] The mathematical theory of information began in a study of probabilistic sequences in natural languages. As a string of words in a natural language increases in length, so the next word becomes more predictable, in the sense that, in general, an increasing number of alternatives can be effectively excluded. They have a lower probability. (This is also described as having a lower 'Cloze value'.[6]) If you read through the sentence I have just written, you

---

[5] Repr. in L. B. Meyer, *Music, the Arts and Ideas*, 2nd edn. (Chicago: University of Chicago Press, 1994), chs. 1, 2, and 3.

[6] See, for a brief discussion, Jerry A. Fodor, *The Modularity of Mind* (Cambridge, Mass.: Bradford Books, MIT Press, 1987), 76 ff.

will appreciate that, as it develops, an adjective, an article, or a noun is to be expected at certain junctures. The sense, too, imposes some limitations. I am not likely to launch, in mid-sentence, into a disquisition on Third World agriculture. These linguistic patterns have analogues in music. The sequence which drives the closing bars of Schubert's Great C major Symphony makes a close on the tonic highly likely, and it becomes more likely, the closer we approach those final chords. Contrariwise, just as metaphors become possible because language generates expectations which a metaphor or any other innovative trope defeats, so musical surprises and jokes become possible within a tonal system which creates expectations which the music then sometimes will confirm and sometimes, teasingly, deny. The principle also applies to musical form. We know a movement will return to the home key; by starting the recapitulation in the wrong key, the composer amuses and delights us by the neatness of the transition. In Hanslick's words, 'The most significant factor in the mental process which accompanies the comprehending of a musical work and makes it enjoyable will most frequently be overlooked. It is the mental satisfaction which the listener finds in continuously following and anticipating the composer's designs, here to be confirmed in his expectations, there to be agreeably led astray.'[7]

Cohen translates Hanslick as describing this phenomenon as a 'pondering of the imagination'; Payzant translates it as a 'musing of the imagination'.[8] Meyer placed a premium on the relative complexity of this, claiming that it is connected with value; however, this does not exhaust the question of what constitutes value; some music delights us by its simplicity, and sometimes simplicity is striking and moving when in opposition to relative complexity.[9] Nevertheless, the fact that music offers us the possibility of anticipating its progress in this way matters; that it is something we value in music is not to be gainsaid; but it is another and more problematic matter as to precisely how it relates to value. Both Hanslick and Meyer present this feature predominantly in terms of anticipation and expectation (though Meyer later came to prefer talk of

[7] E. Hanslick, *On the Musically Beautiful*, trans. Geoffrey Payzant (Indianapolis: Hackett, 1986), 64.

[8] E. Hanslick, *The Beautiful in Music*, trans. Gustav Cohen (Indianapolis: Bobbs-Merrill, 1957), 98; *idem, On the Musically Beautiful*, trans. Payzant, 64.

[9] See R. A. Sharpe, 'Music: The Information-theoretic Approach', *British Journal of Aesthetics*, 11 1971), 385–401.

'implication'). But this is not entirely apposite. Sometimes we may anticipate and be correct, and think that the music is banal. Sometimes we anticipate and are correct, and the music is of immense power. It is a damning judgement on music to describe it as predictable, but it is a recognition of its power to describe it as inexorable. An estimate of the composer's independence and originality is relevant here. A cliché's predictability is no grounds for thinking the music of value. The music of Andrew Lloyd Webber or, especially, Philip Glass might exemplify the first, and the close of the Aria from the Goldberg Variations the latter. Likewise, to follow an argument may not be to be able to predict it; it may be just to see why it leads where it does. But you do not follow entirely without anticipation. Despite these complications and reservations, however, to 'follow music' in this way is to understand it. We must add, too, the anticipation of rhythmic constancy and variation, something relatively neglected in musical analysis. Listeners to Indian music 'keep the tala', so that they are aware of subtle changes in accenting and rhythm which the players introduce.

A crucial test is: Can you sing a continuation of the music? (You may not sing the correct continuation, of course, and in many cases, a subtle tune may delight us in the way Hanslick describes. Such tunes may be teasingly difficult to recall.) In the same way, we might begin a series of numbers, and say to the listener, 'Now go on!' Scruton puts it nicely: 'In a well-formed tonal melody, the notes seem to follow of their own accord, so that if you stop at any point before the end, you leave a musical expectation hanging.'[10]

I spoke of 'inexorability', and of course music varies in the extent to which the listener feels this element of necessity. Such coherence may be high in Bach, Sibelius, or Ockeghem, and low in Mahler, perhaps. The difference between following the first and following the second is a bit like the difference between following an argument and following a story. Charles Rosen has recently pointed out the difference between a classical symphony and a Romantic song-cycle.

The tonality of a movement from a classical symphony ... is perceptible at once: its definition may be postponed for a few seconds at most. The

[10] Roger Scruton, *The Aesthetics of Music* (Oxford: Clarendon Press, 1997) 216.

perception of the large-scale tonal structure of the song cycle is like our experience of reading a novel or moving through a landscape: it is realized and defined progressively.

The contrapuntal possibilities of the theme of a Bach fugue are displayed one by one, but they are already present in the initial bars, and an experienced musician would be able to predict the most important musical developments. The famous dissonant C sharp in bar 7 of Beethoven's *Eroica* symphony may not find its implications fully realized until 397 bars later, but its harmonic significance and its importance in the harmonic framework are immediately felt. In *Die schöne Müllerin*, however, the harmonic structure of the last five songs is defined by the final one, the stream's requiem and lullaby, and consequently the harmonic function of the opening of this set can be perceived only after the fact.[11]

(Rosen's book is full of illustrations of how music is to be followed; his discussion of Schumann's songs is especially interesting in this respect.) It needs to be said, however, that on either model this form of understanding is generally tacit and non-propositional in form.[12]

Fourth, if a teacher points out that by failing to accent a certain phrase, a pupil is failing to bring out a theme, the teacher shows musical understanding that the pupil lacks up to that point. It is necessary, then, that the pupil 'see' that the phrasing is right, and does not just copy it because she has been told to. Again Wittgenstein is adamant that this seeing is not a matter of some specific internal state of the player.[13] When she understands the phrase, she plays it a certain way. Likewise, he draws our attention to the demeanour of somebody who sketches a face with understanding of the expression. His face, his movements, as well as the finished sketch, are what tell us that he draws with understanding. In the same way, a listener may show, perhaps by the inclination of her head or by movements of the body, or certain changes in her expression, that she follows the music. Perhaps just a gesture shows.[14] It has nothing to do with any particular 'internal states' at all.

Fifth, a listener may show her understanding in her ability to identify technical devices such as augmentation, inversion, or musical forms such as sonata-rondo or a mirror fugue. This sort of knowledge is explicit and propositional.

[11] Charles Rosen, *The Romantic Generation* (London: Harper Collins, 1996), 194.
[12] Jerrold Levinson, 'Musical Literacy', in *The Pleasures of Aesthetics* (Ithaca, NY: Cornell University Press, 1996), 39.
[13] Wittgenstein, *Culture and Value*, p. 51e.      [14] Ibid. pp. 69e–71e.

Sixth, a listener may show understanding in recognizing a quotation from another work, or a thematic reference to an earlier movement. Stravinsky regularly quotes other composers. Mahler's use of a nursery rhyme recast in the minor in the slow movement of his First Symphony needs to be recognized for the movement to be more fully understood.[15] Less experienced listeners often see similarities between one work and another, usually a work by a different composer. Often this suggests a failure to recognize the individuality of the work in question, and in that way it is a sign of a sort of musical immaturity. But to see that a later work used an earlier work as a model can show musical understanding.

Seventh, there are still other forms of understanding which involve placing the music in a wider context, hearing the music as an expression of Romanticism, identifying an archaism, or a pastiche, hearing the horn as conveying associations of the hunt or as a symbol for cuckoldry, for example. Perhaps in this category should come the whole vexed question as to how much weight we should attach to programmes of the sort that Romantic composers from Schumann to Mahler attached to both their own and to other composers' music. Is our understanding of Strauss's *Don Juan* enhanced by being told that the don makes three conquests: 'the first is easy and takes only seventy bars in *Allegro molto con brio*', whilst the second is a blonde countess who lives one hour's ride from Seville?[16] If this seems excessive, many of the descriptions of music of Chopin and Beethoven by Liszt and Wagner seem little less fanciful to modern ears. Our musical culture seems to have changed in this respect; we no longer attach such importance to stories; formalism has triumphed, and perhaps we can do little more than recognize this change. (Having said this, there are signs that programmes, under the heading of narrative and drama, are making a come-back.[17])

What we can say is that for music to be a humanist art, the second and third forms of intelligibility are crucial: that we should be able to describe music in expressive terms, and that it should mirror language in our ability to anticipate what will come next and recog-

---

[15] Malcolm Budd, 'Understanding Music', *Proceedings of the Aristotelian Society*, supp. vol. 59 (1985), 233–48.

[16] The German critic, Wilhelm Mauke, quoted in David Randolph's entertaining little book *This is Music* (New York: Mentor, 1964), 46.

[17] See J. Robinson (ed.), *Music and Meaning, passim.*

nize its appropriateness. What does seem to me central is the metaphor of language. To the extent that music can be seen as a language, music is an expressive medium, and in that sense a humanist art.

One point before we continue: information theory also introduced the notion of 'redundancy'; redundancy facilitates communication because it means that in many instances one might miss one word without thereby losing the possibility of construing the whole. The context often helps us to recover the word missed. Thus an experienced lecturer or public speaker deliberately creates redundancy by saying the same thing in different ways, in order that the hearer who is occasionally inattentive, perhaps from extraneous causes, will not fail to catch on. Repetition is essential if the point is central. Naturally, the expert in the field may be so familiar with the various positions possible that the briefest of signposts may enable him to reconstruct the argument. He will also skip-read elementary textbooks, of course.

Now transfer this to music. It is not hard to find analogues of redundancy in music. There may be literal repetition of a figure, or there may be sequence, so that the same figure recurs in succession but rising or falling by a degree of the scale. These devices mean that total concentration by the listener is neither required nor expected. As in any form of comprehension one can miss a bit and still understand in the sense of recognizing the appropriateness of what follows. The more familiar the style, the more easily such lapses can be made up. I cannot improve on Meyer's explanation of the point. He refers to 'those important places in the experiencing of music where the listener's habit responses are able to "take over"—where the listener can pause, albeit briefly, to evaluate what has taken place in the past and to organise this experience with reference to the future'.[18]

I showed earlier in this book how structure uses models drawn from rhetoric, models in which repetition, hence redundancy, is part of the form. Such an element of relative redundancy is also an aid in forming expectations which the music can meet or frustrate. Thus it is the dynamics of key, of harmonic progression, and of the manipulation of material which enable us to feel a sense of arrival when we reach the denouement. To the extent that such a sense of

[18] Meyer, *Music, the Arts and Ideas*, 16.

arrival is connected with probability, it is because we can predict with a degree of certainty how the music will end that we have the sense of arrival, and we can predict because there is a degree of redundancy. Since the technical conception of redundancy and probability are necessarily connected, it should be no surprise that a measure of redundancy means that, given the opening of a phrase, we form an expectation as to how it will continue. The sense of arrival is not markedly different from at the end of a well-constructed plot as in *Twelfth Night* or *Tom Jones*. To follow music in this way requires knowing, for example, what the home key is, even if such knowledge is tacit rather than articulated. The central works of Western musical art are not just patterns, as Kant (who did not understand music) and Kivy (who does) maintain. There is a dynamic feature in the music which we follow, in which redundancy, repetition, or ornamentation is crucial. It is crucial because such music moves towards an end or goal.

The importance of this lies in the fact that music is an art we listen to at a sitting. A mathematical proof does not contain redundancy, but a mathematician follows it, and can pause and reread where he needs to; if he is good enough, he will probably anticipate where the proof is leading just as I may, listening to a philosopher, anticipate what his conclusion will be. Rendundancy in a speech is a gift to the listener, and the same goes for music.

II

My use of the word 'humanist' may look like an annexation. But, if it is, it is an annexation which has some justice on its side. What is important is that, given this definition, we ask what music can be understood in the ways I have outlined, particularly what music can be understood in terms of its capacity to be described in expressive terms and in terms of its capacity to be followed. This must be, in the end, something which depends on how people conversant with a style describe the music composed in it.

For I have, as yet, made no distinctions. I have spoken as though all Western music is 'humanist'. I do not believe this to be true. Not all Western music is intelligible in all the ways I have described. It might seem plausible to think of the hey-day of music as a humanist art as lying between 1500 and 1945; for one thing, this relates humanism in music to the beginning of that humanism in Western culture which owed much to the rediscovery of classical sources; but this is a very rough periodization with many exceptions, particularly in recent music. I do not know precisely when people began to think of music in terms of a language, or the precise weight which the thesis bore, though I suspect that its origins lie with the Florentine Camerata. Certainly it seems that expressive predicates were not applied to pre-Renaissance music with the range to which we have become accustomed.[19] Although medieval writers commonly thought of music as arousing states like pleasure, they did not think of it in expressive terms as we do. When the art of rhetoric was invoked, it is usually the conventional rhetorical gestures which accompany speech which were being referred to.

I quote Stevens:

When words and music come together they have to agree, certainly, but this agreement is primarily a matter of parallel 'harmonies', agreements of phrase and structure, of balance and 'number', so that in song the mind and ear may be 'doubly charmed by a double melody'. Such a view does not exclude from the effects of music emotional experiences of great power (romantic or mystical or any other); indeed it is often invoked to explain them. It does, however, seem to exclude—or, at least, patently and consistently neglects—the close and detailed expressive relations between words and music which we find in the songs of later periods. For this reason a theory of expressive sound closely related to subject-matter, a theory apparently derived from antique rhetoric, has only a limited place in 'the medieval experience of music'.[20]

This, I believe, agrees with our experience. It is hard to find a wide range of expressive predicates which we can use to characterize the music of the Eton Choirbook, for instance. We might describe some of it as elevated or sublime, but it hardly invites the sort of precise description appropriate to nineteenth-century music.

Earlier I suggested that the idea that music is expressive is something of a historical accident, the product of a revival of classical rhetoric (and various socio-economic changes together with certain technological changes in musical instruments were required to bring it to a peak). The decline of rhetoric was followed by the

---

[19] See John Stevens, *Words and Music in the Middle Ages: Song, Narrative, Dance and Drama 1050–1350* (Cambridge: Cambridge University Press, 1986), 368–71, 386–7.     [20] Ibid. 409.

decline of oratory and the decline of the expressive power of Western music, though I think the causes of these changes were independent of one another. The gradual dissolution of tonality, as chromaticism became less and less a means of heightened effect, is like the way in which the continual use of expletives impoverishes both the language and the language-user, leaving the speaker without the power to shock. The way in which Wagner's expansion of the musical vocabulary led to atonalism has often been described, and I shall turn to some of the implications shortly. The increasing chromaticism and the delaying and eventual absence of resolution weakens the implications of harmony until we can no longer form expectations as to what will follow. Consequently, music in the twentieth century on the whole displays a decreasing intelligibility in this second respect. It does not follow, nor is it true, that it is unintelligible in other respects. But in one crucially important way, in our capacity to 'follow' it, it has become steadily less an art which we can understand.

But the question of following music is tricky. I certainly 'follow' music from Purcell to Stravinsky in a way in which I do not follow some medieval music or the music of Stockhausen or Boulez. Yet here is Christopher Page, writing about the virelai 'Joieux de cuer en semellant estoye' by the fourteenth-century composer Solage:

> The counterpoint between the outer parts leads us to expect that 42 will end on a double octave C between Triplum and Tenor. Surely the Tenor will complete its stepwise fall and land on C? It does not. This, and several other possibilities, come into view momentarily, only to disappear in a sudden corona of harmonic colour. The upward motion of the Triplum, reaching b natural, leads us, perhaps, to expect that Solage will *fall* to a Tenor F in 42 from a G; but that does not happen either. In the event, he *rises* to the F from the D below.[21]

Page describes exactly what Hanslick and Meyer describe when they try to characterize 'following music'. Evidently I lack the easy familiarity with the idiom which makes Page's hearing of it a 'pondering of the imagination'. But the story must be more complicated than this. I know Machaut's vocabulary well enough to be able to forecast the way the music will move with a degree of accuracy. But

---

[21] Christopher Page, Notes for 'The Medieval Romantics', Gothic Voices, Hyperion KA 66463; italics original.

I do not feel the same sort of necessity I feel with a Bach fugue. What happens does not seem 'natural' in the same way. What can I say to disarm such apparent falsifications? Evidently I have not internalized that style. In any case, my historical thesis is not intended to be more than a rough-and-ready generalization. Certainly I follow some of the exquisite songs of William Cornyshe or Robert Fayrfax as readily as I do later music, though I do not follow their sacred music in the same way.

The origins of humanism can safely be left to the expert historians of music. My interest is more in its ending, and as grist for this particular mill we have the conceptualization of modern music by Adorno and others. It is a cliché that the development of music through the nineteenth century is a development towards a more concentrated musical language in which repetition plays a smaller part and in which the tonal process becomes more and more something to be hinted at rather than spelt out. Modulations are more abrupt and less prepared. Nevertheless, although there is, for example, little exact repetition in Sibelius's Fourth Symphony, it still needs an unusually incompetent listener to miss the central point and climax of the slow movement (at letter G), which the music approaches and then moves away from. But when we turn to atonal music we find that audibly recognizable repetition of any sort is largely absent. Adorno remarks on the brevity of some of Webern's and some of Schoenberg's works, commenting that 'Their brevity is a direct result of the demand for the greatest consistency. This demand precludes the superfluous', and, a few sentences later, speaks of the disappearance of decoration: 'In this spirit of compression modern music destroys all decorative elements and, therewith, symmetrically extended works.'[22] It should perhaps be said that the modern music of which Adorno speaks is, almost exclusively, that of the Second Viennese School. And, of course, it does not follow from the absence of repetition that there is no way in which this music is intelligible at all. But such music is getting close to mathematics. For in a mathematical proof there is ideally no redundancy. Because it is written down and can be scanned over and over again, it is not beyond our understanding in one sense of understanding; equally, in music, we can identify structural features such as fugue or canon with the aid of the score. But the closer

[22] T. W. Adorno, *Philosophy of Modern Music* (London: Stagbooks, 1994), 37 ff.

music comes to what appears to be Adorno's ideal, a music shorn of repetition, redundancy, decoration, and symmetry, the closer it comes to being an art which can no longer be understood in the sense of 'being followed' aurally. It is no longer an art which can be understood at one or two hearings. As Schoenberg realized, it is close to becoming an art which no longer needs sound at all.[23] Nelson Goodman's disciple, Boretz, draws just this conclusion, that such music does not need to be performed. And, parenthetically, there is music which, through its complexity, makes demands that even the serious listener is unlikely to be able to meet. Much of the music of Elliott Carter may be an example, though, to the extent that the music has immediate rewards as well as rewards for the diligent, its complexity is no criticism.

Still, we must not overemphasize the importance of the initial impact. Certainly, twentieth-century music regularly makes demands upon its listeners which much of the music of the past did not. Atonal music was not expected by its progenitors to be taken in at once; admittedly there is plenty of music of the past which also required rehearing; late Beethoven requires patience and study (though one difference was that by the time of the late quartets, the musical public had 'invested in Beethoven', and was prepared to put in work,[24] much as, I think, more recently they 'invested' in Tippett). In this respect, music makes special demands upon its public; perhaps only poetry and painting parallel it. Whereas it is unusual for anybody to read the same novel, see the same film, play, or opera more than half a dozen times in her life, we live with music. I cannot count the number of times I have heard the Beethoven symphonies live, broadcast, and on record. This is not merely a phenomenon of the era of radio and recording. Much keyboard music is intended for amateurs, and it is only out of this that there grew a corpus of virtuoso music too hard for non-professionals. So amateurs played and heard the 'Forty-Eight' far more frequently than they encountered the products of most of the other arts. Hence music is required to be of such a standing that it not only withstands frequent rehearing, but benefits from it. Much film, fiction, and drama is not like this; it has to meet less stringent

---

[23] Nicholas Cook, *Music, Imagination and Culture* (Oxford: Oxford University Press, 1990), 227.
[24] See Nicholas Cook, *Music: A Very Short Introduction* (Oxford: Oxford University Press, 1998).

requirements, as does much opera, even opera in the repertoire. But, unlike atonal music, the greatest music of the past offered interim payments as well.

The important sense of 'understanding' here is the sense in which we can follow the music. This sometimes shows itself in our making intelligent anticipations of the way it will go and, where this does not occur, at least recognizes the appositeness of what has occurred. But the possibility of anticipation is only much of a possibility to the extent that there is redundancy in the technical sense. Information theory tells me that if I can predict accurately where a cadence will fall, that cadence is redundant and uninformative (though such negative implications do not necessarily carry through to music, as we have seen). What is important here is that this is possible on a *first* hearing, and that this aspect of musical understanding remains constant on any subsequent hearing. We can hear a cadence as leading to a close. This is a phenomenological point. I feel what many have described as 'the gravitational pull' of the music as I hear it. It is not mediated by any intellectual grasp. Now, given a tone-row, it is, of course, possible to predict that it will be developed in various ways, but the tone-row, which is something between a scale and a theme, is determined anew for each composition.[25] So there is nothing which underlies the composition which could allow us to form expectations on a first hearing in the way we can for music based on a shared scale. Tonal music allows a very strong sense of 'following', though there are obviously gradations here. Understanding might just involve recognizing a pattern, though that at least requires repetition. The way in which we 'follow' Debussy differs from the way in which we follow Bach.

A professional musician recently remarked that we listen to serial music as a child listens to music, for sheer sound quality. Curiously, for these most 'intellectual' of composers, there is no way that a musical 'argument' can be followed on the basis of what you hear alone (in contradistinction to memorizing and then *remembering* what comes next). Schoenberg tried to create a language single-handedly, in which no single note was privileged as the tonic is privileged in the music which preceded his. There is no home key which acts as a centre of gravity, but merely a collection of notes

[25] There are many explanations of the principles of dodecaphonic music, but for brevity and clarity it is hard to match Mosco Carner's exposition in 'Alban Berg', in Ralph Hill (ed.), *The Concerto* (Harmondsworth: Penguin, 1952), 364-7.

from which a theme can be plucked and subjected to various transformations. There is no lower level at which the music generates
expectations over and above those which derive from the particular work with its unique thematic context. There is nothing to
compare with the significance of the cadence in tonal music in gen-
erating expectations in the listener, irrespective of the particular
music in which it is used. Serial language does not enable us to
gauge what is likely to come next in a sequence; therefore it cannot
shock us or please us as tonal music can.

I would not want to exclude the possibility that a very experienced musician might identify the tone-row on a single hearing and
then, hearing a fragment, identify it as the beginning of an inversion or a retrogression. He might form expectations and follow the
music in a way which I cannot. Still, the basis for his understanding parallels the way in which I might follow a quartet by Haydn
through identifying the material and looking out for his use of it;
whatever it is, it is not following the music independently of, and
logically prior to, a grasp of the specific thematic material. Now
Christopher Page's understanding of the virelai by Solage might be
of that first form; it might depend upon a knowledge of compositional technique. (Conversely, it might be an anachronistic form of
hearing; the music is being heard in the light of the way we listen
to Bach and others.) If it is based on a general absorption of style,
then, of course, musical humanism in that respect pre-dates the
humanism of the Renaissance. Nor would I want to exclude the
possibility that, as a matter of fact, nobody listens to Schoenberg's
music in a Schoenbergian way. We cannot rid ourselves of listening
with the assumption that a scale of some sort is in the offing, even
though it may not be a scale of the traditional sort. That the atonal
idiom now seems positively homely to the average listener argues
that something like this might be happening. (Probably it has come
to seem familiar because of its use in film scores.[26])

Schoenberg's atonality was heroic; but nobody can create a language single-handedly, nor can anybody create a style that way.
Schoenberg's project was the musical equivalent to the attempt to
create a private language, not so much in the strong sense of a
language which cannot be communicated or is not open to public
check, for anybody can tell whether or not you are using the tone-

[26] See Simon Frith, *Performing Rites* (Oxford: Oxford University Press, 1996), 113,
122.

row consistently. It is, rather, in the sense that it is a scale established by personal fiat. Unquestionably he showed courage in trying to thrust the musical language forward. Nicholas Cook discusses the view, implicit in Adorno, that Schoenberg's ultimate significance lies not in the effect of his music, but in its ethical significance and the personal integrity it displays.[27] The implication is that the music, as sound, is less important. As I have remarked elsewhere, on this assumption we do not need to hear his music, but only to know about it.[28] What is important is Schoenberg's personal odyssey.

It is sometimes argued against the atonalists that our ears are 'naturally' attuned to some form of tonality. We 'naturally' privilege certain tones, and even twelve-tone music will be heard by us in such terms. But the experimental evidence on this seems to me ambiguous. Some work does suggest this conclusion,[29] whilst other work seems to suggest that, once we become used to an atonal piece, we can identify repetitions of a tone-row.[30] Adorno points out that the assumption that the diatonic scale is 'natural' does not square with the fact that there are, and always have been, other scales. He, of course, is inclined to ascribe a sinister political motive to this insistence on what is 'natural'.

In any case, this whole debate is misconceived. It is not so much that the diatonic scale is no more 'natural' than English, Welsh, or German; what matters is that the early acquisition of our mother tongue enables us to form the expectations which make possible the witty or inventive use of language, the usages which defeat our expectations, the very feature of natural languages which parallels our experience of music. Innateness has nothing to do with it. Music does not have to be diatonic; but scales or their equivalent do have to be internalized to the point where expectations can be formed if music is to mirror this aspect of language.

Another point: the memorability of themes which, for ordinary

---

[27] Cook, *Music, Imagination and Culture*, 8.

[28] R. A. Sharpe, 'Culture and its Discontents', *British Journal of Aesthetics*, 28/4 (1988), 306.

[29] See e.g. Lerdahl and Jackendorff's well-known 'Cognitive Constraints on Compositional Systems', in J. A. Sloboda (ed.), *Generative Processes in Music* (Oxford: Clarendon Press, 1988).

[30] The research by Krumhansl and others is reported in John Paynter, Tim Howell, Richard Orton, and Peter Seymour, *Companion to Contemporary Musical Thought* (London: Routledge, 1992), 811.

listeners, not only makes music fascinating, but enables us to pick up the structure at one or more hearings without recourse to a score is also an important ingredient in following music. Adorno, the philosopher of atonalism, speaks with contempt of 'coarsest vulgarities and easily remembered fragments'.[31] But this is to dismiss a feature of music which is central to the way we value it. The strange fact is that it is its memorability—or rather, its half-memorability—which makes us want to hear it again. The urge to repetition is crucial in the arts. So music needs re-identifiability and memorability. I do not drive to work with the catchy melodies of Schoenberg, Boulez, or Berg running through my head, as the music of Britten or Shostakovich might. The music of the former, though it may impress me by its reflection of modern life, its complexity, and its doom-laden angst, cannot have the function that other music does in my life. It will not haunt me in the same way. Of course, music can be worked at, and can reward careful attention; but to ask a listener to work at something with only a remote chance of a reward is asking much of somebody not professionally required to do this. If the music has some initial attractions, which make the task enjoyable, the situation is different. Melody is not the only virtue which makes us value music, but it is so precious to us that its absence from nearly all 'advanced music' is a great loss.[32]

Schoenberg himself wrote despairingly:

[M]usic is only understood when one goes away singing it and is only loved when one falls asleep with it in one's head and finds it still there on waking up next morning ... I always insisted that the new music was merely a logical development of (existing) musical resources. But of what use can theoretical explanations be in comparison with the effect the subject itself makes on the listener? What good can it do to *tell* a listener, 'This music is beautiful', if he does not feel it? How could I win friends with this kind of music?[33]

So, to summarize with a parody of the information-theoretic thesis, redundancy combats unintelligibility. The price of minimiz-

---

[31] Adorno, *Philosophy of Modern Music*, 9.

[32] Nigel Fortune said somewhere that the first great composer whom we esteem for his melodies is Henry Purcell. Though I should think a case could be made out for Monteverdi, the implication is sound. Melody, which means so much to us, is a gift that not all great composers possess.

[33] A. Schoenberg, *Style and Idea*, ed. L. Stein (Berkeley: University of California Press, 1985), 50, 180; discussed by Arnold Whittall, *Music since the First World War* (Oxford: Clarendon Press, 1988), 4.

ing repetition, or sequence, or, indeed, memorability is that you approach unintelligibility in one important respect. Assuming that it makes sense to speak of following music which has minimized repetition, either the demands made upon the listener are unreasonable, or music is approaching an art-form of a different sort, an art-form in which sound and notated score must be simultaneously available for the hearer to be able to understand. It may well be that this is more a return to an older form of music than something radically new. Charles Rosen makes the point that Bach's keyboard music was written for the private player who would see contrapuntal entrances imperceptible to the ear. The listener was assumed to be the performer.[34]

In the other important respect, music of the Second Viennese School is not lacking in intelligibility. We can apply expressive predicates to it, though these predicates tend to belong to the extremes of emotional reactions. Many writers have commented on this. L. B. Meyer describes Schoenberg's music as 'almost hysterically emotional',[35] and Carner describes the free atonal chromaticism of Schoenberg's middle period as expressing 'an excessive degree of emotional tension', and as 'extraordinarily tense, emotionally overcharged, explosive and lyrical in turn, nervous, fragmentary and hypersensitive'.[36] Webern described his own music as 'the music of a madman'.[37] The rhetorical gesture remains central to the effect of such music, and its function is obvious in Schoenberg's *Sprechstimme*.[38] However, simultaneously, the range of predicates which aptly describe such music has moved to the febrile end of the spectrum. The comparisons with the vocal line in ordinary demotic speech are no longer present to the same extent. Except in grief or hysteria, the frequently jagged vocal lines of Berg are not characteristic of the human voice. What is crucial is that the wide range of expressive predicates which we apply to music composed between the Renaissance and roughly 1945, when we talk of music being retiring, hesitant, bold, aggressive, fiery, sad, emotional, unrestrained, has become constricted. Perhaps in the nineteenth century the range of expressive predicates was at its widest. This is not to say that music of that period moves us in special ways or is

---

[34] Rosen, *Romantic Generation*, 6.    [35] Meyer, *Music, the Arts and Ideas*, 243.
[36] Carner, 'Alban Berg', 364, though Ernst Bloch thought it inexpressive.
[37] Quoted by Cook, *Music: A Very Short Introduction*, 21.
[38] A point made to me by Lydia Goehr in conversation.

superior. We may love and value highly music from other periods, but the range of plausible descriptions in terms of expression—minimally metaphorical, defensibly metaphorical, or illuminatingly metaphorical—is slim. The point is that a particular achievement of Western music is historically circumscribed in a way which may be unique in the arts. For a short period in its history, music was a humanist art to a degree which we may not be able to repeat. Granted that atonal music does invite expressive description, I suspect that much of the music of its successors has become less describable in expressive terms. I have the music of Boulez, Stockhausen, Birtwhistle, and Stravinsky's atonal period in mind here, though, as always, such broad historical generalizations are hard to justify. (In another way, such music might be said to be 'humanist', in that its lack of expressive resources exactly reflects the anomie of twentieth-century industrial society, of course.)

## III

Nothing I have said so far implies that music which does not meet all of my conditions for intelligibility may not be good music. It is possible that music should neither invite more than a simple and restricted range of expressive predicates nor be music which can be followed, yet still be music which we value. But the test of quality in music is, to put it very crudely, the test of time. What we expect is that music which perhaps at first seems difficult will, if it is good, gradually reveal its qualities, its individuality, and its coherence, so that what was once the province of a coterie of professionals and semi-professionals becomes music which is loved by the mass of serious music-lovers. We see this in the history of the reception of late Beethoven, of Mahler, Stravinsky, and Bartók. But if the test of music is its survival in popular esteem, then we ought to conclude that the music of the Second Viennese School, with the possible exceptions of Berg's Violin Concerto, *Wozzeck*, and *Lulu*, has failed the test of time. For whereas the music of the other two revolutionary composers of the first half of the twentieth century, Stravinsky and Bartók, is widely loved and sought out, the music of Schoenberg and Webern is not. (In saying this, I do not express a personal opinion. For what it is worth, I do not like the music of Schoenberg, find the music of Berg kitsch—less the poet than the

Puccini of atonalism—but find some of the music of Webern fascinating and moving.) But if we take the usual grounds for assessment, then we should conclude that the official history of twentieth-century music which places atonalism at the centre distorts. (Consequently, I must assume that my liking for Webern is something of a minority interest, just as a passion for the music of Schoenberg or Berg is a minority passion, in that it is not a passion that others will come to share no matter how much they are exposed to the music.) We have taken Schoenberg's self-assessment far too seriously. A history of music in the twentieth century has been constructed around him which affects both our hearing and our valuation of music. On its basis, we approve of late Stravinsky's serial music, perhaps in part because of the 'advanced' features it displays.

Why should the 'official history' make atonalism central? The answer is, by now, obvious. I think that it is because the history was written under the influence of an ideology of music. So we return to the central issues of the latter part of this book and, in the last part of this final chapter, to the question of the ideology of music. I am now in a position to offer a more systematic presentation of that ideology. Any schematic presentation runs the risk of being incomplete, but, with that caveat, I propose that much writing on twentieth-century music makes three ideological assumptions.

First, the assumption of progress: the language of music progresses, bringing with that progression increasing concentration.

Second, the assumption that achievement is independent of progress: music does not evolve in terms of quality. In another sense of progress, music does not progress. To assume that Beethoven was better than Mozart, and Brahms than Beethoven, is evidently wrong. But neither does it regress. Music of quality can be written at any time.[39]

Third, the formalist assumption: the pinnacle of music is abstract music, music which is a purely auditory experience and which can be appreciated without a text, associations, or scene setting.

I suggested earlier that the distinction between what belongs to ideology and what to the work, in so far as that imprecise line can be drawn, lies in the fact that the work has certain features which

---

[39] Compare Ernst Bloch, *Essays on the Philosophy of Music*, trans. Peter Palmer (Cambridge, Cambridge University Press, 1985), 11.

derive from the act of composition within a specific musical culture. A phrase leads to a close, a dissonance asks to be resolved, a movement needs to return to its home key, and so on. It is broader aspects than these which approximate to the ideological. But just as it is extremely difficult to say at what point a particular account of the meaning of a poem becomes a matter of interpretation— that is, of something which we introduce into the study of the poem, rather than find there—so it is difficult to say whether taking a song of Brahms as an expression of romanticism is simply a 'matter of fact' about the song *qua* song, or whether we are already raising issues which properly belong to those interpretative and historical matters which set the music in the context of its history. At what point, we might ask, do we leave questions of intellectual and artistic history that can be settled and enter those regions of dispute and predilection which I have described as ideological? However, the fact that a boundary is hard to draw does not mean that it does not exist.

Not all writers share all the ideological assumptions I listed, but the first is, I think, the most widely held. For part of the ideology of music during the nineteenth and early twentieth centuries was the urge to novelty, the need always to extend a style and to introduce the new.[40] Thus the language of late Beethoven is more difficult, more concentrated, more abstruse, and more discontinuous with the past than that of his first period. Mahler's style is more 'advanced' than that of Schubert, and so on. This view is enshrined in what we might call an 'ideal history', in which the great figures in music march relentlessly forward, constantly making the musical language more complex, and making atonalism the logical end of the historical process. Pierre Boulez expresses this in the most uncompromising way: 'Anyone who has not felt . . . the necessity of the 12 tone language is SUPERFLUOUS. For everything he writes will fall short of the imperatives of our time.'[41]

It was inasmuch as Schoenberg subscribed to this ideology that his own development was inevitable; its inevitability was a consequence of his own agenda. (And, parenthetically, it applies also to jazz—witness the bebop revolution of Parker and Gillespie.)

This ideology agrees very well with a canon based mainly on German and Austrian composers. (A place would need to be found

---

[40] Adorno, *Philosophy of Modern Music*, 32.
[41] See Meyer, *Music, the Arts and Ideas*, 171; capitals original.

for Debussy.) I suggested in an earlier chapter that this was a 'German' ideology, and the degree to which it involves nationalism is very evident in Adorno's writings. His extraordinary animus against Stravinsky is partly due to his assumption that music must be the art of transition, and that music which does not display continual transition cannot be music of the highest order. Presumably he would have objected to Tippett's later music on the same basis. But, more profoundly, the reader quickly forms the suspicion that his deeper objection is that Stravinsky has the temerity to be a radical composer, yet not be a German or an Austrian.

As I have remarked before, since I think that ideology is a universal phenomenon, and since I recognize that I am as much its prisoner as the next man, that Adorno's criticism of Stravinsky is ideologically motivated can hardly be a *particular* objection. If it is a general objection, then who shall escape whipping? It is part of the *condition humaine*. However, I can, consistently with my premisses, object that Adorno's ideology is more flawed than my own, even if I allow, as I do, that, given his background and culture, Adorno could scarcely have viewed the history of music differently. Indeed, the great fascination of Adorno is precisely that he presents, in such a stark and uncompromising way, a view of music history to which anybody of my generation who formed a love of classical music is heir. My criticism is not of Adorno's ideology, but of his apparent ignorance of its ideological nature as well as of its potentially distorting effect.

Naturally, then, the written history of music reflects the canon that forms Adorno's thinking and that of others who share his judgement of the relative value of the great composers. In this, it omits, to a large extent, composers whose influence was great, but whose music has little intrinsic value for us. This history becomes the expression of an ideology, both recounting a sequence and telling us which are the really important figures whose works we should admire.

The ideology has advantages of course. Sometimes we find a composer difficult; if the ideology persuades us to take his music seriously, and not judge him on a single hearing, it gives us time to learn his idiom and reach a considered assessment. If we are still bored or repelled, then we have a difficult judgement to make— the trilemma I alluded to in the preface to this book. Have we failed to prepare ourselves properly, or have we failed to give the music sufficient time? Do we have a blind spot for this particular music? Or is it that this composer is not really very good, after all?

However, the ideology has consequences which are less desirable as well. Like many ideologies, it commits us to judgements which are hard to substantiate. For example, one crucial question is: Is it necessary that music of quality be written by such stylistic entrepreneurs? Bach used to be cited as the great conservative and counter-example to this thesis; though recent scholarship suggests that this is wide of the mark.[42] But there seems to be no overwhelming reason why we should assume quite generally that the best music is composed by entrepreneurs, even though, as we saw in the last chapter, in the criticism of Brahms and Strauss, that there are cases where valid criticism may be based on this premiss. We cannot generalize. It is no criticism of the English madrigalists that they were less advanced than the Italians they took as models, nor a criticism of Purcell's great fantasias for viol consort that they were archaic. And if Bach was indeed the great conservative he was traditionally thought to be, that is not grounds for denigrating his work.

Until recently, we lived in a culture which defined itself as progressive. Various writers have pointed out that, up to the scientific revolution of the seventeenth century, the golden age was placed in the more or less remote past. Technology and the 'new philosophy' placed it in the future. Scientific progress, it was thought, would bring about a new golden age. At the same time, of course, the fact that the arts do not progress in the same sort of way became recognized, and, if Kristeller was right,[43] produced a basis for developing the concept of art in contradistinction to that of science. The claim made on behalf of Shakespeare was that he was the equal of Homer or Virgil, not their superior.

However, to advert to the second thesis, even though the arts did not progress in quality as the language or style developed in refinement, nevertheless there seemed, to the ideologist, no reason to suppose that human achievement in the arts would decline. For Adorno and other commentators, there were political reasons for rejecting the assumption that music might no longer be in a state

---

[42] See Joseph Kerman, *Contemplating Music* (Cambridge, Mass.: Harvard University Press, 1985), 53.

[43] P. O. Kristeller, 'The Modern System of the Arts', *Journal of the History of Ideas*, 12 (1951), 496–527; 13 (1952), 17–46.

of grace. For Adorno values the new music partly because of its reflection of modern life,[44] but also because of its rejection, through its very difficulty for its listeners, of the commercial values of modern society. Modern music might be different and difficult, but it is not inferior. If we reject, as we must, evolutionism in the arts, then it looks like a natural if illegitimate corollary to suppose that musical accomplishment is much of a muchness in standard irrespective of the time at which it is produced.

But this assumption looks suspect. There is no reason to suppose that good music can be written at any time. Music of the past looks something like a matter of peaks and hollows. Compare the seventeenth century with the hundred years from Haydn to Wagner. If I say that Purcell and Monteverdi apart there are no great figures, no doubt I shall have the players of Biber, if not the listeners to Biber, at my throat. But it looks a reasonable enough judgement. The conductor Philip Herreweghe remarked that nothing Lully composed was worth one bar of Purcell, and, if this is an exaggeration, it is pardonable. Equally, there is no reason to suppose that the second half of the twentieth century will produce as much music of quality as the first half. It might do, but, currently, it does not look likely. In retrospect, the important music of the last fifty years may prove to be jazz and rock. Even for the Hegelian, music is relative to a style, and styles wax and wane. They can become used up, and the Hegelian does not have to assume that a new style equal in resources will become immediately available. So the strong assumption, that any age produces music of roughly equal quality, has to be rejected.

Adorno links the assumption of the necessity of progress with the third ideological assumption which came to the fore in the late nineteenth century, and that is the superiority of abstract music to music which sets a text or a drama, accompanies dance, or is accompanied by a programme. Again, Adorno expresses this well; for Adorno, the political significance of twelve-tone music lies in its very isolation: 'the more clearly music defines its formal laws and entrusts itself to them, the more, for the moment, it closes itself off against the manifest portrayal of society in which it has its enclaves'.[45] (The contrary ideology takes the Wagnerian notion of the *Gesamtkunstwerk* as the goal towards which music is moving,

---

[44] Adorno, *Philosophy of Modern Music*, 76.     [45] Ibid. 129 and see 31.

combining a conception of the total work of art with a notion of aesthetic progress.)

But, in fact, it is arguable that Adorno is wrong; he assumes that the music of the Second Viennese School approaches 'pure music'. But there is a good argument for supposing that it requires a more detailed understanding of the *Zeitgeist* than does pre-twentieth-century music, an argument based on the way it is received. There are 'homologies', as they are called: correspondences between the society and the music which it produces. The study of fragmented personalities by Freud and others, so pertinently compared with modern literature by Steven Marcus,[46] and the dramatic presentation of such individuals in works like Berg's *Wozzeck* have become the focus of attention for creative artists, partly because the central topics for the narrative arts have been explored, and partly because of the fertilization of the arts by Freudian studies. It has been a criticism of the school of English music which has been derogatorily described as 'cow-pat' (Vaughan Williams and lesser figures like Finzi and Moeran), that its power depends upon an association with the English countryside, and particularly an idealized picture of the English countryside. Aside from this, it would not move or detain us. Elgar is a much greater figure, but Ken Russell's *Monitor* film, which did so much for the resuscitation of Elgar's music, blatantly trades on connections with the Malverns. What I am suggesting is that the power of the Second Viennese School depends on our combining the music with thoughts about the decline of the Hapsburg empire, with our knowledge of Klimt, Schiele, of German expressionism, of Karl Kraus and of Freud, a milieu which is a million miles away from the cosy sentimentalities of Georgian verse and 'A Shropshire Lad'. It deals with the outermost reaches of human experience, and thereby the least normal. But no more than English music of the time does it stand on its own two feet. Its 'reception', as it would now be called, by its hearers gives the lie to the claim that it represents the peak of formalism.

Music has always been regarded, with some reason, as an art-form for which there can be an 'internal history'—that is, a history which shows how musical styles developed from earlier styles, without reference to the social or political histories of the time. Consequently, an 'internal history' suggests a formalist canon. Of

---

[46] Steven Marcus, *Freud and the Culture of Psychoanalysis* (London: Allen and Unwin, 1984).

course, such a history was always an abstraction. Whether or not musicians can obtain a livelihood from their music locally, or whether they needs must travel, is going to affect the influences that come to bear upon them. And there are many other such economic and social conditions which will affect the development of the art. But it is reasonable at least to say that music is a more enclosed art than any other. You can explain and understand music largely in virtue of the music which the composer heard and which influenced him, and in this respect music differs from the other arts. It is a simple consequence of the fact that music is predominantly a non-representational art. It is certainly true that whereas our understanding of Shakespeare is much enhanced by a knowledge of Elizabethan cosmology, our knowledge of Mozart is little enhanced by a knowledge of the Enlightenment and of the Masonic movement. For most musicians and music-lovers, their ignorance of Mozart's times is hardly a hindrance. What I am suggesting is that there is much twentieth-century music for which this is no longer true. It will not mean much as pure music. I think this is particularly true of Schoenberg, and that it is particularly ironic in his case, since no composer looks more formalistic in his techniques and interests. *Pierrot Lunaire* makes more sense to us as a product of German expressionism. To take a very different and more approachable composer, Shostakovich's particular angst increasingly appears to be an expression of the dreadful years through which he lived, and this knowledge is not irrelevant to the work's impact. By contrast, the impact of Bach is practically immediate. Of course, it may well be that our experience of Bach would be enriched by a greater understanding of the culture from which it came. But it seems a fact that his music has a formal power which much other music lacks.

## IV

I have written as though the two most important respects in which music is intelligible—our capacity to follow it and our capacity to describe it in expressive terms—are independent. But in at least one important way, this is not so. They have the same parentage: both are premissed on an analogy with language. The expressiveness of music is based on certain correspondences with expressive speech. To the extent, then, that music bears such analogies with language, it is an art-form which we can think of as intelligible in two of the most important respects. By parity of reasoning, to the extent it ceases to be analogous in this way, we will no longer think of it as a humanist art in the way I have defined, and it is my belief that a good deal of contemporary music is neither followable nor readily describable in expressive predicates.

Is this a loss? Well, some philosophers have argued that the capacity of music to be, say, poignant gives value to that music. As I argued in the very first chapter, I am not persuaded. Expressive character is not, *tout court*, a positive value. However, I would allow that even if the gravity of the slow movement of Beethoven's 'Eroica' is not, and not even *ceteris paribus* as that clause is usually understood, a reason for valuing it, the fact that it displays gravity *at that point* in the work may well be inextricably bound up with the way we value the work as a whole. So the loss of the special kind of intelligibility given by expressive features is, *ceteris paribus*, a loss of value. But, as I have tried to stress, music which is more 'abstract' or 'objective' may, on other measures, be very fine music. Followability may be a merit in music; but much poor music is followable, and much good music has other virtues.

In an earlier chapter I discussed the way in which the characterization of the precise expressive content of a piece of music converges on the highly particular. It is the exactness which we prize, and this is a matter of the individuality of the music. Whatever general characteristics I appeal to in trying to persuade another listener that a particular piece is good, he can dismiss on the grounds either that they are too general or that he can find works which have that character and are not much good. How do I defend my judgement? Ultimately, I shall reply to the persistent interlocutor that it is just this particular unique, individual piece of music which appeals to me. I do not think that the music which I prize is music which expresses this, that, or the other particular property. It is, *inter alia*, music which bears a special character and an original and unmistakable face. It is inasmuch as it is music which is like nothing else that I value it. What fascinates me about the music of Janáček, Webern, Mahler, Tippett, Shostakovich, Pärt, and Britten is the unmistakableness of their particular voices. If I have an affection for music which expresses the commonplace style in a particularly recognizable form, then it is an affection which does not justify my

according the music of Massenet or Rimsky-Korsakov the highest
places in the pantheon.

Perhaps this fact about our musical values, albeit appearing in
a distorted form, provided the motivation for the widespread
assumption that only advanced music can be music of high quality;
it is, perhaps, natural enough to suppose that originality must
require taking the existing style to new levels of complexity. But
this does not follow. Indeed, what we now lack is a dominant
musical language in which such 'advances' could easily be identified. The ideology of the Second Viennese School is now widely
seen for what it is—ideology! Few now believe that atonalism
is central. Yet no authoritative voice comparable to that of Adorno
or Boulez has come forward to say what most of us now believe:
namely, that we have in contemporary music a multiplicity of
styles no one of which dominates.[47] Contemporary music ranges
from music of extreme complexity to music which is accessible.
Perhaps the important point is that the Adorno–Boulez thesis, that
dodecaphonic music is the only music of quality that can now be
written, looks false. The official history of music on which it is based
is *passé*. However, this does not make me any the more optimistic
about the future for humanism in music. The contemporary music
which can be 'followed' as a Haydn string quartet can be followed,
or which can sustain the range of expressive predicates we can
apply, say, to a symphony of Mahler, sounds marginal. It verges on
the jokey or on pastiche.

If Western music has entered a new non-humanist period, in
which two of the principle conditions for its intelligibility have been
weakened and, with them, the basis for speaking analogically of
music as a language, then we will expect critics to recommend it to
us in new terms. And indeed they do. Commentators tell us about
the wonderful and distinctive sounds we can hear in contemporary
music; they write a lot about textures and the contrast of textures.
The problem is that the fascination of mere sound is too close to
the child's first wonder at music, and too close to our interest in
music from other civilizations.

I do not, of course, preclude the possibility of writing fine music
in a post-humanist setting. But these are hard times for composers;
unlike the novelist or the film-maker, he does not draw on life. The

---

[47] But see Meyer, *Music, the Arts and Ideas*, postlude, 317 ff.

tonal system was neither a language nor a style, but, through its very ubiquity, had some of the features of both. The marginalization of tonality, though inevitable, is, partly through that very inevitability, a tragedy for the art. Present-day composers have been dealt a rotten hand by history.

# Select Bibliography

ADORNO, T. W., *Quasi una Fantasia: Essays on Modern Music*, trans. Rodney Livingstone. London: Verso, 1992.

—— *Philosophy of Modern Music*. London: Stagbooks, 1994.

ALPERSON, PHILIP, 'The Arts of Music', *Journal of Aesthetics and Art Criticism*, 50/3 (1992), 217–30.

—— (ed.), *Musical Worlds; New Directions in the Philosophy of Music*. University Park, Pa.: Pennsylvania State University Press, 1994.

—— (ed.), *What is Music? An Introduction to the Philosophy of Music*. New York: Haven, 1987.

AVISON, CHARLES, *An Essay on Musical Expression*. London, 1775.

BERLIOZ, HECTOR, *Memoirs*, trans. David Cairns. London: Panther, 1970.

—— *The Art of Music*, trans. Elizabeth Cscisery-Ronay. Bloomington, Ind.: Indiana University Press, 1994.

BERMAN, MARSHALL, *All that is Solid Melts into Thin Air*. New York: Verso, 1983.

BLACKING, JOHN, *How Musical is Man?* London: Faber and Faber, 1976.

BLOCH, ERNST, *Essays on the Philosophy of Music*, trans. Peter Palmer. Cambridge: Cambridge University Press, 1985.

BLOOM, HAROLD, *The Western Canon*. New York: Harcourt Brace, 1994.

BONDS, MARK EVANS, *Wordless Rhetoric: Musical Form and the Metaphor of the Oration*. Cambridge, Mass.: Harvard University Press, 1991.

BOOTH, WAYNE C., *The Rhetoric of Fiction*. Chicago: University of Chicago Press, 1961.

BROPHY, BRIGID, *Mozart the Dramatist*. New York: Da Capo, 1988.

BUDD, MALCOLM, 'Belief and Sincerity in Poetry', in Eva Schaper (ed.), *Pleasure, Preference and Value*, Cambridge: Cambridge University Press, 1983, 137–57.

—— 'Understanding Music', *Proceedings of the Aristotelian Society*, supp. vol. 59 (1985), 233–48.

—— *Music and the Emotions*. London: Routledge and Kegan Paul, 1985.

—— *Values of Art*. London: Allen Lane, 1995.

BUJIC, BOJAN (ed.), *Music in European Thought 1851–1912*. Cambridge: Cambridge University Press, 1988.

BURKHOLDER, J., 'Museum Pieces: The Historicist Mainstream in the Music of the Last Hundred Years', *Journal of Musicology*, 2 (1983), 115–34.

BUTLER, GREGORY C., 'Fugue and Rhetoric', *Journal of Music Theory*, 21 (1977), 49–109.

CARNER, MOSCO, 'Alban Berg', in Ralph Hill (ed.), *The Concerto*, Harmondsworth: Penguin, 1952, 362–79.

CASEY, JOHN, 'The Autonomy of Art', in G. Vesey (ed.), *Philosophy and the Arts*, Royal Institute of Philosophy Lectures, vi: *1971–2*, London: Macmillan, 1973, 65–87.

CAVELL, STANLEY, 'Music Discomposed', in *Must We Mean What We Say?*, Cambridge: Cambridge University Press, 1976.

COKER, WILSON, *Music and Meaning*. New York: Free Press, 1972.

COLLINGWOOD, R. G., *The Principles of Art*. Oxford: Oxford University Press, 1978.

CONE, E. T., *The Composer's Voice*. Berkeley: University of California Press, 1974.

COOK, NICHOLAS, *Guide to Musical Analysis*. Oxford: Oxford University Press, 1987.

——*Music, Imagination and Culture*. Oxford: Oxford University Press, 1990.

——*Music: A Very Short Introduction*. Oxford: Oxford University Press, 1998.

COOKE, DERYCK, *The Language of Music*. Oxford: Oxford University Press, 1959.

——*Vindications: Essays on Romantic Music*. Cambridge: Cambridge University Press, 1982.

COOPER, DAVID, *Metaphor*. Oxford: Blackwell for the Aristotelian Society, 1986.

COPLAND, AARON, *The New Music*. London: MacDonald, 1968.

CROCKER, RICHARD, *A History of Musical Style*. New York: Dover, 1966.

DAHLHAUS, CARL, *The Aesthetics of Music*, trans. William Austin. Cambridge: Cambridge University Press, 1982.

DANTO, A. C., 'From Aesthetics to Art Criticism and Back', *Journal of Aesthetics and Art Criticism*, 54/2 (1996), 105–15.

DAVIES, STEPHEN, 'Authenticity in Musical Performance', *British Journal of Aesthetics*, 27/1 (1987), 39–50.

——'Authenticity in Performance, a Reply to James O. Young', *British Journal of Aesthetics*, 28/4 (1988), 373–6.

——*Musical Meaning and Expression*. Ithaca, NY: Cornell University Press, 1994.

——'Musical Understanding and Musical Kinds', in P. Alperson (ed.), *Musical Worlds; New Directions in the Philosophy of Music*, University Park, Pa.: Pennsylvania State University Press, 1998.

DEMPSTER, DOUGLAS and BROWN, MATTHEW, 'Evaluating Musical Analyses and Theories: Five Perspectives', *Journal of Music Theory*, 34/2 (1990), 347–79.

DIPERT, RANDALL, 'The Composer's Intentions: An Examination of their Relevance for Performance', *Musical Quarterly*, 66 (1980), 205–18.

DOE, PAUL, *Tallis*. Oxford: Oxford University Press, 1968.

ENTZENBERG, CLAES, 'Metaphor, Interpretation and Contextualisation', *Danish Yearbook of Philosophy*, 31 (1996), 21–38.

EPSTEIN, DAVID, *Beyond Orpheus*. Cambridge, Mass.: MIT Press, 1979.

FERGUSON, DONALD, *Music as Metaphor*. Minneapolis: University of Minnesota Press, 1960.

FRANKLIN, PETER, *The Idea of Music*. London: Macmillan, 1985.

FRITH, SIMON, *Performing Rites*. Oxford: Oxford University Press, 1998.

FUBINI, ENRICO, *A History of Musical Aesthetics*, trans. Michael Hatwell. London: Macmillan, 1990.

GALLIE, W. B., *Philosophy and the Historical Understanding*. London: Chatto and Windus, 1964.

GIDDENS, ANTHONY, 'Four Theses on Ideology', in A. Kroker and M. Kroker (eds.), *Ideology and Power*, New York: St Martin's Press, 1991, 21–4.

GODLOVITCH, STAN, 'Authentic Performance', *Monist*, 71 (1988), 258–77.

——'Innovation and Conservatism in Performance Practice', *Journal of Aesthetics and Art Criticism*, 55/2 (1997), 151–68.

——*Musical Performance*. London: Routledge, 1998.

GOEHR, LYDIA, *The Imaginary Museum of Musical Works*. Oxford: Clarendon Press, 1992.

GOLDMAN, ALAN, 'Emotions in Music (A Postscript)', *Journal of Aesthetics and Art Criticism*, 53/1 (1995), 59–69.

GOODMAN, NELSON, *Languages of Art*. Oxford: Oxford University Press, 1969.

GORDON, ROBERT, *The Structure of the Emotions*. Cambridge: Cambridge University Press, 1991.

GOULD, GLENN, *The Glenn Gould Reader*, ed. Tim Page. London: Faber and Faber, 1987.

GROSS, JOHN, *Shylock*. London: Chatto, 1992.

GURNEY, EDMUND, *The Power of Sound*. New York: Basic Books, 1966.

HAGBERG, G. L., *Art as Language*. Ithaca, NY: Cornell University Press, 1995.

HANFLING, OSWALD, '"I heard a plaintive melody" (*Philosophical Investigations* p. 209)', in A. P. Griffiths (ed.), *The Wittgenstein Centenary Essays*. Cambridge: Cambridge University Press, 1990, 117–33.

HANSLICK, EDUARD, *Vom Musikalisch-Schonen*. Trans. as *On the Musically Beautiful* by Geoffrey Payzant, Indianapolis: Hackett, 1986, and as *The Beautiful in Music* by Gustav Cohen, Indianapolis: Bobbs-Merrill, 1957.

HINDEMITH, PAUL, *A Composer's World*, The Charles Eliot Norton Lectures 1949–50. New York: Doubleday Anchor, 1961.

HOLLAND, NORMAN, *The Dynamics of Literary Response*. New York: Columbia University Press, 1989.

HOROWITZ, JOSEPH, *Understanding Toscanini*. London: Faber and Faber, 1994.

HOWELL, W. S., *Logic and Rhetoric in England 1500–1700*. Princeton: Princeton University Press, 1956.

—— *Eighteenth Century British Logic and Rhetoric*. Princeton: Princeton University Press, 1971.

HUME, DAVID, 'Of Tragedy', in *Essays Moral, Political and Literary*. London: Grant Richards, 1903.

HURAY, PETER LE and DAY, JAMES, *Music and Aesthetics in the Eighteenth and Early Nineteenth Centuries*. Cambridge: Cambridge University Press, 1981.

INGARDEN, ROMAN, *The Literary Work of Art*, trans. George G. Grabowicz. Evanston, Ill.: Northwestern University Press, 1973.

—— *The Work of Music and the Problem of its Identity*, trans. Adam Czerniawski, ed. Jean G. Harrell. London: Macmillan, 1986.

JAMES, HENRY, *The Critical Muse, Selected Literary Criticism*, ed. Roger Gard. Harmondsworth: Penguin, 1987.

KAMBER, RICHARD, 'Weitz Reconsidered: A Clearer View of Why Theories of Art Fail', *British Journal of Aesthetics*, 38/1 (1998), 33–46.

KENNEDY, GEORGE, *The Art of Persuasion in Greece*. Princeton: Princeton University Press, 1963.

—— *The Art of Persuasion in the Roman World*. Princeton: Princeton University Press, 1972.

KERMAN, JOSEPH, *Opera as Drama*. New York: Vintage, 1956.

—— *Contemplating Music*. Cambridge, Mass.: Harvard University Press, 1985 (also published as *Musicology*, London: Fontana, 1985).

KIRKENDALE, URSULA, 'The Source for Bach's Musical Offering', *Journal of the American Musicological Society*, 33 (1980), 81–141.

KIRKENDALE, WARREN, 'Ciceronians versus Aristotelians on the Ricercar as Exordium, from Bembo to Bach', *Journal of the American Musicological Society*, 32 (1979), 1–44.

KIVY, PETER, *The Corded Shell: Reflections on Musical Expression*. Princeton: Princeton University Press, 1980.

—— 'Secondary Senses and Aesthetic Concepts: A Reply to Professor Tilghman', *Philosophical Investigations*, 4/1 (1981), 35–8.

—— *Sound and Semblance*. Princeton: Princeton University Press, 1984.

—— 'How Music Moves', in P. Alperson (ed.), *What is Music?*, New York: Haven, 1987, 147–63.

—— 'On the Concept of the "Historically Authentic" Performance', *Monist*, 71 (1988), 278–90.

—— *Sound Sentiment*. Philadelphia: Temple University Press, 1989.

—— *Music Alone*. Ithaca, NY: Cornell University Press, 1990.

—— *The Fine Art of Repetition: Essays in the Philosophy of Music*. Cambridge: Cambridge University Press, 1993.

——'Auditors' Emotions: Contention, Concession and Compromise', *Journal of Aesthetics and Art Criticism*, 51/1 (1993), 1–12.

——*Authenticities: Philosophical Reflections on Musical Performance.* Ithaca, NY: Cornell University Press, 1995.

——'Feeling the Musical Emotions', *British Journal of Aesthetics*, 39/1 (1999), 1–13.

KRAMER, LAWRENCE, 'The Musicology of the Future', *Repercussions*, 1/1 (1992), 5–18.

KRAUSZ, MICHAEL (ed.), *The Interpretation of Music.* Oxford: Clarendon Press, 1993.

KRISTELLER, P. O., 'The Modern System of the Arts', *Journal of the History of Ideas*, 12 (1951), 496–527; 13 (1952), 17–46.

LAMARQUE, PETER and OLSEN, STEIN HAUGOM, *Truth, Fiction and Literature.* Oxford: Clarendon Press, 1994.

LASKI, MARGHANITA, *Ecstasy.* London: Cresset Books, 1965.

LEVINSON, JERROLD, *Music, Art and Metaphysics.* Ithaca, NY: Cornell University Press, 1990.

——*The Pleasures of Aesthetics.* Ithaca, NY: Cornell University Press, 1996.

MARCUS, STEVEN, *Freud and the Culture of Psychoanalysis.* London: Allen and Unwin, 1984.

MARK, THOMAS CARSON, 'The Philosophy of Piano Playing: Reflections on the Concept of Performance', *Philosophy and Phenomenological Research*, 41 (1980–1), 299–324.

MARTIN, R. L., 'Musical Works in the Worlds of Performers and Listeners', in Michael Krausz (ed.), *The Interpretation of Music*, Oxford: Clarendon Press, 1993, 119–27.

MATRAVERS, DEREK, *Art and Emotion.* Oxford: Oxford University Press, 1998.

MEYER, L. B., *Emotion and Meaning in Music.* Chicago: University of Chicago Press, 1956.

——*Explaining Music.* Berkeley: University of California Press, 1973.

——*Style and Music.* Philadelphia: University of Pennsylvania Press, 1989.

——*Music, the Arts and Ideas*, 2nd edn. Chicago: University of Chicago Press, 1994.

MIDDLETON, RICHARD, *Studying Popular Music.* Milton Keynes: Open University Press, 1990.

MITCHELL, DONALD, *The Language of Modern Music.* London: Faber and Faber, 1966.

MORGENSTERN, S., *Composers on Music.* London: Faber and Faber, 1968.

NEUBAUER, JOHN, *The Emancipation of Music from Language.* New Haven: Yale University Press, 1986.

NEWCOMB, ANTHONY, 'Once More between Absolute and Program Music:

Schumann's Second Symphony', *Nineteenth Century Music*, 7 (1984), 233ff.

NOVITZ, DAVID, 'Disputes about Art', *Journal of Aesthetics and Art Criticism*, 54/2 (1996), 153–63.

NOZICK, ROBERT, *Philosophical Explanations*. Cambridge, Mass.: Belknap Press, Harvard University Press, 1981.

—— *The Examined Life*. New York: Simon and Schuster, 1989.

PARRY, C. H., *The Evolution of the Art of Music*. London: Kegan Paul, Trench, Trubner, 1896.

PAYNTER, JOHN; HOWELL, TIM; ORTON, RICHARD; and SEYMOUR, PETER (eds.), *Routledge Companion to Contemporary Musical Thought*. London: Routledge, 1992.

PENELHUM, TERENCE, 'Pleasure and Falsity', *American Philosophical Quarterly*, 1 (1964), 81–91.

PIKE, LIONEL, *Beethoven, Sibelius and 'the Profound Logic'*. London: Athlone Press, 1978.

PRICE, KINGSLEY (ed.), *On Criticising Music*. Baltimore: Johns Hopkins University Press, 1981.

RADFORD, COLIN, 'Emotions and Music: A Reply to the Cognitivists', *Journal of Aesthetics and Art Criticism*, 47 (1989), 69–76.

—— 'Muddy Waters', *Journal of Aesthetics and Art Criticism*, 49 (1991), 242–52.

RAFFMAN, DIANA, *Music, Language and Mind*. Cambridge, Mass.: Bradford Books, MIT Press, 1993.

RANDOLPH, DAVID, *This is Music*. New York: Mentor, 1964.

RANUM, P., 'Audible Rhetoric and Mute Rhetoric: The 17th Century French Sarabande', *Early Music*, 14/1 (1986), 22–34.

RETI, RUDOLPH, *The Thematic Process in Music*. London: Faber and Faber, 1961.

RIDLEY, AARON, *Music, Value and the Passions*. Ithaca, NY: Cornell University Press, 1995.

—— 'Musical Sympathies: The Experience of Expressive Music', *Journal of Aesthetics and Art Criticism*, 53/1 (1995), 49–57.

ROBINSON, JENEFER, 'The Expression and Arousal of Emotion in Music', *Journal of Aesthetics and Art Criticism*, 52/1 (1994), 13–22.

—— (ed.), *Music and Meaning*. Ithaca, NY: Cornell University Press, 1997.

ROBINSON, IAN, *The Survival of English*. Cambridge: Cambridge University Press, 1973.

ROSE, PAUL LAWRENCE, *Wagner*. London: Faber and Faber, 1992.

ROSEN, CHARLES, *Sonata Forms*. New York: Norton, 1980.

—— 'Music a la Mode', *New York Review of Books*, 23 June 1994, 55–62.

—— *The Romantic Generation*. London: Harper Collins, 1996.

ROWELL, LEWIS, *Thinking about Music*: Amherst, Mass.: University of Massachusetts Press, 1983.

SAATELA, SIMO, 'Aesthetics as Grammar'. Uppsala University, Department of Aesthetics, 1998.

SAID, EDWARD, *Musical Elaborations*. New York: Columbia University Press, 1991.

SAVILE, ANTONY, *The Test of Time*. Oxford: Clarendon Press, 1982.

SCHERCHEN, HERMANN, *The Nature of Music*. London: Dobson, 1950.

SCHOENBERG, ARNOLD, *Style and Idea*, ed. L. Stein. Berkeley: University of California Press, 1985.

SCRUTON, ROGER, *Art and Imagination*. London: Methuen, 1974.

—— *The Aesthetic Understanding*. London: Methuen, 1983.

—— 'Notes on the Meaning of Music', in Michael Krausz (ed.), *The Interpretation of Music*. Oxford: Clarendon Press, 1993, 193–202.

—— *The Aesthetics of Music*. Oxford: Clarendon Press, 1997.

SESSIONS, ROGER, *The Musical Experience of Composer, Performer and Listener*. Princeton: Princeton University Press, 1950.

—— *Questions about Music*. Cambridge, Mass.: Harvard University Press, 1970.

SEYMOUR, PETER, 'Oratory and Performance', in Paynter *et al.* (eds.), *Companion to Contemporary Musical Thought*, London: Routledge, 1992, 913–19.

SHARPE, R. A., 'Music: The Information-theoretic Approach. *British Journal of Aesthetics*, 11 (1971), 385–401.

—— 'Type, Token, Interpretation and Performance', *Mind*, 88 (1979), 437–40.

—— 'Performing an Interpretation: A Reply', *Mind*, 91 (1982), 112–14.

—— *Contemporary Aesthetics*. Brighton: Harvester Press, 1983; Aldershot: Gregg Revivals, 1991.

—— 'Solid Joys or Fading Pleasures', in E. Schaper (ed.), *Pleasure, Preference and Value*, Cambridge: Cambridge University Press, 1983, 86–98.

—— 'The Private Reader and the Listening Public', in Jeremy Hawthorn (ed.), *Criticism and Critical Theory*, London: Edward Arnold, 1984, 15–28.

—— 'Culture and its Discontents', *British Journal of Aesthetics*, 28/4 (1988), 305–16.

—— 'Moral Tales', *Philosophy*, 67 (1992), 155–68.

—— 'What is the Object of Musical Analysis', *Music Review*, 54/1 (1993), 63–72.

SHAW, G. B., *Shaw's Music*, ed. Dan H. Laurence, 3 vols., London: Bodley Head, 1981.

SLOBODA, J. A. (ed.), *Generative Processes in Music*. Oxford: Clarendon Press, 1988.

SPARSHOTT, FRANCIS, 'Music and Feeling', *Journal of Aesthetics and Art Criticism*, 52/1 (Winter 1994), 23–36.

STECKER, ROBERT, *Artworks*. University Park, Pa.: Penn State University Press, 1997.

STEINER, GEORGE, *On Difficulty and Other Essays*. Oxford: Oxford University Press, 1978.

STEVENS, JOHN, *Words and Music in the Middle Ages: Song, Narrative, Dance and Drama 1050–1350*. Cambridge: Cambridge University Press, 1986.

——'Music, Number and Rhetoric in the Early Middle Ages', in Paynter *et al.* (eds.), *Companion to Contemporary Musical Thought*, London: Routledge, 1992, 885–910.

STORR, ANTHONY, *Music and the Mind*. London: Harper Collins, 1992.

STRAVINSKY, IGOR, *Autobiography*. London: Calder and Boyars, 1975.

——and CRAFT, ROBERT, *Expositions and Developments*. London: Faber and Faber, 1962.

TANNER, MICHAEL, 'Understanding Music', *Proceedings of the Aristotelian Society*, supp. vol. 59 (1985), 215–32.

TARUSKIN, RICHARD, *Text and Act*. Oxford: Oxford University Press, 1995.

THOM, PAUL, 'The Corded Shell Strikes Back', *Grazer Philosophische Studien*, 19 (1983), 93–108.

——*For an Audience*. Philadelphia: Temple University Press, 1993.

THOMPSON, JOHN B., *Ideology and Modern Culture: Critical Social Theory in the Era of Mass Communication*. Cambridge: Polity Press, 1992.

TILGHMAN, B. R., 'Aesthetic Descriptions and Secondary Senses', *Philosophical Investigations*, 3/3 (1980), 1–15.

——*But Is It Art?* Oxford: Blackwell, 1984.

TOLSTOY, LEO, *What is Art? and Essays on Art*, The World's Classics. Oxford: Oxford University Press, 1930.

TOMLINSON, GARY, *Music in Renaissance Magic*. Chicago: University of Chicago Press, 1993.

TORMEY, ALAN, *The Concept of Expression*. Princeton: Princeton University Press, 1971.

TREITLER, LEO, *Music and the Historical Imagination*. Cambridge, Mass.: Harvard University Press, 1989.

——'Language and the Interpretation of Music', in Jenefer Robinson (ed.), *Music and Meaning*, Ithaca, NY: Cornell University Press, 1997, 23–56.

TRILLING, LIONEL, *Sincerity and Authenticity*. Oxford: Oxford University Press, 1972.

URMSON, J. O., 'The Ethics of Performance', in Michael Krausz (ed.), *The Interpretation of Music*, Oxford: Clarendon Press, 1993, 157–64.

WALKER, ALAN, *A Study in Musical Analysis*. London: Barrie and Rockliff, 1962.

——*An Anatomy of Musical Criticism*. London: Barrie and Rockliff, 1966.

WALSH, STEPHEN, *The Music of Stravinsky*. London: Routledge, 1988.

WALTON, KENDALL, 'What is Abstract about the Art of Music?', *Journal of Aesthetics and Art Criticism*, 46 (1988), 351–64.

WEBB, DANIEL, *Observations on the Correspondence between Music and Poetry*. London, 1769.

WEBER, WILLIAM, 'Mass Culture and the Reshaping of European Musical Taste', *International Review of the Aesthetics and Sociology of Music*, 88 (1977), 5–22.

WEITZ, MORRIS, 'The Role of Theory in Aesthetics', *Journal of Aesthetics and Art Criticism*, 15 (1956), 27–35.

WHITALL, ARNOLD, *Music since the First World War*. Oxford: Oxford University Press, 1988.

WILLIAMS, PETER, 'The Snares and Delusions of Musical Rhetoric: Some Examples from Recent Writings on J. S. Bach', in Peter Reidemeister and Veronica Gutmann (eds.), *Alte Musik: Praxis and Reflections*, Winterthur: Schola Cantorum Basiliensis, 1983, 230–40.

WITTGENSTEIN, L., *Philosophical Investigations*. Oxford: Blackwell, 1953.

——*Culture and Value*, trans. Peter Winch. Oxford: Blackwell, 1980.

——*Remarks on Philosophical Psychology*, i, trans. G. E. M. Anscombe and G. H. Von Wright. Oxford: Blackwell, 1980.

WOLTERSTORFF, N., *Works and Worlds of Art*. Oxford: Clarendon Press, 1980.

YOUNG, JAMES O., 'The Concept of Authentic Performance', *British Journal of Aesthetics*, 28/3 (1988), 228–38.

# Index